Tinderbox

U.S. Foreign Policy
and the Roots of Terrorism

Stephen Zunes

Zed Books   London

Cover design by Matt Wuerker and Erica Bjerning
Photo Bush and Sharon by Win McNamee, Reuters NewsMedia Inc/
    Corbis
Photo Flaming Barricades in West Bank by Yola Monakhov, Reuters
    NewsMedia Inc/ Corbis
Photo Helicopter and US aircraft carrier by Jim Hollander, Reuters
    NewsMedia Inc/ Corbis

Published outside North America by Zed Books Ltd,
7 Cynthia Street, London N1 9JF.

A catalogue record for this book is available
from the British Library.

ISBN 1 84277 258 9 hb
ISBN 1 84277 259 7 pb

Published in the U.S. by
Common Courage Press
Monroe, ME

Printed in the USA.
This edition not for sale in North America

First Printing

To my parents, John and Helen,
who were responsible for my early education
about the Middle East, U.S. foreign policy,
and how ordinary concerned citizens
could make a difference
in the struggle for peace and justice.

Acknowledgements

There are many who made this book possible, particularly Greg Bates of Common Courage Press.

Many thanks to Joel Beinin, Eric Hoogland, Noam Chomsky, Asad AbuKhalil and Philip Mattar for reviewing all or parts of the manuscript and providing critical feedback. Thanks also to Carolyn McCoy, Tom Hewitt and Suzanne Green for their special assistance in making the manuscript possible.

I am particularly grateful for those I have known over the years who, from a variety of political perspectives and experiences, have enhanced my understanding of the Middle East. These include Cherie Brown, Noam Chomsky, Ned Hanauer, Scott Kennedy, Jill Crystal, Ron Young, Allan Solomonow, Phyllis Bennis, John Duke Anthony, Alan Kellum, Deborah Gerner, Matti Peled, Peretz Kidron, Asad AbuKhalil, Edward Azar and, in particular, my parents John and Helen Zunes.

I am indebted to the efforts of the Foreign Policy in Focus Project for making it financially feasible for me to take a full-year sabbatical that made this book possible. Credit also goes to the University of San Francisco Faculty Association (American Federation of Teachers) for their successful efforts in recent contract talks with the university preserving adequate sabbatical pay.

Special appreciation also goes to the co-directors of the Foreign Policy in Focus Project: Martha Honey of the Institute for Policy Studies and Tom Barry of the Interhemispheric Resource Center. Several segments of this book originally appeared in Foreign Policy in Focus publications.

Other segments of this book appeared in articles of mine originally published in *Middle East Policy*, *Arab Studies Quarterly*, *The Progressive*, *Peace Review*, *Global Dialogue*, *Foreign Service Journal*, *Current History*, and *New Political Science*, as well as in briefs from the Center for Policy Analysis on Palestine. Some other segments originally appeared as parts of chapters from *The Middle East at the Crossroads: A Survey of Contemporary International Relations*, edited by Manochehr Dorraj (University Press of America, 1999); *The United States and Human Rights: Looking Inward and Outward*, edited by David Forsythe (Lincoln: University of Nebraska Press,

2000); and *Bridging a Gulf: Peacebuilding in West Asia*, edited by Majid Tehranian (I.B. Taurus, 2002).

After promising my family that I would spend this long-awaited sabbatical year as a househusband and primary parent, the unfolding international crises resulted in my spending much of the time researching and writing this book. As a result, my most deep and sincere appreciation goes to my beloved partner Nanlouise Wolfe and our children Shanti, Kalila and Tobin for their patience and understanding.

Stephen Zunes
September 2002

Contents

1,000

Foreword

by Richard Falk

With each passing day, American foreign policy seems to be spinning further out of control. Briefly, in the immediate weeks following the September 11 attacks, the efforts by the U.S. government to restore the security of its citizens by addressing effectively the persisting challenge of mega-terrorism posed by the Al-Qaeda network commanded worldwide support and respect. But as the White House and Pentagon discloses by stages their policy it has increasingly seemed more like a prescription for catastrophe and insecurity than a prudent response of real benefit to the well-being of American citizens, much less to the peoples of the world more generally.

From the outset of the American official reaction to these devastating attacks on its prime symbols of economic and military power, there were many signs of trouble: the immediate embrace of a war mode via a nationalist logic thereby marginalizing the United Nations; the stated visionary goal of destroying "terrorism" everywhere; the White House diktat that those governments that do not join with the U.S. in the global campaign would be treated as allies of "the terrorists;" the arrogant insistence that America was leading the forces of goodness in a holy war against the arrayed forces of evil. President Bush in his State of the Union Address on January 29, 2002 extended the reach of War on Global Terror to encompass "the axis of evil" countries of Iraq, Iran, and North Korea, making it clear that the super-hawks in the Pentagon were carrying the day in shaping the scope of the response to September 11. Extending the American war goals beyond Al-Qaeda to include a series of sovereign states that were not linked to the September 11 attacks and were far more threatened than threatening, is to embark on a geopolitical project of dangerous immensity, and to do so by way of aggressive war.

Beyond this, in March of 2002 a leaked Department of Defense document reveals a new willingness by the U.S. government to plan for wide potential uses of nuclear weapons, not as deterrents, but in warfighting situations, and most provocatively, against a series of named countries. This unprecedented embrace of nuclearism is bound to give rise to profound anxiety throughout the world, confirming the worst fears about the destructive and dangerous drift of the brand of unilateralism being pursued by the Bush Administration. Such an arrogant form of militarist geopolitics menaces the entire world.

While these disturbing indications of a mounting world order crisis were accumulating, the Palestine/Israel encounter was entering its bloodiest phases ever, with both sides daily relying on Crimes Against Humanity to inflict as much harm as possible on the respective civilian societies of their enemy. Israel with its superior firepower deployed tanks and helicopter gunships against defenseless Palestinian refugee camps and undefended towns, creating a spectacle of oppressive brutality rarely, if ever, seen before in the long gory history of military occupation. The Israeli Prime Minister, Ariel Sharon, responsible for a whole string of past abuses throughout his long career amounting to war crimes, actually had the chilling temerity to tell the Israeli Knesset that the violence could not end until more Palestinians had been killed: "The aim is to increase the number of losses on the other side. Only after they have been battered will we able to conduct talks." It needs to be remembered that the other side is not an army, but an occupied helpless and impoverished civilian society!

As shocking as are these developments, the scandalous American reaction still manages to startle the moral imagination by its perversity. The U.S. government has during these bloody days consistently singled out Yasir Arafat and the Palestinian Authority to blame for the escalating violence, and has endorsed the outrageous Israeli view that their struggle is as much against terrorism as is the American response to Al-Qaeda. It is the intention of this absurdly distorted view of terrorism to give a green light to state terrorism even if it is engaged in directly targeting civilian society with heavy weapons. There is little doubt that such policies are plunging the world into a snake pit of chaos and depravity.

Perhaps most frightening of all are the metaphorical connections between what is happening on the ground between Israeli and Palestinians, and the global implications of U.S. foreign policy in the aftermath of September 11. We are caught in a maelstrom of violence and visionary politics that could soon transform the world into one bloody wasteland that might begin to reproduce the current realities of the Palestinians entrapped in Gaza and the West Bank. Gurus of the American establishment, such as Bernard Lewis or Thomas Friedman, are urging policies and approaches that are leading in such directions. They are suggesting that what went wrong on September 11 reflected an underlying inability of the Arab world to make a successful transition to modernity, provoking an extremist backlash that will not subside unless crushed by American military power, and beaten into renewed submission. Such sinister advice is seductive, as it situates all the responsibility on the Islamic Other, while totally exonerating the American Self. Such advocacy is reinforced by a surge of chauvinist patriotism that only celebrates America as it is, and refuses to consider what America should or could be.

It is against such a background that one welcomes this fine and prescient book by Stephen Zunes, which surgically explains and clarifies what has truly gone wrong with American policy in a manner that challenges impressively the false reassurances of the conventional wisdom that weaves the myth of American innocence in relation to the terrorist backlash of September 11. Zunes provides us with an unblinkered understanding of the terrorist challenge, the Palestinian ordeal, and a panoramic view of the wider failings of U.S. policy in the Middle East. His assessment goes well beyond critique to offer a plausible alternative course of policy and action for the U.S. government to follow so as to abandon its current futility. Zunes convincingly discloses the deep roots of discrediting opportunism and immorality in U.S. foreign policy that has led this country to where it finds itself today. He provides telling examples of our own frequent reliance on our own brands of "terrorism" to promote strategic and ideological goals as in relation to the contras in Nicaragua during the 1980s or with respect to the anti-Soviet phases of Afghan resistance when Osama bin Laden was our trusted and valued friend and ally. Zunes also shows how much our policies toward Israel/Palestine have proceeded with a brazen disregard for international law, the authority of the United Nations, especially Security Council resolutions, and the protection of human rights.

The analysis offered by Zunes also helps answer that haunting question that stumped George W. Bush so visibly after September 11: "Why do they hate us?" Bush pridefully and awkwardly asserted that they hated us because we are a free and successful democracy, while Zunes shows far more convincingly that the anti-American resentment in the Arab world arises from the peoples of the region enduring an endless series of humiliations, impositions, and exploitations, and not just in relation to the Israel/Palestine encounter, but with respect to the maintenance of cruel sanctions against the people of Iraq for more than a decade, by propping up corrupt regimes resented by their own citizenry, and by a domineering oil-driven geopolitics that ignores human well-being.

In effect, Zunes portrays America taking over from the colonialists, and doing the same sort of dirty work to the peoples of the region, whether in the context of ensuring access to cheap oil for promiscuous energy consumption in rich countries or backing up the cruel Israeli refusal to provide Palestinians with their legitimate rights, above all, their right of self-determination. What distinguishes this powerful analysis from other critiques of American foreign policy in the Middle East is that you need not accept the principled part of Zunes' assessment to be persuaded by his overall argument that the U.S. government is pursuing a path that is self-defeating and will ultimately rebound to undermine its strategic interests in the region. What is more, Zunes is at pains to insist that the quality of American support for Israeli official policies is having the effect of weakening the legitimate core of Israel's search for security as a prosperous sovereign state living at peace with its neighbors and at ease with itself. In this important respect, those who ardently support Israel, and identify with its struggle, would do well to ponder his central contention that the "friendship" being tendered by the U.S. government includes a poisoned chalice!

Stephen Zunes devotes most of the book to developing this intriguing mixture of critical and pragmatic argument, but he does not stop there. He outlines an alternative line of U.S. policy based on respect for law and morality, support for the UN, and an overall commitment to global justice in economic, political, and cultural relations. Of course, Zunes is not naïve enough to think that the persuasiveness of his argument will by itself alter the behavior of the American leviathan, or even make a dent in the monolithic mainstream media that has been so active in orchestrating both the war against global terrorism and the one-sided interpretation of the Palestinian/Israeli conflict. What Zunes hopes for and believes in is the growth of a grassroots movement here and abroad that will mobilize the American people to challenge for their own sake the disastrous drift of current U.S. foreign policy, especially as it is being so murderously enacted in the Middle East, but also as it is being projected with respect to the war of terrorism, the use of nuclear weapons, and the militarization of space.

To move ahead in these directions is more imperative now than ever before in American history. Zunes, more than anyone else at the moment, can in this book help awaken Americans and others to the pragmatic and principled necessity, and rapidly disappearing opportunity, to move out from the gathering shadows of doom that threatens all of us on this planet. To be sure, this opportunity remains a live possibility. But with the passage of time, the obstacles mount, and soon the challenge will seem all but insurmountable.

—Richard Falk
Princeton

Introduction

What created the anger and the resulting horror of September 11, 2001? Will current U.S. policy in the Middle East intensify or diminish it? Americans are asking these questions with unprecedented concern and interest.

Throughout the centuries, Western empires from the Romans to the British have tried to impose their order on the region. For certain periods of time they have succeeded, only to find themselves at the receiving end of a popular and oftentimes violent backlash. Proponents of U.S. policy argued that this would not be the case with the United States, since Americans entered the region eschewing colonial ambitions, championing the rule of law and the authority of the United Nations, and seeking economic growth and political stability. America stood out as a singular and responsible overseer, so went this argument, in using its military and economic power to insure stability and security in the face of despots, terrorists and religious extremists.

Critics of the U.S. role, on the other hand, point out that America's overbearing power has created widespread resentment among those from the Middle East and elsewhere in the Islamic world. The chief complaints revolve around U.S. support for what are seen as repressive and corrupt regimes, the exploitative practices by American oil companies and other corporations, the prejudicial use of the United Nations, the arming and bankrolling of a militaristic and expansionist Israel, destabilization efforts against internationally recognized governments, as well as direct military intervention.

It was widely assumed following the collapse of the Soviet Union and the American triumph in the Gulf War that, for good or for ill, the United States had become the unchallenged outside power in the Middle East. Or so it seemed until the planes crashed into the World Trade Center that September morning.

Whatever the nature of the U.S. role in the Middle East, there is little question regarding the strategic importance of the region. For more than 4000 years, the Middle East has been contested by competing great powers. At the intersection of three continents and the source of most of the world's petroleum reserves, there is perhaps no region that the United States considers more important. The State Department has described the Middle East as "a stupendous source of strategic power, and one of the greatest material prizes in world history...probably the richest economic prize in the world in the field of foreign investment."[1] President Dwight Eisenhower described the Middle East as the most "strategically important area in the world."[2] Furthermore, the Middle East is the destination of the majority of American arms exports and is therefore considered extremely important for politically influential arms manufacturers.

American officials are no longer concerned that the region might fall to Soviet influence, yet the United States also has had a longstanding concern about the influence of indigenous movements that could potentially challenge American interests. There is a perception of an ongoing threat from radical forces—both Islamic and secular—as well as concern over the instability that could result from any major challenges to the rule of pro-Western regimes, even if led by potentially democratic movements.[3] This has resulted in a policy where the United States generally has supported the maintenance of the status quo regardless of a given regime's level of commitment to democracy or human rights.

The allied Gulf monarchies are guardians of valuable oil reserves to which the United States seeks access, not just to supplement American reserves, but—as some would argue—as a means of maintaining a degree of leverage over the import-dependent European and Japanese markets.[4] Though without oil, Turkey, Egypt and Morocco are populous, strategically located, and traditionally sympathetic to U.S. interests in the region. The tiny but powerful state of Israel is one of America's most important strategic allies in the world today.

In addition to those countries that are seen as strategic assets, the Middle East is also the home of some of the United States' most prominent adversaries of recent years, including Iraq, Iran, Libya, Sudan and Syria. That list has now expanded to include Al-Qaeda, the shadowy network led by Osama bin Laden responsible for the infamous attacks of September 2001 that resulted in the deaths of more than 3000 Americans in the largest mass killings on American soil since the Civil War.

The United States has demonstrated its ability to accomplish short-term strategic objectives in a dramatic fashion, such as the military operations during the fall of 2001 that overthrew the Taliban government in Afghanistan, destroyed the major Al-Qaeda bases in that country and killed and captured many of its fighters. Yet, what will be the likely long-term success of this primarily military response to the threat of terrorism? The answer may be found by taking into account the dramatic militarization of the Middle East in recent decades, actively encouraged and aided by successive American administrations.

A core argument in subsequent chapters is this: the more the United States has militarized the region, the less secure the American people have become. All the sophisticated weaponry, brave fighting men and women, and brilliant military leadership the United States may possess will do little good if there are hundreds of millions of people in the Middle East and beyond who hate us. Even though only a small percentage of the population supports bin Laden's methods, there will still be enough people to maintain dangerous terrorist networks as long as his grievances resonate with large numbers.

As most Muslims recognize, bin Laden is not an authority on Islam. He is, however, a businessman who—like any shrewd businessman—knows how to take a popular fear or desire and use it to sell a product: in this case, anti-American terrorism. The grievances expressed in his manifestoes—the ongoing U.S. military presence in the Gulf, the humanitarian consequences of the U.S.-led sanctions against Iraq, U.S. support for the Israeli government, and U.S. backing of autocratic Arab regimes—have widespread appeal in that part of the world. A survey by the *Wall Street Journal* found that even among wealthy élites in Islamic countries—many of whom had business or other ties with the United States—there was an enormous amount of anger and dismay about these very policies.[5] British novelist John LeCarre may have been right when he observed in the aftermath of the September 2001 terrorist attacks, "What America longs for at this moment, even more than retribution, is more friends and fewer enemies."[6]

As a result, despite the initially successful outcome of the military response against the Al-Qaeda network and its Taliban supporters in Afghanistan, it is likely that new terrorists will take their place. Even fanatics need reasons to expose themselves and others to deadly peril. The only way out of this hellish spiral begins with a critical examination of what has prompted the rise of such a fanatical movement.

Many disagree that such examination is needed. There are those who argue that Osama bin Laden's political agenda should not be taken any more seriously than that of Oklahoma City bomber Timothy McVeigh, the 1960s cult leader Charles Manson, or any other mass murderer.[7] Certainly there is some merit to this argument; anyone who would be willing to sacrifice thousands of innocent lives for any reason is psychopathic and is unlikely to be reasoned with or appeased through negotiations. There is lit-tle question that Usama bin Laden's ideology is apocalyptic and his meth-ods are genocidal. Indeed, his worldview is closer to that of European fas-cists of the 1930s than leftist Third World revolutionaries of the 1960s and 1970s who inspired many of my generation in the West.

An important distinction should be made, however: Terrorists whose political grievances have little political appeal—such as those on the far left and far right that have periodically arisen in relatively open societies like those in Western Europe and the United States—can be suppressed relatively easily. By contrast, terrorist groups whose agendas reflect those of systematically oppressed populations—such as Palestinian Arabs, Sri Lankan Tamils, or Northern Ireland Catholics—are far more difficult to control without also addressing their underlying political grievances. Osama bin Laden and his network may be more like the latter, only on a regional scale. Indeed, with the dramatic rise of radical Islamic movements worldwide and the growing Arab Diaspora, the threat is global.

There was nothing karmic about the events of September 11, 2001. Whatever the failings of a government in its foreign policy, no country deserves to experience such a large-scale loss of innocent lives. Yet the hope of stopping extremists who might resort to such heinous acts in the future rests in part on the willingness of Americans to recognize what gave rise to what the British daily newspaper *The Independent* headlined as "the wickedness and awesome cruelty of a crushed and humiliated people."[8] To raise these uncomfortable questions about U.S. foreign policy is difficult for many Americans, particularly in the aftermath of the attacks. Perhaps we were afraid to ask the right questions because we feared the answers. However, it could not be more important or timely.

Critical to addressing any political grievance in a responsible manner is the development of democracy. The first chapter exposes how the United States systematically has discouraged the development of greater political pluralism and civil society in the Middle East through the support of auto-cratic regimes and occupying armies.

Very much related to the Middle East's lack of political freedom and stability is the militarization of the region, including the large-scale U.S. transfer of armaments and direct military intervention. The deleterious impact of such policies on these countries' political, social and economic development is the subject of the second chapter, as are American con-cerns over the potential development of weapons of mass destruction by Iran and Iraq.

Central to the militarization of the Middle East is U.S. involvement in the Persian Gulf, including the conflict with Iran, the Gulf War, and the subsequent sanctions, air strikes and threats of an invasion against Iraq. This is the focus of Chapter Three.

The grievances of the Palestinians and their supporters can be understood best in light of the recent history of relations between the United States and Israel, particularly the close strategic partnership between these two countries. Chapter Four shows how U.S. policy has brought neither justice for the Palestinians nor security for Israel, both of which are crucial for peace and stability in the region.

With these chapters as a backdrop, Chapter Five examines how U.S. policies, both consciously and inadvertently, have encouraged the rise of dangerous and reactionary Islamic movements in Afghanistan, Lebanon, Palestine and elsewhere.

Chapter Six looks at how the U.S. strategy for combating terrorism has largely failed to counter the threat and may actually encourage the very forces the United States hopes to overcome.

Finally, how can we resolve the mess we have in no small part helped to create? Is there a contradiction between the ethical principles with which most Americans identify and legitimate U.S. security interests? The seventh and final chapter briefly outlines a new Middle East policy that actually could enhance American security interests in this vital region.

In critically examining how U.S. Middle East policy has contributed to the rise of terrorism, this does not imply that there are not other actors in the Middle East and elsewhere who also share responsibility for the dangerous escalation in terrorist violence of recent years. Given that most readers of this book are Americans, however, it is particularly important to understand how our government has contributed to the rise of terrorist groups like Al-Qaeda.

The tragedy of September 11, 2001 has reminded us that decisions by our government relating to countries far away indeed can have a major impact here at home. It is hoped that this book will enable its readers to become more informed citizens and thereby be able to contribute to the debate on future directions for United States policy in the Middle East.

Santa Cruz, California
September 2002

Chapter One

The Suppression of Human Rights

More than forty years ago, President John F. Kennedy observed that "Those who make peaceful evolution impossible will make violent revolution inevitable."[1] Despite disastrous consequences from ignoring this advice in the subsequent decades of the Cold War in such regions as Southeast Asia, Latin America and Africa, American policy makers may now be making the same tragic mistake in the Middle East. In aiding and abetting political repression, the United States has helped create the very forces that now threaten American security. Though U.S. support for repressive governments has widespread bipartisan support in Washington, history has shown repeatedly that such policies end up being counter to American interests over the long term.

The standard reason given by U.S. officials and many pundits in the American media for what motivated the attacks of September 11, 2001 is the terrorists' hatred of liberty and of democracy. According to President George W. Bush, "They hate...democratically elected government. They hate our freedoms—our freedom of religion, our freedom of speech, our freedom to vote and assemble and disagree with each other."[2] Though Americans have reason to be proud of their country's democratic institutions and individual liberties, the unfortunate reality is that U.S. policy in the Middle East has tended not to promote freedom, but to support authoritarian governments and occupation armies. The contradiction between the democratic ideals with which most Americans identify and the perceived exigencies of superpower status is certainly not unique to current U.S. policy in the Middle East, yet its significance is rarely appreciated.

Attention to human rights by successive American administrations has always been relative to the perceived strategic importance of the country in question: the more important an allied regime is strategically, the less attention is given to human rights. Unfortunately for people living under the rule of Middle Eastern governments allied to the United States, their location makes their countries of great strategic value in the view of American policy makers. There is a price to pay for such priorities, however.

Terrorism rarely rises out of democratic societies. When it does, terrorist groups are usually suppressed fairly easily, since few people agree with the terrorists' assertion that armed resistance is the best way to force needed political changes, especially when the targets are non-combatants. By contrast, it is no coincidence that political movements dedicated to advancing their cause through violence tend to arise within countries where governments hold power through violence. The United States plays a major role in propping up repressive governments which, in turn, has led to a terrorist backlash. Most Middle Easterners do not see American democracy at work, but they do see "Made in USA" on tear gas canisters and bomb casings used against civilians.

For example, the autocratic regime in Saudi Arabia maintains its grip on power in part through the Saudi National Guard (SANG), which has been accused of widespread human rights abuses against suspected opponents. SANG, whose primary function is internal security, is almost entirely armed, trained and managed by the United States, largely through a network of military contractors. It may be no coincidence that what many believe to be Al-Qaeda's first terrorist attack, a November 1995 bombing that killed five American servicemen, was targeted at a U.S.-operated SANG training center in Riyadh.

Barely a month after the September 11 attacks, Great Britain's prestigious *Financial Times* observed, "For a long time after the Gulf War, the U.S. assumed its allies in the region—most of which are authoritarian regimes—could impose their views on their people. The error of this approach has become apparent."[3]

Moral Twists in the Pretzel of U.S. Policy

Many Americans question whether democracy is even possible in the Middle East, believing that human rights abuses are the inevitable outgrowth of authoritarian forms of government that are required and reinforced by cultural norms. Attitudes underlying these questions minimize the importance of democracy and human rights to Middle Eastern peoples and the desire of Middle Eastern peoples to encourage democratization and improve the human rights records of their governments. Such American assumptions at times harbor somewhat racist overtones. For example, widespread misunderstandings in the West of Islamic principles regarding human rights have minimized popular sympathy with victims of human

rights abuses in many of these countries. A crude kind of structural-func-
tionalism[4] and pseudo-sensitivity appears to underline the belief that the
lack of better human rights records by Middle Eastern governments is
somehow a cultural phenomenon that no policy shift by the United States
could alter. Even some otherwise reputable scholars, such as Harvard
University's Samuel Huntington, will go to some lengths to dismiss the
potential for democracy in the Islamic world.[5] It is not inaccurate to gen-
eralize that there has tended to be a greater tolerance for autocratic rule
and a lesser emphasis on individual liberties in the Islamic world than in
the West. However, there is also a strong belief in a social contract between
ruler and subject that gives the people the right to resist if the rule is
unjust.[6] Furthermore, international human rights covenants routinely violated by Middle Eastern governments are based upon the Universal
Declaration of Human Rights, deemed universal because it does reflect an
international consensus. Given that most Middle Eastern governments
have signed the International Covenant on Civil and Political Rights,
which is based upon the Universal Declaration, these governments are
legally bound to uphold its principles. Furthermore, individual Arabs and
Muslims do not like being detained, denied due process, tortured and murdered for their political beliefs by repressive governments anymore than do
their Western Christian and Jewish counterparts.

Even though democracy and individual liberty is not common in the
Arab-Islamic world, the emphasis in the West on cultural or religious
explanations tends to minimize other factors that are arguably more salient.
These include the legacy of colonialism, high levels of militarization, and
uneven economic development, much of which can be linked in no small
part to the policies of Western governments, including the United States.
There is a tragic convenience to an American policy that strengthens the
police and military of repressive Arab regimes, better enabling them to
crush incipient human rights movements, only to then claim that the lack
of freedom in these countries is evidence that their people do not really
want it. As the examples discussed throughout this book illustrate, these
arms transfers and the diplomatic and economic support systems provided
by the United States play an important role in keeping these regimes in
power by strengthening the hand of the state and supporting internal
repression.

A further irony is that American political leaders then use the dictatorial orientation of these Arab regimes as an excuse for supporting the
government of Israel, which also suppresses Arab peoples demanding

democracy and human rights. Domestic political groups in the United States allied with Israel—along with sympathetic individuals in politics, academia, and the media—have frequently played upon stereotypes of the "authoritarian nature" of Arab societies as reasons why the United States should continue large-scale military and economic support of the Israeli government. Egyptian human rights activist Hafez Abu Saada expressed the sentiment of many Arab democrats when he noted the implicit racism in U.S. policy that believes in "Democracy for the Jews, but not for the Arabs."[7] In a speech before a joint session of Congress when he was Israeli prime minister, Benyamin Netanyahu argued that the lack of democracy in the Arab world meant, "the proper course for the democratic world, led by the United States, is to strengthen the only democracy in the Middle East." He therefore insisted that it would be wrong to pressure the Israeli government to compromise further in the peace process or improve its human rights record in the occupied territories, since Israel is part of "the united front of democracy, led by the world's greatest democracy, the United States." [8]

There also appears to be a kind of self-righteousness regarding Western concepts of individual liberty that has only exacerbated misunderstandings between the United States and Middle Eastern countries on the subject of human rights. One example is the reaction over the 1989 Iranian religious opinion that effectively sentenced Indian-British author Salman Rushdie to death as a result of passages deemed offensive in his novel *Satanic Verses*.[9] Despite the impression given in the frenzy of Western media coverage over the episode, Iran was the only government in the entire Muslim world to support the *fatwa*. Similarly, there was also widespread support of Rushdie by Muslim authorities, who argued that he had the right to offend anybody, and—while Muslims had a right to be upset—a death sentence was beyond the jurisdiction of temporal authorities.[10] While Rushdie's previous and arguably better works were generally successful, *Satanic Verses* became a colossal best seller. At a time when public readings of texts offensive to Jews and Christians would not be considered appropriate in the United States, such readings of *Satanic Verses*, that was offensive to Muslims, became widespread. The negative feeling in the Islamic world towards this reaction in the West was not because they believed the *fatwa* by Iranian authorities was appropriate. Rather, what bothered many Muslims was that Western governments and intellectuals would so vigorously defend Rushdie while ignoring the growing demand for greater political liberalization and democracy in these countries in the face of thousands of prisoners of conscience detained, tortured and murdered by

Western-backed Muslim governments. A survey of media coverage in the United States showed far more attention on the Rushdie episode than on all other issues of human rights and democracy in the region for several preceding years combined.[11] It is noteworthy that during the thick of the international reaction to the Rushdie affair, the U.S.-backed Saudi government executed a man for alleged apostasy with scarcely a murmur of protest.

Human Rights:
Transforming a Moral Issue into a Political Tool

Human rights violations by foreign governments and their lack of democratic institutions generally get the most attention in the United States when a given administration has called attention to them in order to mobilize domestic and international opinion against a regime the U.S. government opposes.[12] However, every administration in recent years has also had to address, at least to some degree, the less expedient phenomenon of responding to public and Congressional pressure regarding the lack of democracy and human rights in allied countries. Oftentimes, such official responses would constitute little more than lip service and damage control, but—since at least the 1970s—it has been difficult to ignore completely. Most of the pressure has stemmed from grassroots movements, sometimes amplified by sympathetic segments of the media and members of Congress. The resulting debates have covered world regions ranging from East and Southeast Asia, to Eastern Europe, to Latin America and to Africa, and have been particularly vehement regarding regimes that directly receive arms and economic assistance from the U.S. government.

Yet despite this surge in debate over human rights policy, the very region that receives the largest amount of American arms and aid has been notably absent from the public debate: the Middle East. Not only has there been mostly silence from traditional human rights advocates in Congress, there has not been much in the way of grassroots pressure, either. This relatively docile response is not because the problem is small. A large majority of countries in that region lack democratic institutions and engage in a consistent pattern of gross and systematic human rights violations. In addition, three major recipients of U.S. aid—Morocco, Israel and Turkey—have conquered all or parts of neighboring countries by force, engaged in ethnic cleansing, and continue to subjugate the population of these occupied territories in defiance of the Geneva Convention and the United Nations.

Despite the poor human rights situation in the Middle East, with the exception of certain intellectual circles and the most committed human rights activists, there has been little effort among American activists to support pro-democracy movements in the Middle East. These struggles have not captured the imagination of the grassroots organizations in recent decades to the extent of human rights movements in Latin America, southern Africa, the Philippines, or even East Timor. While established human rights groups such as Amnesty International and Human Rights Watch have generally given a proportional amount of attention to human rights abuses in the Middle East, it has not resulted in the same level of popular activism as have similar movements regarding other parts of the world. This gives the United States little incentive to change its policy of supporting repressive governments.

In other parts of the world, even where there may have been widespread repression, the United States has insisted that competitive elections and other legal structures are an adequate indicator of democracy. This is why even in the case of El Salvador in the 1980s—where, despite formal competitive elections, government-backed death squads murdered tens of thousands of dissidents—the country was labeled a "democracy" by the U.S. government and much of the American media. The Middle East is more problematic, however, since some of America's closest allies are absolute monarchies without even the pretense of democratic institutions. As a result, successive administrations and the media have frequently labeled such governments as "moderate," even if there was nothing particularly moderate in their level of despotism. The term is used primarily in reference to governments that have been friendly to the United States and its foreign policy goals in the Middle East; it has also been used in reference to governments that have been relatively less hostile towards Israel and U.S.-led peace initiatives. In either case, there is virtually no correlation between this label and a given government's record on democracy and human rights. This is how Saudi Arabia, a fundamentalist and misogynist theocracy that engages in widespread human rights abuses, is labeled so frequently in the United States as a "moderate" Arab regime.

Unlike Saudi Arabia, most Middle Eastern states do have elections. They are usually formalities, however, the primary purpose of which is to ratify the existing leadership. The smaller emirates of the Persian Gulf, that generally eschew any kind of formal elections, traditionally maintained legitimacy through the *majlis* system, which provides for the direct petitioning of grievances to royalty. In addition, monarchical succession was not automatic to the eldest son or any single member of the royal family;

the successor was chosen by a consensus of tribal elders based on his qual-
ifications. It was the British, who dominated the Gulf region during the
nineteenth and twentieth centuries, that helped ossify the sheikly system
to a largely inherited position. With the addition of strong American backing in subsequent years, several of these Arab monarchies have evolved
from their relatively open traditional tribal governing structures to ones
more closely resembling modern bureaucratic authoritarianism. As a result,
human rights abuses have increased in a number of these countries and the
legitimacy of these governments is being challenged to a growing degree
from within. Popular resentment cannot help but expand beyond the
regime in question to its chief foreign patron as well.

As with other parts of the world, the U.S. government will often
downplay the human rights abuses of its allies and exaggerate the abuses of
its adversaries. To cite some recent examples: in the State Department's
annual human rights report, the description of the Sultanate of Oman was
changed, as a result of pressure from department superiors, to downplay the
authoritarian nature of the regime.[13] For example, in the 1991 report,
Oman is described as "an absolute monarchy;" a more recent report simply
refers to the sultanate as "a monarchy without popularly elected representative institutions."[14] More recently, the 2000 human rights report noted
how Egypt's military courts "do not ensure civilian defendants due process
before an independent tribunal." However, thanks to pressure from above,
all references to these unfair tribunals were dropped from the 2001 report
even though they continue.[15] The State Department has even allowed
Israeli officials to review and edit its human rights report on Israeli practices in the occupied territories prior to publication, substantially toning
down the original analysis.[16] Even Iraq had its lack of democracy and poor
human rights record downplayed by U.S. officials during its invasion of
Iran in the 1980s. Only after its invasion of Kuwait in 1990 was the record
corrected and Iraq's violations prominently exposed.

One of the more striking examples of the U.S. government's lack of
concern for human rights regards the Universal Declaration of Human
Rights, which is recognized in U.S. courts (and elsewhere) as "customary
international law" and as the "authoritative definition" of standards of
human rights. Article 13 of the Universal Declaration, perhaps the most
famous part of the document, guarantees the right of individuals to leave
and return to their own country. The Clinton Administration, in a break
with previous administrations, ended U.S. support for its universal applica-
tion, such as in the annual confirmation of United Nations General

Assembly Resolution 194 guaranteeing the right of return for Palestinian refugees.[17] Even before the United States formally reversed its stance, American officials rarely mentioned it, emphasizing only the first part (the right to leave) regarding Soviet Jews or other victims of oppression in Communist countries. When the issue involved allied governments, however, the right of return was notably omitted.[18]

Rampant double standards also fuel resentment of the United States. American officials have condemned Iraqi repression of its Kurdish minority—at least since the 1990 Iraqi invasion of Kuwait. Meanwhile, just to the north, the United States has armed the Turkish armed forces in their repression of its Kurdish minority. Strict enforcement of reactionary interpretations of Islamic law by Iranian authorities are highlighted as examples of the perfidy of that regime, while even more draconian measures enacted in Saudi Arabia are downplayed or even rationalized as inherently part of their culture. The right of self-determination for Kuwaiti Arabs while under Iraqi occupation was vigorously defended, but not the right of Palestinian Arabs under Israeli occupation or Sahrawi Arabs under Moroccan occupation. Martial law in NATO ally Turkey during the 1980s was largely supported, while martial law in the Warsaw Pact nation of Poland during that same period was strongly condemned and resulted in U.S. sanctions. The United States has publicly advocated the overthrow of Saddam Hussein so the people of Iraq could choose their own leaders,[19] but this right to choose their own leaders is something virtually no other Arab people have ever known, including those who live under regimes supported by the U.S. government.[20]

U.S. aid to Israel has generally increased as the government's repression in the occupied territories has worsened.[21] Similarly, aid to Morocco increased as that country's repression in occupied Western Sahara and even within Morocco itself continued unabated.[22] The United States largely welcomed the 1992 military coup in Algeria that nullified that country's first democratic elections.[23] American forces failed to stop widespread repression, even lynchings, of Palestinian residents of Kuwait immediately after the country's liberation from Iraq; these anti-Palestinian pogroms, in reaction to some Palestinian residents collaborating with Iraqi occupation forces, constituted collective punishment based on ethnic origin, a particularly serious violation of international law.[24]

Rather than encourage democratization in the Middle East, the United States has reduced—or maintained at low levels—its economic, military, and diplomatic support of Arab countries that have experienced substantial liberalization in recent years. For example, Jordan received large-scale U.S. support in the 1970s and 1980s despite widespread repression and authoritarian rule. In the early 1990s, when it became perhaps the most democratic country in the Arab world—with a relatively free press, opposition political parties, and lively debate in a parliament that wielded real political power within a constitutional monarchy—the United States suspended foreign aid.[25] Similarly, aid to Yemen was cut off within months of the newly reunified country's first democratic election in 1990.[26] The official explanation for the cutoff of U.S. support for these two countries was because of their failure to support the United States in its war against Iraq. However, the reason these governments could not back the American war effort was because their leaders—unlike those of their more autocratic Arab neighbors that supported the war—needed to be responsive to their citizenry, who generally opposed the war, *because* they had relatively open political systems. By contrast, American support for dictatorial regimes—such as Egypt, Saudi Arabia and the smaller Gulf emirates that backed the U.S.-led war effort—increased during this period.

As *Newsweek* magazine observed, in reference to Pakistan, "It may be a good thing that Pakistan is ruled by a friendly military dictator rather than what could well be a hostile democracy."[27] As British journalist Robert Fisk noted, "Far better to have a Mubarak or a King Abdullah or a King Fahd running the show than to let the Arabs vote for a real government that might oppose U.S. policies in the region."[28]

Even with repressive regimes the United States does not support, calls for a change in government do not mean the United States is necessarily interested in democracy. For example, despite public announcements of support for democratic change in Iraq, Richard Haas, former Director of Middle East Affairs on the National Security Council, observed, "Our policy is to get rid of Saddam, not his regime."[29]

Despite worldwide trends toward democracy and greater individual freedom throughout the world, the United States has helped perpetuate the rule of absolute monarchs in the Persian Gulf through billions of dollars in military sales and generous arrangements for economic investments. Many Arabs oppose these corrupt royal families to the point that they were not sorry to see the Kuwaiti government temporarily overthrown by Iraqi forces in 1990. Saudi Arabia, meanwhile, has demonstrated outright hostility towards democratic trends in neighboring Yemen—the only republic on the Arabian Peninsula—with no apparent American objections.

In recent years, the United States has rationalized its support for autocratic regimes in the Middle East, North Africa and Central Asia as a regrettable but necessary means of suppressing the Islamic opposition. In many respects, this policy closely parallels the decades of support during the Cold War of repressive right-wing governments in the name of anti-Communism. The result is similar, however: the lack of open political expression only encourages large segments of the oppressed populations to ally with an underground—and often violent and authoritarian—opposition movement. In Islamic countries, that often means extremist Islamic groups. As Hafez Abu Saada, secretary general of the Egyptian Organization for Human Rights said, "Politics is prohibited in this society in general, but the government can't close the mosque."[30] Furthermore, the lack of a free press means that for many Muslims who do not believe the official media, the only alternative source of information comes through the Internet and other anonymous alternative sources, exposing them to extremist propaganda, including conspiracy theories, without any credible countervailing sources of information.

Rather than disliking American democracy, most Middle Easterners are envious of it and are resentful that the American attitude seems to be that they are somehow not deserving of it. The anti-terrorist coalition the United States has built for its military response to the September 2001 attacks—centered around alliances with the absolute monarchy in Saudi Arabia, the military regime of Pakistan and the crypto-Communists that rule Uzbekistan—has been labeled "Operation Enduring Freedom." It's an irony lost on few Middle Easterners.

Supporting Repression in Islamic Countries

Saudi Arabia

One of the many ironies in U.S. Middle East policy is that a nation founded in one of the world's first republican revolutions is now the major backer of the world's few remaining absolute monarchies. For the past twenty years, the United States has been on record that it is willing to use military force to repel not just external aggression against U.S. allies in the Gulf, but internal challenges as well. There is little question that U.S. economic and military support has kept the hereditary rulers of the Middle East in power as despots far longer than a more natural evolution of social change would have otherwise allowed. When U.S.-trained SANG forces crushed an anti-regime uprising in 1981, President Ronald Reagan declared "I will not permit [Saudi Arabia] to be an Iran," referring to the successful uprising that had ousted the U.S.-backed Shah two years earlier.[31]

The most important American ally in the Islamic world is the kingdom of Saudi Arabia, which is run exclusively by a royal family that allows no public dissent or independent press. Those who dare challenge the regime or its policies are punished severely. There is no constitution, no political parties and no legislature. It was under such an environment of repression that bin Laden and most of his followers first emerged.

Support for these family dictatorships has been a prevailing theme of U.S. policy for several decades, a view shared by the British when they were the dominant outside power. According to Harold Macmillan, who served as prime minister in the late 1950s and early 1960s, it is "rather sad that circumstances compel us to support reactionary and really rather outmoded regimes because we know that the new forces, even if they begin with moderate opinions, always seem to drift into violent revolutionary and strongly anti-Western positions."[32] More bluntly, F. Gregory Gause III, a contemporary specialist on Saudi Arabia at the University of Vermont, noted how "The truth is the more democratic the Saudis become, the less cooperative they will be with us. So why should we want that?"[33]

British-based journalist and author Dilip Hiro describes how the United States does not support democracy in the Middle East because "it is much simpler to manipulate a few ruling families—to secure fat orders for arms and ensure that oil price remains low—than a wide variety of personalities and policies bound to be thrown up by a democratic system." In particular, says Hiro, elected governments might reflect the popular sentiment for "self-reliance and Islamic fellowship."[34]

Indeed, to link arms transfers with the human rights records of America's Middle East allies, for example, would lead to the loss of tens of billions of dollars worth of sales for American arms manufacturers, which are among the most powerful special interest groups in Washington. It could also risk the hundreds of billions of dollars that the Saudis have invested in the American economy. With the exception of Israel, none of America's allies in the region could really be considered democracies, yet none require democratic institutions in order to fulfill American strategic objectives. Most observers acknowledge that close strategic cooperation with the United States tends to be unpopular in Arab countries, as are government policies that devote large amounts of public expenditures towards the acquisition of weapons, most of which are of American origin. Were these leaders subjected to the will of the majority, they would likely be forced to greatly reduce arms purchases from and strategic cooperation with the United States. In short, democracy among Middle Eastern countries is seen as potentially damaging to American policy goals.

Uzbekistan and Central Asia

Central Asia offers a particularly ironic twist in U.S. policy. In some cases—such as Uzbekistan, Tajikistan and Turkmenistan—the United States has allied with old-line Communist Party bosses from the Soviet era who are still in power as a means of countering the growth of Islamic movements in those countries. (This contrasts with previous decades, when the United States supported such Islamic movements to counter the Communists.) This comes despite the fact that, in part because of the strong Sufi influence, most Islamic movements in Central Asia—with the notable exception of the Islamic Movement of Uzbekistan (IMU)—are actually fairly progressive and moderate as compared with some of their Middle Eastern and North African counterparts.

In the case of Uzbekistan—the United States' closest ally in the region—the radical orientation of its Islamic opposition is a direct result of the Karimov regime's imprisonment and torture of nonviolent Muslims who dared to worship outside of state controls. Attacks by the dictatorship's armed forces against the IMU have resulted in widespread civilian casualties, not just within Uzbekistan, but also in neighboring Tajikistan and Kyrgyzstan. Amnesty International documented widespread human rights violations during the 2001 counter-insurgency campaign, where "villages were set on fire and bombed, livestock were killed, houses and fields destroyed."[35] However, the U.S. State Department saw the Karimov regime's actions quite differently, declaring "The United States supports the right of Uzbekistan to defend its sovereignty and territorial integrity from the violent actions of the IMU, and commends the measures in the course of the current incursions to minimize casualties and ensure the protection of innocent civilians."[36]

Egypt

The United States has traditionally justified its support for authoritarian regimes on the grounds that the alternatives would be worse: during the Cold War, the fear was from forces of the left and, more recently, it has come from anti-American Islamists. However, the United States is also quite willing to support Middle Eastern governments that suppress liberal democratic movements. A particularly vivid example of this lack of concern for democracy involves Egypt, by far the largest Arab country. In May

2001, the increasing authoritarianism of U.S.-backed dictator Hosni Mubarak was demonstrated in the quick conviction of Dr. Saad El-Din Ibrahim and twenty-seven associates in what was widely seen as a serious blow against Egypt's burgeoning pro-democracy movement. Dr. Ibrahim and his colleagues served with the Ibn Khaldun Center for Developmental Studies, a think tank dedicated to the promotion of civil society in Egypt and throughout the Arab world. In 2000, the Egyptian government shut down this internationally renowned center, known for its study of applied social sciences in Egypt and the Arab world. Its monthly publication, *Civil Society*, had been an important source of information and analysis for scholars across the globe. The Center had also engaged in the monitoring of elections and providing workshops in civic education. For these activities, Dr. Ibrahim was sentenced to a seven-year jail term. The closure of the center and the jailing of its staff was clearly intended to deter other academics from pursuing similar research and related activities, thereby limiting the free exchange of ideas crucial to advancing political pluralism in Egypt and other Arab countries. The convictions were the latest in a series of repressive government measures against other Egyptian scholars, democrats, and human rights activists, as well as gays and feminists. The Ibn Khaldun Center advocated just the kind of liberal democratic values that U.S. foreign policy supposedly upholds, yet there was little reaction from the Bush Administration until August 2002, when it was announced that no additional foreign aid allocations would be considered until his release. This did not affect current foreign aid, however, and no additional allocations were under consideration anyway.

Egypt's corrupt and autocratic government is the second largest recipient of U.S. economic and military assistance in the world, surpassed only by Israel. Concerns by pro-democracy groups in Egypt and human rights organizations in the United States that such aid is only making further repression possible have been rejected by the State Department, which still insists such aid is necessary to "push the peace march forward."[37] As long as the Mubarak regime knows that U.S. aid will flow regardless of its violations of internationally recognized human rights, there is little incentive for political liberalization. The growing anti-American sentiment in Egypt stems not as much from U.S. support for Israel as it does from U.S. support for Mubarak's dictatorial rule.

Turkey

Turkey is another Middle Eastern country where the United States has aided conflict and repression. For over fifty years, the Turkish republic has received large-scale military, economic, and diplomatic support from the United States. It was U.S. support of the pro-Western government of Turkey in the late 1940s—along with its neighbor and historic rival Greece—against perceived Soviet-instigated communist threats that many historians point to as the origins of the Cold War. At NATO's southeastern flank, Turkey's strategic location relative to both the former Soviet Union and the Middle East made that country, after Israel and Egypt, the largest recipient of U.S. foreign aid—primarily military—in recent decades. Direct grants of armaments were phased out only as recently as 1998; arms sales to and ongoing strategic cooperation with Turkey continues.

Turkey has yet to acknowledge its genocide against its Armenian population over eighty years ago in which over one million civilians were slaughtered. In order to appease its Turkish client, the U.S. government has refused to publicly acknowledge that the genocide even took place, despite the widespread historic documentation of the atrocities.

On several occasions the United States has had to intervene diplomatically to prevent war from breaking out between Turkey and Greece, most recently during a 1998 clash over disputed islands in the Aegean Sea. Such a war between two heavily armed and relatively developed nations would not only be a frightening scenario on humanitarian grounds, but could seriously destabilize the entire region. Avoiding such a war between these two U.S. allies has been a major concern of successive U.S. administrations going back several decades. The major flash point has been the island nation of Cyprus, located in the eastern Mediterranean Sea just west of Lebanon, where nearly 80 percent of the population is ethnically Greek. Soon after Cyprus gained independence from Great Britain in 1960, the United States sought to partition the island along ethnic lines, which was strongly opposed by both the Cypriot and Greek governments. In 1967, the United States backed a coup by right-wing Greek army officers—led by the military's CIA liaison Colonel George Papadopoulos—that toppled Greece's democratic government. In turn, the Greek junta backed a coup in 1974 by right-wing ethnic Greeks in Cyprus who sought to unify the country with Greece, a scenario that Turkey feared would threaten the island's ethnic Turk minority. Within days, Turkish troops, armed with American weapons, seized the northern 40 percent of the country and engaged in a campaign of ethnic cleansing against the Greek population. As many as 2000 civilians were killed. The United Nations Security Council condemned the invasion and called for Turkey's immediate withdrawal.[38] However, the United States blocked the imposition of international sanctions to force the Turks to pull out. Congress immediately cut off aid to Turkey in response to the invasion and occupation, but aid was restored three years later after strong pressure from President Jimmy Carter on the grounds that a resumption of aid would make it easier to convince the Turks to withdraw. Decades later, however, Turkish troops remain, still occupying much of the northern part of the country—now declared an independent Turkish Cypriot state but not recognized by any country besides Turkey—and the island remains divided.

The Greek Cypriots are not the only victims of U.S.-backed Turkish armed forces. The fifteen million strong Kurdish minority, located primarily in the eastern part of the country, has suffered enormously under Turkish rule. There have been periods when simply speaking the Kurdish language or celebrating Kurdish festivals has been severely repressed. In addition to being denied basic cultural and political rights, Kurdish civilians have been the primary victims of a Turkish counter-insurgency campaign ostensibly targeted at the Kurdish Workers Party (PKK), a Marxist-led guerrilla group fighting for greater autonomy. The Turkish regime has capitalized on the PKK's use of terrorism as an excuse to crush even nonviolent expressions of Kurdish nationalism. The United States has been largely silent regarding the Turkish government's repression but quite vocal in condemning what it sees as Kurdish terrorism.

The Clinton Administration justified its eleven-week bombing campaign of Yugoslavia in 1999 on the grounds that atrocities such as the Serbian repression of the Kosovar Albanians must not take place "on NATO's doorstep."[39] Ironically, similar ethnic-based repression on an even greater scale had been already taking place for a number of years *within* a NATO country. During the 1980s and 1990s, the United States supplied Turkey with $15 billion worth of armaments as the Turkish military carried out widespread attacks against civilian populations in the largest use of American weapons by non-U.S. forces since Israel's 1982 invasion of Lebanon. Most of this took place during President Bill Clinton's first term. Over 3000 Kurdish villages were destroyed and over two million Kurds became refugees in an operation where more than three-quarters of the weapons were of U.S. origin. The fifteen-year war cost over 40,000 lives. [40]

The Kurds are a nation of more than 25 million people divided among six countries. Their struggle for self-determination has been hampered by the sometimes bitter rivalry between competing nationalist groups, some of which have been used as pawns by competing regional powers. While Iraqi repression against the Kurds has at times received coverage in the U.S. media, the situation for Turkish Kurds during the past decade has been even worse, but has gone relatively unnoticed since the human rights abuses have been committed by a strategic ally of the United States. Human Rights Watch, which has also criticized the PKK rebels for serious human rights violations, has documented how the U.S.-supplied Turkish army was "responsible for the majority of forced evacuations and destruction of villages."[41]

On several occasions, thousands of Turkish troops have crossed into Iraqi territory to attack Kurdish guerrillas and civilians there as well. These incursions have taken place in areas that, since 1991, were declared by the United States to be "safe havens" for the Kurds. These Turkish attacks have been far greater in scope than Saddam Hussein's 1996 forays into Iraqi Kurdistan that resulted in large-scale U.S. air strikes in response. By contrast, when it came time to respond to Turkey's assaults, President Clinton stood out as the only international leader to openly support the Turkish regime. According to then-State Department spokesman Nicholas Burns, "Turkey's an ally. And we have no reason to question the need for an incursion across the border."[42]

The United States provided a major boost for Turkey's fight against the Kurds in 1998 when the Clinton Administration successfully pressured Syria to expel PKK leader Abdullah Ocalan. In February the following year, the United States assisted Turkish intelligence agents in locating Ocalan in Kenya, where he was kidnapped, brought to Turkey and initially sentenced to death. Despite what most observers saw as prejudicial treatment, the Clinton State Department refused to question the fairness of the proceedings. Since then, a cease-fire, a more moderate PKK leadership and a lessening of Turkish repression has given some hope for a peaceful settlement to the conflict, though hundreds of nonviolent Kurdish dissidents remain in jail.

The denial of the degree of Turkish repression has continued under the Bush Administration. In an interview on July 14, 2002 with CNN Turkey, Deputy Secretary of Defense Paul Wolfowitz declared that "one of the things that impresses me about Turkish history [is] the way Turkey treats its minorities."

Such pandering to the Turkish government was rationalized during the Cold War as necessary to back a key ally that bordered the Soviet Union. Today, while this veneer is gone, the policy continues.

Western Sahara

Yet another example where the United States has directly contributed
to violations of human rights and international law is Western Sahara, located along Africa's Atlantic coast on the western extreme of the Arab-Islamic
world. Just prior to the scheduled end of colonial administration in 1976, the
territory—then known as Spanish Sahara—was partitioned between
Morocco and Mauritania. Spain had promised the country independence,
but pressure from Morocco and the United States forced the Spanish government, in the midst of its own delicate transition period to democratic rule,
to back away from its commitment. Instead, in November 1975, the
Spaniards signed the Madrid Accords, which granted Morocco administration of the northern two-thirds of the colony and Mauritania the remainder.
The United States was concerned about the possible leftist orientation of an
independent Western Sahara and that the failure to meet Moroccan territorial demands might result in the overthrow of Morocco's King Hassan II, a
strong American ally who had barely survived two recent coup attempts.

The Polisario Front, the nationalist movement that had until then
been battling Spain for independence, rejected the accords, so Morocco
had to seize the territory by force.[43] The United Nations Security Council
passed a resolution deploring the invasion, calling for the withdrawal of
Moroccan forces and a negotiated settlement. However, as a result of
French and American objections, no enforcement mechanisms, such as
economic sanctions, were included.

Morocco's invasion, which included widespread attacks on civilians,
forced the majority of the population into exile in a desert region of neighboring Algeria. Nearly 170,000 Sahrawis now live in a series of refugee
camps southeast of Tindouf where they have been granted effective autonomy by the Algerian government. The Polisario, meanwhile, continued
their fight for independence, battling both Moroccan and Mauritanian
occupation forces. In 1976, the Polisario Front proclaimed the creation of
the Sahrawi Arab Democratic Republic (SADR), commonly known as
Western Sahara. Over 75 nations have since recognized Western Sahara as
an independent state, and the Organization of African Unity, the United
Nations General Assembly, and the World Court have all called on
Morocco to respect the Sahrawis' right to self-determination. In 1980,
Mauritania signed a peace treaty with the Polisario and renounced sovereignty over its share of Western Sahara, but Morocco simply annexed the
Mauritanian segment as well. In subsequent years, Morocco has sent tens
of thousands of Moroccan settlers into the territory, in direct violation of

the Fourth Geneva Convention, which forbids the transfer of civilian population onto territories seized by military force.[44] The remaining Sahrawis are now a minority in their own country and are subjected to severe repression for openly opposing the Moroccan occupation. Long considered an important Western ally and a bulwark against Communism, France and the United States came to Morocco's assistance. Under the Reagan Administration, the already substantial U.S. support for the Moroccan war effort launched under President Carter was greatly expanded to include direct assistance in counter-insurgency operations and dramatic increases in military aid, efforts that effectively reversed the tide of the war in Morocco's favor. Part of Morocco's military successes was the construction—with U.S. assistance—of a heavily-fortified sand wall that eventually reached 1500 miles long, designed to prevent Polisario penetration into Moroccan-occupied territory. The wall led to a war of attrition. The conflict resulted in more than 10,000 deaths prior to a cease-fire going into effect in 1991.

A peace plan agreed to that year between Morocco and the Polisario, and endorsed by the UN Security Council, called for a referendum that would give the Sahrawis the choice of independence or incorporation into Morocco. Refugees were to be repatriated to take part in the voting along with Sahrawis still living in the territory. The roster of eligible voters was to have been based on a 1974 Spanish census. Most observers predicted a solid vote in favor of independence.

However, the referendum has been delayed repeatedly due to Moroccan insistence on greatly expanding the eligible electorate to include large numbers of Moroccans. Meanwhile, Moroccan occupation forces have continued their suppression of pro-independence activists, interference with UN peacekeeping forces, violations of the cease-fire, and widespread fraud and intimidation during the voter identification process. According to the Los Angeles Times, "The problems have been exacerbated by the evident unwillingness of the United States to put much pressure on King Hassan."[45] Given that the status quo appeared to be in their favor, the Moroccans had no apparent reason not to simply delay the process at every turn. While it would have been politically problematic to pull out of the process, they clearly hoped that by continually prolonging it, the United Nations would give up on an interminable process which was costing the world body a lot of money and resources and was simultaneously wearing down the Polisario.

This strategy appears to be working. Even under the rule of Hassan's more liberal-minded successor Mohammed VI, Morocco seems determined to continue its occupation and colonization of Western Sahara. The United States is supporting an effort that would cancel the referendum and grant the Sahrawis limited autonomy under Moroccan rule for a five-year period based on a formula that would likely lead to the country's complete absorption into the highly-centralized kingdom within five years. As a result, the Polisario is threatening to return to war and serious human rights abuses in the occupied Western Sahara continue.

Supplying Repression from Israel

Israel has by far the strongest democratic institutions of any country in the Middle East. Unfortunately, such respect for individual freedom and human rights is largely restricted to areas within its internationally recognized borders and primarily to its Jewish citizens. Indeed, Israeli occupation forces in the Palestinian-populated West Bank and Gaza Strip are perpetrating some of the worst human rights violations taking place in the Middle East today. As an important American ally, however, criticism of U.S. support for Israeli repression is extremely difficult within mainstream political discourse in the United States.

However, U.S. support for Israel in the face of its poor human rights record is a major source of anti-American sentiment throughout the Arab and Islamic world. Human rights violations by the Israeli government have traditionally upset Muslims more than comparable or even worse human rights violations by Islamic governments. This comes in part because many Muslims see Israel as a colonial-settler state created in the interests of Western imperialism. There is also concern over the religious significance of Jerusalem, the third holiest city in Islam, being under what they view as a foreign occupation. The economic and political burdens from the Palestinian Diaspora on other Arab countries, combined with anger over the trauma from exile and the oppression of occupation experienced by the Palestinians, has made this perhaps the single most important issue in international politics for most of the world's Muslims. Added to this is the tendency for some Muslim governments, particularly in the Arab world, to use the plight of the Palestinians as a means to distract their populations from domestic concerns.

Many United Nations reports and resolutions critical of Israeli human rights violations, while in the most part valid, have lacked credibility because these efforts were supported by some of the world's most tyrannical states.[46] Even in the United States, some groups that raise concerns about Israeli human rights violations have been noted for their failure to also criticize Arab regimes that violate human rights. Such organizations may sometimes attract followers who do not uphold a universal concern for human rights, but carry a hidden—and sometimes not-so-hidden—anti-Israel or even anti-Semitic agenda.

As a result, many Americans sympathetic with Israel are concerned that making even legitimate criticisms of Israel's human rights record may in some ways encourage anti-Semitism or lead to accusations of harboring such motivations. When a number of peace and human rights organizations, politicians, and academics with a strong universal commitment to democracy and human rights have raised the issue of human rights violations by Israel or the subject of democratic rights for Palestinians, they have been subjected to unfair denunciation.[47] As a result, critics of Israel's human rights record and of U.S. complicity in Israeli repression in the occupied territories are even more on the margins of political discourse than are those who criticize U.S. support of its repressive Arab allies. In addition, because Israel's leadership has publicly endorsed Western values regarding democracy and human rights and has created exemplary democratic institutions for its Jewish citizens that surpass any other Middle Eastern country, it is hard for many Americans to understand why the human rights policies of a democracy in a region dominated by dictatorships should be challenged. Furthermore, while there are certainly widespread Israeli violations of the Universal Declaration of Human Rights against Arab populations under their control, Israel's most egregious violations of human rights generally fall under the Geneva Convention, which is less likely to be cited by those raising issues of human rights.

Soon after fighting broke out between Palestinians and Israeli occupation forces in the fall of 2000, Human Rights Watch—while critical of the Palestinians on several counts—emphasized, "Israeli security forces have committed by far the most serious and systematic violations." Furthermore, Human Rights Watch documented "excessive and indiscriminate use of lethal force, arbitrary killings, and collective punishment, including willful destruction of property and severe restrictions on movement that far exceed any possible military necessity." Subsequent reports have documented the destruction of hundreds of Palestinian homes and other property, including thousands of olive trees. These reports have also criticized the Israeli government for failing to protect unarmed Palestinians from attacks by right-wing Jewish settlers squatting on Palestinian land,[48] many of whom are American émigrés. Similar reports have been issued from Amnesty International, the Palestinian human rights group Al-Huq and the Israeli human rights group B'tselem.

The U.S. position regarding these ongoing human rights violations is revealing. In the early months of the Palestinian uprising, then-Secretary of State Madeleine Albright claimed that Israeli occupation forces were simply defending themselves and that the young Palestinians throwing rocks at them had placed Israel "under siege."[49] As concerns by human rights groups on the situation in the Israeli-occupied territories has increased, both houses of Congress have backed a series of bipartisan resolutions that have defended Israeli policies and placed the blame for the violence exclusively on the Palestinians.

Calls grew—from the Palestinians, Islamic countries, the Europeans and others—for the UN Security Council to send an international peacekeeping force to the occupied territories to separate the sides and put an end to the violence. Public opinion polls showed a majority of Israelis in support of such an idea,[50] but the United States made clear it would veto any such effort. As an alternative, Human Rights Watch—echoing similar calls by Amnesty International, the UN Human Rights Commission, and other human rights groups—called on the UN Security Council to "immediately establish a permanent international presence in the West Bank and Gaza to monitor and report regularly on the compliance by all parties with international human rights and humanitarian law standards."[51] However, the same week the Human Rights Watch report containing the recommendation was released, the United States cast the lone dissenting vote in the Security Council authorizing the establishment of just such an unarmed human rights monitoring group, thereby vetoing the measure.

In October 2000, just weeks after the Palestinian uprising began, the Clinton Administration approved the largest sale of military helicopters in the past decade to Israel. Similar helicopters had been used in some of the worst Israeli atrocities of the preceding weeks, including an attack just the day before against an apartment complex in Gaza. A Pentagon official was quoted as saying that U.S. weapons sales do not carry a stipulation that the weapons cannot be used against civilians and that the United States would not second guess an Israeli commander who orders such attacks.[52] An October 19, 2000 report from Amnesty International criticized the United States for providing these new military helicopters.[53] The following week, after a series of scathing human rights reports from reputable non-governmental organizations criticizing Israeli actions, Congress approved a foreign aid allocation of $2.82 billion to Israel, which critics charged was essentially rewarding the government for its repression. Not a single amendment was offered to make the aid conditional on Israel ceasing its human rights abuses. Furthermore, as an apparent rejoinder to Amnesty International and other human rights groups, the House of Representatives passed a resolution by a vote of 365-30 expressing its "solidarity with the state and people of Israel at this time of crisis." The resolution resolved that the House "condemns the Palestinian leadership for encouraging the violence and doing so little for so long to stop it."[54] No solidarity with the Palestinians then under attack or criticisms of Israeli violence was forthcoming.

Since the right-wing Prime Minister Ariel Sharon came to power in February 2001, Israeli human rights abuses have increased further. The Israeli government has dispatched assassination squads, ranging from individuals with rifles to U.S.-supplied helicopter gun ships with missiles, to kill Palestinian activists. Some of these Palestinians have been wanted terrorists associated with radical Islamic groups responsible for the murder of Israeli civilians. Others have been civilian political leaders of Islamic organizations, members of left-wing groups, activists in the ruling Fatah party, and still others were targeted for no apparent reason. One target was a teacher at a Catholic school who had been working closely with Israeli teachers on developing a joint conflict resolution curriculum.[55] There have also been a number of innocent bystanders killed as well. Princeton international law professor Richard Falk, an American Jew who served on a fact finding commission dispatched to the occupied territories at the behest of the United Nations General Assembly during the winter of 2001, expressed concerns over Israel's "seemingly random hit list." The commission noted that such assassinations "are grave breaches of the Fourth Geneva Convention, Article 147, and of international humanitarian law." [56] Some Bush Administration officials have criticized the assassination squads, though Vice-President Dick Cheney, in an interview in the summer of 2001, appeared to be supportive of the practice, arguing that "in some cases, I suppose…it is justified."[57] Senator Joseph Biden, chairman of the Senate Foreign Relations Committee, has openly defended the Israeli use of these extra-judicial killings. Biden, the Democratic Party's chief foreign policy spokesman, argued "I don't believe this is a policy of assassinations" since "this is in effect a declared war…by an organization that decided that it is going to do all it can to damage civilians and others within Israel."[58] Senator Charles Schumer and other leading Democrats have also voiced their support of what amounts to the utilization of death squads by the Israeli government.

The United States takes a very different attitude, however, if Palestinians assassinate Israelis. For example, on August 27, 2001, Israeli occupation forces—using a U.S.-supplied helicopter gunship and missiles—assassinated Abu Ali Mustafa, head of the far-left Popular Front for the Liberation of Palestine in his office in Ramallah. Seven weeks later, four PFLP militants assassinated Rehavam Zeevi, head of the far-right Moledet Party—who had been serving as Israeli Tourism Minister—in retaliation. Regarding Mustafa's murder, the State Department issued only a mild statement reiterating its opposition to Israel's assassination policy. By contrast, President Bush personally condemned Zeevi's murder, criticized the Palestinian Authority's handling of the situation and demanded that the assassins be punished. He furthermore expressed his understanding for Israel's six-week siege of Palestinian President Yasir Arafat's offices in Ramallah in the spring of 2002 on the grounds that the PFLP suspects had sought refuge there. Referring to the "Zeevi Five," Bush noted how "these people are accused of killing a cabinet official of the Israel government. I can understand why the prime minister wants them brought to justice." He added, "They should be brought to justice if they killed this man in cold blood."[59] Arafat finally agreed to have the PFLP assassins—along with the PFLP leader Ahmed Saadat—jailed in return for the Israelis lifting the siege of his Ramallah office, convicting them in a quick secret trial in his compound while surrounded by Israeli tanks. While refusing to bring in American forces to the West Bank to try to separate the sides and end the violence, President Bush did deploy American servicemen to help guard the prisoners. By contrast, there were no American demands to bring to justice the Israelis responsible for Mustafa's assassination. Similarly, there was no U.S. criticism of the 1988 Israeli assassination of a member of Arafat's cabinet, Defense Minister Khalid al-Wazir in Tunisia, much less a demand that those responsible for his murder be brought to justice. (An investigation by the Israeli newspaper *Maariv* revealed that the leader of the seaborne command center that oversaw al-Wazir's murder was Israel's then-deputy military chief Ehud Barak, who would later become Israeli prime minister.)[60]

As the uprising continued, the Palestinian resistance escalated to include armed attacks by Palestinian militiamen against Israeli occupation forces and settlers as well as terrorist attacks by extremist Islamic groups against Israeli settlers and against civilians inside Israel. Israeli repression increased as well, including killings of scores of Palestinian paramedics and other medical workers seeking to rescue the wounded in riots where the

Israelis had responded with lethal force. In December 2001, the United States vetoed a UN Security Council resolution strongly condemning Palestinian terrorism because it also criticized Israeli policies of assassinating Palestinian dissidents and imposing collective punishment against civilian populations. The United States was the only dissenter within the 15-member world body.

Violence on both sides escalated still further in 2002, including Israeli incursions into Palestinian urban areas and an increase in suicide bombings inside Israel. Following a particularly deadly series of Palestinian terrorist attacks in late March 2002, there was a dramatic escalation of Israeli repression, as the Israeli Defense Forces (IDF) attacked most major Palestinian urban areas in the West Bank, including refugee camps. The Bush Administration largely supported the Israeli offensive, even as hundreds of civilians were killed and thousands of young men were detained without charge amid widespread reports of torture. According to Amnesty International,

> ...the IDF acted as though the main aim was to punish all Palestinians. Actions were taken by the IDF which had no clear or obvious military necessity; many of these, such as unlawful killings, destruction of property and arbitrary detention, torture and ill-treatment, violated international human rights and humanitarian law. The IDF instituted a strict curfew and killed and wounded armed Palestinians. But they also killed and targeted medical personnel and journalists, and fired randomly at houses and people in the streets. Mass arbitrary arrests were carried out in a manner designed to degrade those detained.[61]

However, the U.S. House of Representatives categorically rejected Amnesty International's findings. On May 2, by a vote of 352-21, they declared that "Israel's military operations are an effort to defend itself...and are aimed only at dismantling the terrorist infrastructure in the Palestinian areas."[62] This was widely interpreted as an attack against the credibility of Amnesty International, winner of the 1977 Nobel Peace Prize. In an apparent retort to growing demands by peace and human rights groups to suspend military aid to Israel, the resolution called for an *increase* in military aid, which many of these activists felt was, in effect, rewarding Israel for its repression.

That same day, the U.S. Senate, in a 94-2 vote, passed a similar resolution, again referring to the Israeli assault on Palestinian towns and refugee camps as "necessary steps to provide security to its people by dismantling the terrorist infrastructure in the Palestinian areas."[63] Both resolutions stressed their support for Israel's military offensive in the West Bank.

According to a joint statement by Senators Diane Feinstein and Mitch McConnell, co-sponsors of an amendment which would block Palestinian officials from entering the United States and other steps to keep the Palestinian Authority out of the peace process, "Israel has done no less—and certainly no more—than what any country would do to defend itself....Israel's military operation has been one based on specific intelligence information, with specific military goals—to act directly against terrorists...—and carried out with considerable restraint."[64] This statement, like the resolutions, came after journalists' cameras were finally allowed into the refugee camps and urban areas targeted by the Israeli assaults and the widespread destruction to the civilian infrastructure was apparent even to casual viewers of the evening news. Still, House Minority Leader Dick Gephardt, proclaimed that, in supporting the Israeli government's offensive, "We will stand for freedom."[65]

For Arabs and Muslims throughout the world, these resolutions—passed with such overwhelming bipartisan majorities—and statements by political leaders of both major political parties are indicative of the United States' lack of concern for basic human rights. In fact, it came across to millions of observers in the Arab and Islamic world as an act of racism: the majority of liberal Democrats—most of whom were on record in support of human rights in Guatemala, East Timor, Colombia, Tibet, and elsewhere—had decided, in a situation where the victims of human rights abuses were Arabs, to instead throw their support to the perpetrator of the human rights abuses. In fact, one of the two sponsors of the House resolution was California Democrat Tom Lantos, who is the long-time chairman of the Human Rights Caucus.

The most serious human rights abuses during Israel's spring 2002 offensive were against the Jenin refugee camp, where Israel claimed there were a number of terrorist cells operating. U.S.-supplied Apache helicopters and F-16 fighter jets pounded Jenin for eight days, with Israeli infantry shooting their way into the densely populated camp. The result was a humanitarian disaster, where scores of civilians were killed and Palestinian officials and some international observers alleged that a massacre of hundreds took place. The Israelis did not allow any journalists into the occupied refugee camp for two weeks and even barred ambulances and rescue workers, despite widespread casualties. In addition, Israeli occupation forces barred civilian convoys—including those consisting of Israeli human rights activists—from bringing in water, medications and food.[66]

On his visit to Israel and the West Bank in the immediate aftermath of the assault, Secretary of State Colin Powell asked to view the site of a Palestinian terrorist attack in Jerusalem that killed six Israeli civilians, but refused to go to see Jenin. He did state, however, that while there may have been isolated incidents of killing civilians, no massacre took place in Jenin. (This was virtually the same response that Powell gave in 1968 when, as an Army major, he was asked to investigate charges of a massacre in the Vietnamese hamlet of My Lai. His cover-up succeeded for more than a year until a soldier from the unit wrote a letter to a Congressman revealing, as confirmed by a subsequent investigation, that American forces had murdered as many as 500 civilians, including women, children and elderly people.)[67]

In response to demands by human rights organizations that the UN dispatch a team to investigate the alleged massacre, some Muslim states drew up a resolution in the Security Council to organize such an inquiry. U.S. ambassador to the United Nations John Negroponte threatened to veto the proposed investigation, however, arguing that the Bush Administration did not believe it should be done through a Security Council resolution.[68] However, Israeli Foreign Minister Shimon Peres stated that Israel would actually accept such an investigation if the language of the resolution was toned down. Not wanting to appear to take a more obstructionist position than the Israelis, the Bush Administration reversed its position and drew up its own resolution calling for an investigation, which passed the Security Council unanimously on April 19. Secretary General Kofi Annan appointed a prestigious team headed by former Finnish president Martti Ahtisaari and including an impressive team of international civil servants with expertise ranging from human rights to forensic science and included William Nash, a retired U.S. Army Major General, as their military advisor.

Israel objected to the makeup of the commission, however, and refused to allow them to investigate unless more military and counter-terrorism experts were included. In response, the Secretary General added four additional military and police experts and three additional forensics experts. Israeli officials then raised at least a half dozen new conditions, including demands that the mission also investigate Palestinian terrorism, that Israel control submission of documents and testimony to the commission, that it have the power to review and comment on Palestinian testimony, that soldiers and officials be guaranteed immunity from any future prosecution, and that the team not make any public "observations" or "conclusions." Traditionally, the United Nations has not allowed countries subjected to such investigations to change the makeup of the mission of such investigative teams. In fact, the United States has responded to similar objections to the makeup and mission of UN inspection teams by the government of Iraq by bombing that country. However, on April 29, the United States promised the Israelis that it would support their refusal to allow the UN team to investigate. U.S. National Security Advisor Condoleeza Rice conveyed to Prime Minister Sharon a personal message from President Bush that the United States "will be with you the entire way."[69] This may be the first time that a sponsor of a UN Security Council resolution ended up blocking its implementation within a matter of days.

On May 7, the UN General Assembly voted on a resolution condemning Israel for its assaults against Palestinian civilians, particularly in the Jenin refugee camp, and for its refusal to cooperate with a fact-finding team initiated by Secretary-General Kofi Annan. In addition, the resolution emphasized the importance of civilian safety and well-being throughout the Middle East and condemned all acts of violence and terror resulting in deaths and injuries among Palestinian and Israeli civilians. The United States was one of only four countries in the 189-member body voting in opposition. (In addition to Israel, the only others voting "no" were the tiny island states of Micronesia and the Marshall Islands, both former trust territories of the United States heavily dependent on U.S. foreign aid.) This came despite a public opinion poll that week that showed that more than three-quarters of the American public believed Israel should allow the United Nations to investigate.[70]

During Israel's April 2002 offensive, UN High Commissioner for Refugees Mary Robinson reiterated her call for an end of the suicide bombings as well as an end to the occupation. She particularly criticized the Israelis for placing 600,000 Palestinians under a strict curfew for most of the month and the destruction of Palestinian medical, religious and service institutions in contravention of international law, as well as the use of Palestinian civilians as human shields. Robinson, a former president of Ireland, had been one of the most visible and effective commissioners in the history of the UN's Human Rights Commission. In response to her criticisms of America's most important Middle East ally, however, the United States—which has veto power over the re-appointment of top UN officials—forced her to step down at the end of her term.

For the past decade, the United States has claimed that the Geneva Convention pertaining to conduct by occupying powers does not apply to

Israel. For example, in a UN General Assembly vote in December 2001 reaffirming the applicability of the Geneva Convention to the Israeli-occupied territories supported by 165 countries, the United States—along with Israel, Micronesia and the Marshall Islands—were the only "no" votes cast. In addition, the United States has backed Israel's refusal to allow investigators from the UN Commission for Human Rights to investigate the human rights situation in the occupied territories. The United States also boycotted the meeting of the Fourth Geneva Convention that month at which Israel was reprimanded by 114 states—including Great Britain and other EU nations—for its "grave breaches" of the Geneva Convention, including indiscriminate and disproportionate use of violence against Palestinian civilians, among others.[71]

Over the past thirty-five years, the United States has been one of only three dissenting votes in the General Assembly criticizing Israeli human rights abuses at least six times and one of only two dissenting votes at least eight times. In the Security Council, the United States has been the sole dissenting vote, thereby vetoing resolutions critical of Israeli human rights violations, on at least eighteen occasions.

Understanding "Our Commitment to Freedom"

To those in the Arab and Islamic world, U.S. defense of Israeli repression against their Palestinian brethren is perhaps the most sensitive of a whole series of grievances regarding American callousness towards internationally-recognized human rights in the Middle East. Yet it is the U.S. support of repression by regimes of Islamic countries that Muslims know the best. Morocco and Turkey, like Israel, have utilized American weapons in the occupation and repression of other peoples. Uzbekistan, Saudi Arabia, Egypt and other Islamic countries have suffered under autocratic rule maintained, in varying degrees, through American military, economic and diplomatic support.

In a major White House speech on U.S. policy towards the Israeli-Palestinian conflict in June 2002, President Bush insisted that democratic governance and an end to violence and corruption must be a prerequisite for Palestinian independence. This came across as particularly ironic, given that his administration—as well as previous administrations—has so strongly supported a series of violent, corrupt and autocratic regimes throughout the Middle East and beyond. Millions of people watched the president of the United States demand that the Palestinians create a democratic political system based upon "tolerance and liberty"[72] while at the same time befriending other Middle Eastern governments that are among the most intolerant and autocratic regimes in the world. It was ironic that President Bush specifically criticized the Palestinian Authority's lack of a fair judicial system. It was the same infamous State Security Court he criticized, which has carried out some of the worst human rights abuses, that was established with strong U.S. support and was once praised by Vice President Al Gore when he visited Jericho in 1994.[73]

Until the extent of the repression and the American complicity in the repression is recognized, it will be difficult to understand the negative sentiments a growing number of ordinary people in the Islamic world have towards the United States. Therefore, self-righteous claims by American leaders that the anger expressed by Arabs and Muslims towards the United States is because of "our commitment to freedom"[74] only exacerbates feelings of ill-will and feeds the rage manifested in anti-American violence and terrorism.

Chapter Two

The Militarization of the Middle East

As the Cold War began to thaw in the late 1980s, Georgi Arbatov, long-time Director of the Soviet Union's Institute for the Study of the USA and Canada, promised, "We are going to do something terrible to you—we are going to deprive you of an enemy."[1] However, he clearly underestimated the ability of successive U.S. administrations to find new enemies. The principal targets of American antipathy in recent years have been Middle Eastern: Libya's Muammar Qaddafi and Iran's Ruhollah Khomeini in the 1980s and Iraq's Saddam Hussein and the international terrorist Osama bin Laden subsequently. In many respects they have been ideal enemies: they are presented as the personification of evil, the prototype of the irrational Third World megalomaniac needing to be vanquished by the civilized forces of world order. Typical of this perspective was the speech that President George W. Bush gave before the United Nations General Assembly two months after the September 11 terrorist attacks. He declared that the U.S.-led war against terrorism was nothing less than a choice between "the dignity of life over a culture of death," of "lawful change and civil disagreement over coercion, subversion and chaos," and he predicted ultimate success with "courage defeating cruelty and light overcoming darkness."[2]

This world view has been put forward by successive generations of American intellectuals who have built upon the theme of seventeenth century Puritan leader John Winthrop that the United States is the "city on the hill,"[3] bringing enlightenment, civilization and the rule of law to the world, serving as a beacon of progress. This self-perception closely parallels themes from the old Westerns of the man in the white hat riding into town to vanquish the bad guys, using violence in an appropriate manner in order to bring stability, order and justice.

During the Cold War, the United States' targets were often popular national liberation struggles with which at least some progressive segments of the American population could express qualified support. These new enemies of the post-Cold War era, by contrast, have tended to be tyrants and thugs, despised by the left as much as by the right. In this context, it is easy for many Americans to fall into a smug self-righteousness, often bordering on racism, towards these dark-skinned foes. When the enemy is undeniably a terrorist or a despot, the American self-perception is not that of imperialists but as liberators of oppressed peoples. The killing of thousands of innocent civilians and unwilling conscripts in the process of battling such foes is neatly camouflaged by talk of "smart bombs" and valiant efforts to avoid such "collateral damage."

The demonization of these Middle Eastern figures has been utilized in large part to deflect attention away from the enormous harm done to a country's population resulting from war and economic sanctions. The suffering of 22 million Iraqis from the destruction of the country's civilian infrastructure during the Gulf War and the subsequent sanctions is given far less attention by U.S. policy makers or the news media than the oppressive and violent actions of a vicious dictator. The deaths of thousands of Afghan civilians from American bombs and the resulting refugee flow in the onset of winter was given far less attention than the hunt for a single Saudi exile hiding in the mountains. The nefarious nature of such leaders makes them tempting targets for self-righteous anger, thereby making it easy to ignore the fact that wars and sanctions allegedly targeted against these individuals are in fact directed against entire nations.

Pursuing such policies requires the support or acquiescence of the American public, who has historically been skeptical of foreign military entanglements and has expressed a strong preference for peace. For countless years, militarists have justified going to war and spending their countries' resources on armaments in the name of peace. World War I was defended as "the war to end all wars." The Vietnam War was rationalized as a means to bring the country "a generation of peace."[4] The MX missile, a dangerous first-strike weapon now banned by international treaty, was labeled "the Peacekeeper."[5] The Reagan Administration's massive nuclear arms buildup was justified as providing "peace through strength." Today, the U.S. government continues to send billions of dollars worth of military aid every year to the Middle East—already the most heavily militarized region in the world—"in support of regional stability and a comprehensive peace between Israel and its neighbors."[6] These rationalizations are not that far off from the maxim in George Orwell's famous novel, 1984, that "war is peace." [7]

Such militarization in the name of defending freedom ignores a crucial historic fact: In recent decades, the vast majority of dictatorial regimes that have been overthrown came not as a result of foreign military intervention or armed revolution, but from massive nonviolent resistance by ordinary citizens demanding their freedom. Every society requires the obedience or acquiescence of its citizens to function. If that is systematically withdrawn and challenged through protests and the establishment of parallel institutions, the regimes will either be forced into significant reforms or they will fall. This is how Communism fell in Eastern Europe and how dictatorships were toppled in such diverse countries as the Philippines, Bolivia, Malawi, and Serbia. Virtually all of these democratic revolutions have resulted in demilitarization and a decline in regional tensions.[8] The Islamic world has seen a disproportionate number of successful unarmed insurrections in recent decades, including Bangladesh, Indonesia and Mali.[9] Despite the return of authoritarian rule, massive nonviolent resistance also toppled such dictatorships as the Shah of Iran (1979), the Nimieri regime in Sudan (1985), and Zia al-Huq's regime in Pakistan (1988.) As far back as the 1920s, Khan Abdul Ghaffar Khan led the tribesmen of colonial India's Northwest Frontier in a nonviolent resistance campaign against British colonialism through a group called Khudai Khidmatgar, or "Servants of God." Their successes led Mahatma Gandhi to recognize them as his most effective and disciplined "nonviolent soldiers."[10] Khan and his followers were Pushtuns, who are the largest ethnic group in Afghanistan.

Not only are Americans quick to believe violent stereotypes of Muslims and others in the Third World, there is also a propensity to ignore the many ways the United States has made the nonviolent resolution of conflicts more difficult. What many Americans seem to forget, but most people in the Middle East and elsewhere know all too well, is this: the United States and its allies in the "war on terrorism" manufacture and sell the vast majority of the world's weapons and possess virtually all of the world's weapons of mass destruction. Either directly or through allied regimes to which they provide weaponry and financial support, these "civilized" Western powers are responsible for most of the major human rights violations and war crimes of recent decades. As a result, the idea that America's anti-terrorism campaign is a simple struggle between good and evil is very difficult for many Muslims and others in the Third World to appreciate.

Fueling the Arab-Israeli Arms Race

Peace agreements between antagonists have historically promoted varying degrees of demilitarization. A reduced threat of war normally results in lower levels of military spending and arms procurement. However, in the case of U.S.-brokered agreements between Israel and its neighbors, it has resulted in just the opposite. Consider the following:

- The 1978 Camp David agreement between Israel and Egypt, heralded as a breakthrough peace treaty, was actually more of a tripartite military pact. Its provisions included more than five billion dollars in military and economic aid to the two signatories. It was originally designed as a one-time payback to the two parties for agreeing to sign the accords. However, each year since, the United States has continued allocating this sizable military and economic assistance package to the Israeli and Egyptian governments. Since 1978, Egypt has received approximately $1.2 billion annually in military assistance, while Israel has gotten at least $1.8 billion annually.

- Following the 1996 peace agreement between Israel and Jordan, the United States sent an additional $200 million to Israel and an additional $75 million to Jordan, as well as training and support for modernizing the Jordanian armed forces that had been cut off five years earlier. This apparently helped persuade the Arab monarchy, which had resisted signing a separate peace agreement with Israel without further resolution to the Israeli-Palestinian conflict, to agree to the U.S.-brokered deal.[11]

- In a supplemental foreign aid package passed by Congress following the signing of the 1998 Wye River redeployment agreement between Israel and the Palestinian Authority, the United States sent $1.2 billion in additional military aid to Israel. This came in addition to the $1.8 billion already earmarked in military assistance to that government that year. Even top Israeli military officials privately acknowledged that there was no justification for such massive amounts of aid for such a minor redeployment, which consisted of less than 14% of the West Bank, particularly since most of the aid project was earmarked for strategic weapons. The arms package included an additional $200 million worth of armaments to Jordan, even though Jordan was not even a party to the agreement.[12]

The trend in U.S. aid to Israel over the past twenty-five years raises some interesting questions in light of Israel's security situation then and now. During most of the 1970s, Israel was faced with the following: Egypt's massive and well-equipped armed forces threatened war. Syria's military was expanding rapidly with advanced Soviet weaponry. Jordan still claimed the West Bank and stationed large numbers of troops along its lengthy border and demarcation line with Israel. Iraq was embarking upon its vast program of militarization.

Today, Israel's security position is markedly improved. Israel has a longstanding peace treaty with Egypt and a large demilitarized and internationally monitored buffer zone keeping this once formidable foe's army at a distance. A gradually demilitarizing Syria has been weakened by the collapse of its Soviet patron and is now willing to live in peace with Israel in return for the occupied Golan Heights, Syrian territory seized by Israel in 1967. Jordan has signed a peace treaty with fully normalized relations. Iraq's armed forces were devastated during the Gulf War and remain crippled under strict international sanctions.

Yet United States military aid to Israel is much higher than it was during the 1970s, either remaining steady or actually increasing each year since. Even more striking, the United States sent essentially no military aid to Israel prior to 1967, when the country was most vulnerable strategically. Virtually all U.S. military aid sent to Israel came only after its quick and decisive victory in the Six Day War that June when it proved itself to be more powerful than any combination of Arab armies.

The U.S. government and leaders of both American political parties have consistently argued that aid to Israel should either be increased or kept at current levels. Yet if the real concern for such military assistance is to provide adequate support for Israel's defense, why are they not calling instead for providing sufficient aid levels to maintain Israel's security needs, which presumably would have declined as the peace process with neighboring countries moved forward and Soviet military assistance to hostile Arab regimes dried up? Is there something other than a commitment to meeting Israel's legitimate defense needs that drives this relentless militarization?

Matti Peled, the late Israeli major general and Knesset member, noted in the early 1990s that, as far as he could tell, the $1.8 billion figure for annual American military support was arrived at "out of thin air."[13] He noted that this was far more than Israel needed to replenish stocks, was not apparently related directly to any specific security requirements, and had remained relatively constant in the preceding years. He argued that he and other Israeli military leaders saw the aid package as little more than a U.S. government subsidy for American arms manufacturers. For example, during this period the United States was helping Israel develop a sophisticated anti-missile defense system. The project was far more complicated and costly than it needed to be because the United States insisted that it be a mobile system, even though Israel—a small country—recognized that a simpler and less expensive fixed system would adequately meet their needs.

This benefit to American defense contractors is multiplied by the fact that every major arms transfer to Israel creates a new demand by Arab states—most of which can pay in hard currency from oil exports—for additional American weapons to respond to Israel. In a telling incident that suggests Peled had accurately captured the dynamics of the situation, Israel announced in 1991 its acceptance of a proposal by arms control advocates that would freeze arms exports to the Middle East. For Israel, this made sense from the point of view of its defense needs: given its significant qualitative superiority in weapons and having the only major domestic arms production capability in the region that could expand its dominance still further, the proposal was to its advantage. However, the United States, the very country most adamantly claiming its concern for Israel's defense, effectively blocked the proposal.

In late 1993, a bipartisan group of 78 senators wrote President Clinton insisting that U.S. military aid to Israel must be maintained despite significant advances in the peace process. They justified it on the grounds of massive arms procurement by Arab states, neglecting to note that 80% of those arms transfers to those Arab regimes were also from the United States. Were these senators, who represented more than three-quarters of the upper house of Congress, really concerned about Israeli security, they would have voted to block these arms transfers to the Gulf monarchies and other Arab regimes. However, it appears that the priority of both the executive branch and Congress in recent decades has not been Israeli security, but maintaining the flow of American arms exports. These distorted American priorities have even influenced the Israelis themselves: for example, Israel did not actively oppose the 1992 sale of 72 highly sophisticated F-15E jet fighters to Saudi Arabia. The reason was simple: in return for Israeli acquiescence, the senior Bush Administration offered yet another increase in U.S. arms transfers to Israel.[14]

Militarization serves interests beyond those of arms manufacturers who benefit from U.S.-funded military aid to Israel, Egypt and Jordan and

U.S.-subsidized arms sales to the wealthy Arab monarchies of the Gulf. Israel, conservative Arab states, and the United States all share an interest in curbing radical nationalist and Islamic movements and preserving the regional status quo—by military force if deemed necessary. In addition, for the Israelis, Arab militarism serves as an excuse for continued repression in the occupied territories and resistance to demands for territorial compromise since it can buttress their claim that a buffer zone is required to protect themselves against powerful Arab armies. For autocratic Arab leaders, the perceived threat from Israeli militarism serves as a pretext for their lack of internal democracy and inability to address badly needed social and economic reforms. (It is noteworthy how until 1993, the United States refused to even talk with representatives of the Palestine Liberation Organization—the de facto government-in-exile for the Palestinians—or include them in the peace process, supposedly due to their hostility towards Israel. Yet, during those decades, the United States was sending billions of dollars' worth of armaments annually to Arab monarchies of the Gulf that took a harder line towards Israel than did the Palestinians)

The resulting arms race has been a bonanza for U.S. arms manufacturers, which may be a major explanation for the inordinate amount of U.S. military aid to Israel. Much attention has been given to the clout of pro-Israel Political Action Committees (PACs) and their alleged role in convincing members of Congress to support these taxpayer-funded arms transfers to Israel. However, contributions by PACs affiliated with military contractors far surpass the pro-Israel PACs. For example, during the 1999-2000 election cycle, just slightly over $2 million in campaign contributions came from the pro-Israel PACs, while PACs affiliated with the arms industry came close to $5 million.[15] This clout is enhanced through the additional inducement of creating jobs and bringing federal dollars into key states and congressional districts.

The Real Costs of Arms Transfers

The significance of U.S. arms transfers to the region becomes apparent in looking at the figures: For Fiscal Year 2003, 72% of U.S. foreign aid allotted to the Middle East was military as opposed to just 28% for economic development. The $3.8 billion in military aid is well over 90% of what the United States gives the entire world.[16] Even more startling is that, on top of this aid, there is the far larger sum of arms purchases, totaling $6.1 billion in 2001, over half of the world's total.[17] The United States gave or sold more arms to the Middle East than all other arms exporters combined, totaling more than $90 billion since the Gulf War.[18] Weapons and their delivery systems are America's number one export to the Middle East, totaling nearly one-third of all exports to the region.[19]

Joe Stork, while serving as director of the Middle East Research and Information Project, argued that the ongoing Middle Eastern arms race continues for three reasons: 1) arms sales are an important component of building political alliances, particularly with the military leadership of recipient countries; 2) there is a strategic benefit coming from interoperability, of having U.S.-manufactured systems on the ground in the event of a direct U.S. military intervention; and, 3) arms sales are a means of supporting military industries faced with declining demand in Western countries.[20]

One revealing episode came in a 1993 off-the-record seminar with Assistant Secretary of State Richard Murphy, top Saudi officials, and the vice-chairman of the board of Morgan Guaranty (a major lender to the Saudi regime), where it was acknowledged that arms transfers had little to do with the objective security needs for the kingdom.[21]

U.S. officials insist that the Saudis alone are responsible for their purchases. Yet underneath this convenient claim of Saudi sovereignty that supposedly absolves the United States of any responsibility in the arms purchases and their deleterious effects lies a practice which can be traced as far back as the 1940s. It is the U.S Defense Department that routinely defines the kingdom's security needs, often providing a far more pessimistic analysis of the country's security situation than more objective strategic analyses. Conveniently, these alleged needs lead directly to purchases of specific U.S. weapons.[22]

As Robert Vitalis, director of the Middle East Center at the University of Pennsylvania, observed,

> If the billions have not been useful to the Saudis, they were a gold mine for Congresspersons compelled to cast pro-Saudi votes, along with cabinet officials and party leaders worried about the economy of key states and electoral districts. To the extent that the regime faces politically destabilizing cutbacks in social spending, a proximate cause is the strong bipartisan push for arms exports to the Gulf as a means to bolster the sagging fortunes of key constituents and regions—the "gun belt"—that represents the domestic face of internationalism.[23]

These military expenditures place a major toll on the fiscal well-being of Middle Eastern countries. For example, the rather stagnant economies of Middle Eastern countries in the past decade can be explained in large part by the enormous militarization following the Gulf War. At that time, the U.S. Arms Control and Disarmament Agency noted how military expenditures for Middle Eastern countries came to 54.8% of combined central government expenditures, a full 20.1% of gross national product. Force ratios—representing the number of people under arms per thousand— stood at 13.5% for the Middle East, nearly twice that of industrialized countries and well over three times that of most Third World countries.[24] Vitalis and other senior observers believe that debt financing in Saudi Arabia to pay for the arms purchases is threatening the kingdom's fragile social pact of distributing oil rents to favored constituents and regions.[25]

A very important factor, often overlooked, is that a number of Middle Eastern states—such as Egypt, Jordan, Tunisia and Morocco, among others—are highly dependent on Saudi Arabia for financial assistance. As Saudi Arabia suffers a financial crisis resulting in large part from its arms acquisitions, it becomes less generous, leading to serious budget shortfalls throughout the Arab world. Furthermore, much of the Saudi aid that remains is being used to finance arms purchases by Egypt and to subsidize Morocco's occupation of Western Sahara.[26] The result is that these arms sales may be causing more instability and threatening these countries' security interests more than they are protecting them.

Even Middle Eastern countries that do not have to buy their American weapons suffer the economic consequences. For example, most of the foreign aid the United States sends to Israel does not go to ordinary Israelis. It returns to U.S. arms manufacturers to produce weapons for the Israeli military and to American banks in the form of interest payments on previous loans for weapons. Meanwhile, in Israel, U.S. arms transfers cost the Israelis two to three times their value in maintenance, spare parts, training of personnel, and related expenses. It drains their economy and further ties them into an economic dependence on the United States. Such additional costs add further to the burden of other Middle Eastern states that purchase arms.

The implications of these ongoing arms purchases are ominous on several levels. For example, one of the most striking but least talked about for the Middle East is the "food deficit," the amount of food produced relative to demand. With continued high military spending—combined with rapid population growth and increased urbanization—the resulting low investments in agriculture have made this deficit the fastest growing in the world. Malnutrition in the Middle East is on the increase and could worsen substantially in the coming years if current trends continue. Ultimately the largest number of civilian casualties, social disorder and resulting anti-American sentiment may result from weapons systems and ordinance that are never actually used in combat.

The End of Security

Whatever the effects of such militarization on the Middle East, U.S. military policy has important implications for security at home. With the end of the Cold War threatening to result in a dramatic reduction in the Pentagon budget, the senior Bush Administration embarked on a "regional strategy" based on the prospect of periodic clashes with emerging Third World powers. The result was the adoption of a military posture, essentially confirmed by the Clinton Administration in its 1993 "bottom-up" review. This strategy rested on the assumption that the United States must maintain enough force to fight two simultaneous major regional wars on the scale of the 1991 Gulf War in response to surprise attacks from middle-level military powers with no allied forces to support the American side. To fight such a war, it is argued, requires standing combat personnel totaling 1.4 million and the air, naval and land-based equipment to support them. While most independent observers see such a scenario as at best extremely unlikely, it has been adopted as the basis for maintaining high levels of military spending since the early 1990s. Assessments since the terrorist attacks and the war against Afghanistan in the fall of 2001 have resulted in plans to expand U.S. military capabilities in the Middle East and beyond even further.

The scenarios of what is needed to maintain U.S. security interests for the current administration and its two predecessors were developed by Pentagon planners who had a vested interest in maintaining a large military establishment despite the end of the Cold War. According to strategic analyst Michael Klare, in his review of the military budget in the mid-1990s,

> To justify this vast expense, the Clinton Administration must be able to demonstrate that the United States is indeed threatened by potent foreign enemies. Hence the periodic alarms in Washington over the military power and aggressive designs of Iraq, Iran, Libya and North Korea. Only when Congress and the American people can be shown an authentic—and sufficiently menacing—threat on the horizon will they be prepared to subsidize indefinitely a cold-war-level military establishment.[27]

It is to control these "rogue states" of the Middle East, along with North Korea, that the United States justifies a military budget of close to $400 billion. This figure is higher, even adjusted for inflation, than the level of military spending during most of the Cold War, including the final military budgets of such Republican presidents as Dwight Eisenhower,

Richard Nixon and Gerald Ford. This is the basis of why, when faced with unprecedented needs for domestic spending, Americans are warned of an imminent threat from an "axis of evil" emanating from what in reality are isolated Third World countries struggling to meet the most basic needs of their own populations.

There is a tendency to define security in terms of a given country's strengths and interests. With the United States as the world's dominant political, economic and military power, it is not surprising that security has been defined in ways that promote America's perceived interests. This comes in spite of evidence that such an assessment may be at odds with the interests of the countries of the region itself, including the United States' ostensible allies. There is also a broader general phenomenon—certainly not unique to the United States—to define security principally in terms of military hardware. From the American perspective, if it is U.S. military hardware, all the better. While the economic imperatives promoting the arms trade are probably not the primary motivator of U.S. policy in the Middle East, the political and economic power of American arms exporters does make it difficult to challenge these assumptions. Indeed, it is rather striking how arms transfers to the Middle East have taken place without any consistent strategy or basic mission priorities and with little regard for coalition warfare.[28]

Yet, the current situation may be untenable. For example, regarding the Persian Gulf, the stronger the U.S. military presence and the stronger the American strategic ties are with the six Arab monarchies of the Gulf Cooperation Council (GCC), the more likely Iran and Iraq will feel threatened. Hard-line elements in Iraq and Iran will point to these ties to depict GCC countries as puppets of American imperialism. Ongoing close strategic cooperation between the United States and the GCC provokes both a genuine fear and a convenient excuse by Iran and Iraq to continue their own quests for further militarization and discourages these potentially hostile regimes from pursuing mutual security agreements and a de-escalation of tensions.

The blame does not rest exclusively with the United States. Great Britain and France, among others, are very much involved in promoting the regional arms race through major arms sales to Arab states, particularly those of the GCC. More importantly, there are élites within these countries who support such large-scale arms transfers for their own reasons, including career-enhancement, ideological precepts and/or personal financial gain. A U.S. policy that colludes with and encourages such tendencies does not enhance the genuine security interests of any nation. Meanwhile, there are also political leaders within such countries as Iraq, Iran, Syria and Libya who are quite willing to draw upon their regimes' revolutionary heritage to promote militarism, nationalism and hostility to foreign powers in response to a perceived American military threat.

The more weapons and the more sophisticated weaponry the United States has sent to the region, the more threatened the United States and its interests have become. History has shown, most clearly in the case of the Shah's Iran, that unrestricted military and diplomatic support of unpopular and corrupt governments creates a situation where the opposition links the abuses of the regime with its chief foreign supporter, such as the United States. Such resentment is likely to remain if and when such opposition groups come to power. These hostile successor regimes would also find themselves in possession of vast quantities of American arms sent to the previous allied government that could eventually be used against American soldiers or civilians. Such a scenario may now be unfolding in Saudi Arabia, in the other Gulf monarchies, in Tunisia, in Egypt and in Morocco, where unconditional U.S. support for autocratic rulers is creating enormous resentment amidst increasingly radicalized opposition forces. For example, a secret CIA memo circulated at the National Security Council and State Department that was leaked to the press in the spring of 2002 noted how the "culture of royal excess" in Saudi Arabia "has ruled over the kingdom with documented human rights abuses.... Democracy has never been part of the equation." The study also reportedly describes the House of Saud as an "anachronism" that is "inherently fragile" and that there were "serious concerns about long-term stability."[29]

Al-Qaeda believes that the Saudi regime is corrupt and evil in large part because the royal family has squandered its wealth for personal consumption and exotic weaponry while most Arabs suffer in poverty. They are further angered by the regime's tendency to persecute those who advocate for more ethical priorities. They are angry with the United States, therefore, for propping up such a regime. The U.S.-Saudi alliance, in Al-Qaeda's view, further illustrates the depravity of the Saudi rulers in their decision to allow American troops on what they see as sacred Saudi soil in order to keep the regime in power. Such a regime is anti-Islamic, from their perspective, and therefore needs to be overthrown.

Unfortunately for these Islamic radicals, the United States has dedicated itself for more than a half century to perpetuate the Saud family's hold on power. In 1945, President Franklin D. Roosevelt met with King

Abel-Aziz ibn Saud, the founder of the modern Arabian kingdom that now bears his family's name, and forged the alliance that remains to this day: in return for open access to Saudi oil, the United States would protect the royal family from its enemies, both external and internal. So, the first challenge, in the eyes of Al-Qaeda, is to oust the United States from the region since it is the U.S. military that is keeping the corrupt Saudi regime in power. Given that Al-Qaeda is no match for the United States militarily, they therefore rationalize for the use of terrorism.

As a result, even putting aside moral arguments against backing such regimes as Saudi Arabia, there are serious questions as to whether the large-scale arms transfers and ongoing U.S. military presence in the Gulf really enhances American security interests. Rather than protecting the United States from its enemies, these policies appear to be creating enemies.

What, then, is the United States trying to protect itself and its allies from by militarizing the region to such a degree? In recent years, it has been Saddam Hussein's Iraq. However, Iraq not only had much of its military equipment destroyed during the Gulf War and subsequent air strikes, it does not have access to spare parts due to a strict military embargo first imposed in 1990. Iraq's armed forces are barely one-third their pre-war strength. Even though they have not been required to reduce their conventional forces under post-war restrictions imposed by the United Nations Security Council, the destruction of their weapons and their economic difficulties have led to a substantial reduction in men under arms. The navy is virtually nonexistent, and the air force is just a fraction of what it was before the war. Military spending by Iraq is barely one-tenth of its levels in the 1980s.[30] Furthermore, Iraq never has had an effective system of support, sustainability or supplies for its military outside of its now blocked dependence on foreign imports.[31] Saddam Hussein became a threat to his neighbors in the 1980s only because of foreign military aid, and such military aid is no longer forthcoming. Though there are widespread calls internationally to liberalize or eliminate the current sanctions on civilian goods for humanitarian reasons, there are no serious calls for ending the military embargo against the country. As a result, there is little reason to believe that Iraq would pose a credible threat to its neighbors in the foreseeable future through conventional arms.

The biggest concern raised by U.S. officials, however, is non-conventional weaponry.

Nuclear Apartheid: the Solution or the Cause?

The cease-fire agreement imposed on Iraq by the UN Security Council at the end of the Gulf War in 1991 included unprecedented infringements on Iraq's sovereignty, particularly regarding the dismantling of weapons of mass destruction (WMD) and related facilities. UN Security Council resolution 687, among other things, provided for the destruction, removal or rendering harmless all Iraqi nuclear, chemical and biological weapons capability, including both the weapons themselves and facilities for research, development and manufacturing, as well as eliminating ballistic missiles with a range of over 100 miles. In order to follow through on such a disarmament program, the Security Council set up the United Nations Special Commission on Iraq (UNSCOM), that would be allowed free access to inspect and destroy such weaponry. The United States and its allies in the UN argued that such stringent measures were a reasonable response to a regime that had indicated its ability to develop and utilize WMDs and commit acts of aggression against its neighbors. Even Arabs who shared American concerns about the Iraqi regime, however, were disturbed that the United States had succeeded in getting the world body to single out this Arab nationalist government for such special restrictions, given U.S. support for Israel, which they point out has done the same thing.

The U.S.-led militarization of the Middle East is repeatedly justified in the name of defending the security interests of the United States. However, U.S. military prowess is many times greater than all potential Middle Eastern adversaries combined. Furthermore, the United States is located on the opposite side of the planet from the Middle East, far out of range of potentially hostile militaries, none of which have much in the way of power projection beyond a few hundred miles of their borders. As a result, the greatest single fear for United States security stemming from the Middle East is the possibility that a government or group hostile to the United States will somehow obtain a nuclear weapon and seek to use it against the United States. Despite desperate efforts by the Bush Administration to justify the creation of a nuclear missile defense program of dubious efficacy, the primary threat of such an attack comes not from missiles but from less conventional forms of delivery, such as from being smuggled into the country. Putting aside questions of plausibility or method, however, the United States commitment to non-proliferation has been quite inconsistent:

Abandoning decades of efforts to promote nuclear non-proliferation, the Clinton Administration in the 1990s moved toward a policy of "counter-proliferation," signaling that the preferred response to the problem had become that of military force. Related to this was a de-emphasis on export controls and other preventative measures. For example, the nuclear program of Iraq—the Middle Eastern country about which the United States has expressed the greatest concern—was made possible through imports from the West of so-called "dual-use" technologies, having civilian applications but also capable of producing nuclear weapons or delivery systems. Yet President Clinton's Secretary of Defense, William Perry, argued before Congress that it was a "hopeless task" to control such dual use technology, arguing that "it only interferes with a company's ability to succeed internationally."[32] This Clinton Administration position, upheld by its successor, is in direct contradiction to the position taken by United Nations inspectors in Iraq, who called for "strict maintenance of export controls by the industrialized nations" to prevent the Iraqi regime from once again developing its nuclear program.[33]

The United States has raised concerns about Iran's nuclear ambitions as well. As far back as 1995, the United States began putting heavy pressure on the Russian government over its sale of civilian nuclear technology to the Islamic Republic and this was still a major point of contention between the two governments during the May 2002 summit conference in Moscow. There have also been dire warnings regarding Iranian intentions by President Bush in his 2002 State of the Union address and subsequently. However, it is highly unlikely that the nuclear reactor built by Moscow—quite legal under the Nuclear Non-Proliferation Treaty (NPT)—would help Iran create an atomic bomb. The reactor would be capable of producing only low-grade nuclear material and Iran lacks much of the necessary infrastructure for weapons production. Most foreign diplomats based in Teheran appear to agree that Iran's motivations are entirely peaceful.[34] Furthermore, Iran has allowed inspectors from the International Atomic Energy Agency to visit any location in Iran on request, which they have done on several occasions, inspections that "did not detect any activities in violation of Iran's NPT obligations."[35] While there are certainly environmental, economic and other reasons to be concerned about nuclear power development in Iran or anywhere else, this has not been the concern of the U.S. government. In fact, the United States is obligated under the NPT to allow signatory states in good standing (which includes Iran) to have access to peaceful nuclear technology, which the United States has gone to great lengths to try to limit. In addition, the

United States—like the other existing nuclear powers—is obliged under the NPT to take serious steps towards nuclear disarmament, something that both Republican and Democratic administrations have steadfastly resisted.

Interestingly, Russia is not the first country to transfer nuclear technology to the Iranians: Throughout the 1970s, the U.S. government encouraged American companies to sell nuclear reactors to the Iranian government, then under the dictatorial rule of the Shah.[36] Even more so than the mullahs now in power, the shah's megalomania led many to fear his goals were to divert the technology for military purposes.

The United States has long employed a double standard with regard to non-proliferation, having few problems with nuclear weapons development by its allies in the region, such as Israel, which is believed to have over 300 warheads along with sophisticated medium-range missiles. Israel has long stated that it would not be the first to introduce nuclear weapons into the Middle East, which is a rather disingenuous commitment given that U.S. planes and warships have been bringing nuclear weapons into the region since the 1950s. Israel is generally believed to have become a nuclear power by 1969. The newly elected President Richard Nixon and his chief foreign policy advisor Henry Kissinger privately endorsed Israel's program that year. They quickly ended the regular U.S. inspections of Israel's Dimona nuclear center. This was of little consequence, however, since these "inspections" were *pro forma* and not taken seriously. (President Lyndon Johnson demonstrated his lack of concern over the prospects of Israel becoming a nuclear power by rejecting calls that one of the early major weapons sales to Israel be conditioned on Israel signing the NPT.) The Nixon Administration went to great lengths to keep nuclear issues out of any talks on the Middle East. Information on Israeli nuclear capabilities was routinely suppressed. The United States even supplied Israel with krytrons (nuclear triggers) and supercomputers that were bound for the Israeli nuclear program.[37] Under the Carter Administration, which took the threat of nuclear proliferation somewhat more seriously than others, the issue of Israel's development of nuclear weaponry was not raised publicly. When satellite footage of an aborted nuclear test in South Africa's Kalahari Desert gave evidence of a large-scale presence of Israeli personnel at the test site, the Carter Administration kept it quiet.[38] Two years later, when a U.S. satellite detected a successful joint Israeli-South African atomic bomb test in the Indian Ocean, the Carter Administration rushed to squelch initial media reports. According to Joseph Nye, then-Deputy Under Secretary of State, the Carter Administration considered Israel's nuclear weapons program a low priority.[39]

The Reagan Administration made an effort to keep information on Israel's nuclear capability from State Department officials and others who might have concerns over nuclear proliferation issues.[40] The senior Bush Administration sold at least 1500 nuclear "dual-use" items to Israel, according to a report by the General Accounting Office, despite NPT requirements that the United States not help another country's nuclear weapons program "in any way."[41] Meanwhile, for many years, Congress has made it clear to the Nuclear Regulatory Commission and other responsible parties that they did not want to have anything revealed in an open hearing related to Israel's nuclear capability. While most U.S. restrictions against foreign aid to new nuclear states have been written in such a way as to exempt Israel, a public acknowledgment might still have jeopardized U.S. economic and military assistance. Outside of Washington, top Israeli nuclear scientists had open access to American institutions and many leading American nuclear scientists had extended visits with their counterparts in Israel, in what has been called "informational promiscuity" in the seepage of nuclear intelligence.[42] In addition, given the enormous costs of any nuclear program of such magnitude, it would have been very difficult for Israel to develop such a large and advanced arsenal without the tens of billions of dollars in unrestricted American financial support. More than simply employing a double standard of rebuking enemies for developing nuclear weapons while tolerating development by its allies, the United States has, in effect, subsidized nuclear proliferation in the Middle East.

The U.S. encouragement of nuclear weapons development by Israel fits with another disturbing development in recent years: the apparent U.S. belief that it is legitimate for the United States or an ally to maintain its regional nuclear monopoly through force. In 1981, the Israeli air force attacked Iraq's French-built Osirak nuclear power plant, an operation made possible by the U.S. decision to supply Israel with high-resolution photographs of Iraq from the KH-11 satellite, data that no other nation was allowed access to, as well as through U.S.-supplied F-16 fighter bombers. Though the U.S. government publicly condemned the bombing, in private, according to investigative journalist Seymour Hersh, "Reagan was delighted...[and] very satisfied." Publicly, the U.S. suspended the delivery of four additional F-16s fighter-bombers to the Israeli air force. Two months later, that suspension was quietly lifted.[43]

Such an attitude was not just that of a conservative Republican administration. Less than ten years after the Israeli air strikes, the U.S. House of Representatives—in an effort led by liberal Democrats—passed a resolution endorsing the Israeli attack on Iraq and calling for the United States to seek the repeal of UN Security Council resolution 487 that condemned it.[44]

The irony is that Israel's action may have spurred Iraq's effort to procure nuclear weapons rather than curbed it. Not only was the Osirak reactor not the focal point of Iraq's nuclear weapons program, the Israeli attack likely encouraged the Iraqis to take greater efforts to evade detection of their primary nuclear development facilities.[45]

Israel's air strikes at Osirak paled in comparison with the much wider bombing attacks against suspected Iraqi nuclear-related sites ten years later by the United States during the Gulf War. Like the Israeli bombing, they violated both the spirit and the letter of the Nuclear Non-proliferation Treaty, and were the final demonstration of the United States' lack of support for law-based approaches to this problem. They were also a reflection of the unilateralist view now even more apparent in U.S. foreign policy that advocates military action rather than reliance on international organizations, international law, or diplomacy. Such a policy delegitimizes traditional international safeguards against nuclear proliferation in favor of an international anarchy where regional nuclear powers can launch pre-emptive attacks against potential rivals at will. To cite two examples, subsequent to the U.S. bombing of suspected Iraqi nuclear facilities, both the South Korean and Indian governments began talking openly about taking unilateral actions against North Korea and Pakistan, respectively. Tragically, such lawless attacks, ostensibly aimed at preventing proliferation in other countries, create the very insecurity that motivates governments to develop their nuclear programs in the first place. Such attacks will likely set back rather than promote the cause of nuclear non-proliferation.

The subsequent U.S.-led embargo and periodic air strikes against Iraq have been justified as necessary to enforce UN Security Council resolution 687, which calls for the destruction of Iraq's weapons of mass destruction and capability of producing such weapons in the future. However, the resolution places this demand on Iraq within the context of ridding weapons of mass destruction from the entire region. The United States, however, rejects such a formula, preferring a kind of nuclear apartheid where the United States and Israel can maintain their nuclear arsenals in the region, but Iraq and other Islamic countries are effectively barred from developing such weapons of mass destruction.

Furthermore, throughout the years of controversy regarding UNSCOM inspections of Iraq's potential weapons of mass destruction, the Iraqis have allowed the UN's International Atomic Energy Agency to continue regular inspections of Iraqi facilities. No evidence of a renewal of Iraq's nuclear program has been found.

Given the risks inherent in unilateral military action and other problems with U.S. nuclear policy in the Middle East, why does the United States not pursue a more comprehensive program of nuclear non-proliferation? One answer may be that the primary concern of the United States is not preventing nuclear proliferation per se but preventing a challenge to its military domination in the post-Cold War world. With American strategic planners moving away from the prospects of a major East-West confrontation to ones involving medium-intensity warfare against Third World regional powers, the desire for maintaining a nuclear monopoly by the major powers and certain allies like Israel becomes all the more important.

Concern over the prospects of nuclear proliferation also serves as a pretext for the ongoing U.S. military presence in the region and for attacking countries like Iraq that challenge this American dominance. Instead of seeing the potential acquisition of nuclear weapons by Arabs or Iranians as an inevitable reaction to the American failure to support global nuclear disarmament, the United States—by labeling it as part of the threat from international terrorism—can justify its military interventionism in the Middle East.

Nuclear weapons are inherently weapons of terror, given their level of devastation and their non-discriminate nature. Indeed, the nuclear arms race between the United States and the Soviet Union during the Cold War was often referred to as "the balance of terror." Many people outside the United States see the atomic bombings of two Japanese cities in 1945 as among the greatest acts of terrorism in world history. American concerns, however, are not about the ability of the United States to threaten other countries with nuclear weapons but how others might threaten the United States. This can make it possible to portray American attacks against far-off countries as acts of self-defense.

To cite one example, during the fall of 1990, following Iraq's takeover of Kuwait, the senior Bush Administration was struggling—with only limited success at that point—to rally a reluctant American public to support going to war. In November, Bush Administration officials noticed that public opinion polls indicated that the possibility of an imminent Iraqi procurement of nuclear weapons was the only issue that would lead a majoriry of Americans to support the war.[46] At that point, the Bush Administration started issuing alarmist reports regarding Iraq's nuclear potential, an issue that had not been seriously addressed until then.

Whatever the actual motivations for professed American concerns regarding nuclear proliferation, is non-proliferation in the Middle East even possible? Ironically, Iran and Iraq have endorsed calls for a nuclear-free zone in the Middle East, which has been opposed by the United States. Even if such pronouncements by the Iraqis and Iranians proved less than sincere, U.S. support for the concept would provide far greater legitimacy to efforts to control any potential nuclear threat from Iran and Iraq than does current policy. In effect, the United States insists that nuclear weapons in the Middle East should be the exclusive domain of itself and Israel. Such a stance will most likely lead not to acquiescence, but to a rush by other nations to counter this perceived American-Israeli threat, as witnessed by Iraq's ambitious nuclear program, aborted by the Gulf War and subsequent inspections.

Even worse, such a policy increases the likelihood that an extremist group—with or without government support—might some day procure and detonate a nuclear weapon against the United States.

The "Poor Man's Nuclear Bomb": The Threat from Chemical and Biological Weapons

How seriously should Americans take concerns that a country like Iraq might obtain weapons of mass destruction? Based on recent history, it appears the government's answer is based upon what the current U.S. relationship with that country might be at a particular time.

When ABC television news correspondent Charles Glass revealed sites of Iraq's biological warfare programs in early 1989, when the United States was quietly supporting Iraq, the Defense Department denied the facts presented and the story essentially died.[47] Glass observed that it was not until a few years later—following Iraq's invasion of Kuwait, a U.S. ally—that the State Department began issuing briefings on those same sites.

Similarly, the March 1988 massacre at Halabja—where Iraq government forces massacred upwards to 5000 civilians in that Kurdish town by gassing them with chemical weapons—was downplayed by the Reagan Administration, even to the point of claiming that Iran, then the preferred American enemy, was actually responsible. The Halabja tragedy was not an isolated incident, as U.S. officials were well aware at the time. UN reports in 1986 and 1987 documented Iraq's use of chemical weapons, which were confirmed both by investigations from the CIA and from U.S. embassy staff who visited Iraqi Kurdish refugees in Turkey. However, not only was the United States not particularly concerned about the ongoing repression, the use of chemical weapons and the potential use of nuclear and biological weapons, the United States actually was supporting the Iraqi government's procurement effort of materials necessary for the development of such an arsenal. It is in this light that current U.S. concerns over Iraq's possession of WMDs ought to be considered.

During the 1980s, American companies, with U.S. government backing, supplied Saddam Hussein's government with much of the raw material for Iraq's chemical and biological weapons program as well as $1 billion worth of components necessary for the development of missiles and nuclear weapons. A Senate committee reported in 1994 that American companies licensed by the U.S. Commerce Department had shipped large quantities of biological material usable for weapons production in Iraq. A major task of UNSCOM after the Gulf War was to destroy the very weapons the United States had helped to build. This report noted that such trade continued at least until the end of the decade, despite evidence of Iraqi chemical warfare against Iranians and against Iraqi Kurds.[48] Much of this trade was no oversight. It was made possible because the Reagan Administration took Iraq off of its list of countries supporting terrorism in 1982, making them eligible to receive such items. This re-designation came in spite of Iraq's ongoing support of Abu Nidal and other terrorist groups.[49]

It was no secret to the Reagan Administration that Iraq was using chemical weapons. A *New York Times* report shows that the U.S. Defense Intelligence Agency provided detailed military assistance in a 1988 Iraqi military offensive against Iran in which they knew Iraq would likely use chemical weapons. According to Colonel Walter Lang, the senior intelligence officer at the time, "The use of gas on the battlefield by the Iraqis was not a matter of deep strategic concern."[50] In an ironic twist of history, George Bush, who as vice president was a strong supporter of U.S. backing for Iraq, would later—as president—emphasize how Saddam Hussein had "used chemical weapons against his own people" as a major justification for going to war against the country.[51]

As late as December 1989, just eight months prior to Iraq's designation as an enemy for having invaded Kuwait, the Bush Administration pushed through new loans to the Iraqi government in order to facilitate U.S.-Iraqi trade.[52] Meanwhile, according to a 1992 Senate investigation, the Commerce Department repeatedly deleted and altered information on export licenses for trade with Iraq in order to hide potential military uses of American exports.[53] Such policies raise serious questions as to why, if Iraq is currently such a danger to American security as U.S. policy makers have been claiming, did the United States help facilitate the development of its military capability and its acquisition of weapons of mass destruction?

The sincerity of the U.S. obsession with Iraq's potential threat to the region during the most recent decade is weakened by the fact that Iraq's military, including its real and potential weapons of mass destruction, was significantly stronger in the late 1980s than it is today. Iraqi dictator Saddam Hussein once really was a threat when he had his full complement of medium-range missiles, a functioning air force and a massive stockpile of chemical and biological weaponry. Yet, from the Carter Administration through the Reagan Administration through the first half of the senior Bush Administration, the United States dismissed any potential strategic threat to the point of coddling Saddam's regime with economic subsidies and military support. Why then, beginning in late 1997, when Iraq had only a tiny percentage of its once-formidable military capability, did the United States suddenly portray Iraq as an intolerable threat? It is no surprise, under these circumstances, that so many Americans, rightly or wrongly, suspected President Clinton of manufacturing the crisis to distract the American public from the sex scandal then surrounding his office. Indeed, the December 1998 bombing campaign began on the very day of his scheduled impeachment by the House of Representatives, which, in response, postponed the vote.

A review of the chronology leading up to that American military campaign is revealing.

In November 1997, the temporary Iraqi banning of American participants from UNSCOM inspection teams led the United States to mobilize its armed forces for a major bombing campaign, which was suspended when the Russians were able to negotiate an agreement where the Iraqis rescinded the ban. Soon thereafter, the Clinton Administration began to raise concerns about Iraq's refusal to allow UNSCOM inspectors to visit so-called "presidential sites," a liberally-defined series of buildings and grounds across the country that Iraq claimed were used by government officials. The United States and some UNSCOM officials believed that the reason for the Iraqi restrictions was that anthrax and other biological warfare agents might be under production within some of those sites. The Iraqis, by contrast, saw granting unfettered access by inspectors as yet another intrusion on their sovereign rights. Given that a number of prominent American political leaders from both parties had called openly for assassinating Saddam Hussein, the Iraqi leader's reluctance to allow Americans into presidential palaces also may have been a result of concerns that such access would make him and other top officials personally vulnerable. Furthermore, the Iraqis had complained that, despite a stated policy of avoiding staffing UNSCOM with experts from "intelligence providing states," there was a disproportionate number of Americans involved in the inspections, whom—the Iraqis noted periodically—deliberately prolonged the process and potentially provided information to the U.S. military.[54]

Even those in the West dubious of Iraq's alleged concerns were suspicious of American motivations in raising the issue: Though such Iraqi restrictions on these "presidential sites" had existed since the beginning of the sanctions regime nearly seven years earlier, the United States announced only in January 1998 that it had become an intolerable violation of UN Security Council resolution 687 that might necessitate a sustained bombing campaign against Iraq. By February, a large-scale U.S. military assault seemed likely. However, United Nations Secretary General Kofi Annan was able to broker a deal late that month that met the United Nations' insistence that the sites be open to UN inspectors, but with an additional diplomatic presence in recognition of the sites' special status.

At the end of October, Iraq imposed new restrictions on UNSCOM as a result of revelations that the United States was illegally using UNSCOM as a vehicle for spying on the Iraqi government.[55] On November 10, in response to pressure from President Clinton, UNSCOM chairman Richard Butler announced his decision to pull UNSCOM out of Iraq without the required authorization from the Security Council. Iraq then reversed itself and agreed to allow the inspectors to resume their activities. The United States, however, was eager to launch military action, particularly by mid-December, in order to take advantage of overlapping American military units on rotation in the Persian Gulf, which made it a particularly auspicious time for major air strikes. Clinton's National Security Advisor Sandy Berger met with Butler on November 30, when the UNSCOM director was instructed to provoke Iraq to break its agreement to fully cooperate with UNSCOM. Without consulting the UN Security Council as required, Butler announced to the Iraqis that he was nullifying previously agreed-upon modalities dealing with sensitive sites that limited the number of UNSCOM inspectors. He chose the Baath Party headquarters in Baghdad as the site to demand unfettered access, a very unlikely place to store weapons of mass destruction but one very likely to provoke a negative reaction. The Iraqis refused to allow the large group into their party headquarters, but did allow them unrestricted access to a series of sensitive military installations. At that point, Butler and the Clinton Administration unilaterally ordered the UNSCOM inspectors out of Iraq. Back in New York, American officials then helped Butler draft a report blaming Iraq exclusively for the impasse in a late night session at the U.S. Mission across from the United Nations.[56] As the UN Security Council was meeting in an emergency special session on how to implement a unified response to Iraq's non-cooperation, the United States—with support from Great Britain—launched an unauthorized four-day series of sustained air strikes against Iraq in what became known as Operation Desert Fox. In response, Iraq forbade UNSCOM from returning. To this day, the U.S. government claims that UNSCOM inspectors were "expelled from Iraq" by Saddam Hussein as a means of bolstering the American claim that the Iraqis must have something to hide, namely their alleged development of weapons of mass destruction.

In reality, in the aftermath of the 1991 Gulf War and the subsequent inspections regime, virtually any aggressive military potential by Iraq was destroyed. Before UNSCOM was withdrawn, its agents reportedly oversaw the destruction of 38,000 chemical weapons, 480,000 liters of live chemical-weapons agents, 48 missiles, six missile launchers, 30 missile warheads modified to carry chemical or biological agents and hundreds of related equipment with the capability to produce chemical weapons. In late 1997, Butler reported that they had made "significant progress" in tracking Iraq's chemical weapons program and that 817 of the 819 Soviet-supplied long-range missiles had been accounted for. There were also believed to be a couple of dozen Iraqi-made ballistic missiles unaccounted for, but these were of questionable caliber.[57] UNSCOM was unable to come up with any evidence that Iraq had been concealing prohibited weapons since October 1995.[58]

Early UNSCOM inspections revealed evidence of the production of large amounts of biological agents, including anthrax, and charged that Iraq had vastly understated the amount of biological warfare agents it had manufactured. In response, UNSCOM set up sophisticated monitoring devices to detect chemical or biological weapons, though these were dismantled after the American and British bombing raids of December 1998.[59] Still, though in the past Iraq certainly produced both chemical and biological agents, the United States never has unable to present any credible evidence that Iraq currently has biological weapons or other WMDs.

Indeed, U.S. officials have admitted that there is no evidence that Iraq has resumed its nuclear, chemical or biological weapons programs.[60]

Even in the unlikely event that Iraq was able and willing to engage in the production or deployment of nuclear or chemical weapons, it would almost certainly be detected by satellite or air reconnaissance and destroyed in air strikes.

The development of biological weapons, by contrast, is much easier to conceal due to the small amount of space needed for their manufacture. However, there are serious questions as to whether the alleged biological agents could be dispersed successfully in a manner that could harm troops or the civilian population, given the rather complicated technology required. For example, a vial of biological weapons on the tip of a missile would almost certainly be destroyed on impact or dispersed harmlessly. Israeli military analyst Meir Stieglitz, writing in the Israeli newspaper *Yediot Ahronot*, noted "there is no such thing as a long-range Iraqi missile with an effective biological warhead. No one has found an Iraqi biological warhead. The chances of Iraq having succeeded in developing operative warheads without tests are zero."[61] Furthermore, as mentioned above, there is no evidence that Iraq's Scud missiles and launchers even survived the Gulf War. Indeed, UNSCOM reported in 1992 that Iraq had no launchers for their missiles or even any engines.

Frightening scenarios regarding mass fatalities from a small amount of anthrax assumes that the Iraqis have developed the highly sophisticated means of distributing them by missile or aircraft. To become a lethal weapon, highly concentrated amounts of the spores must be inhaled and then left untreated by antibiotics until the infection was too far advanced. For the attack to be successful, the winds would have to be just right, no rain would fall, the spray nozzles would not clog, the population would not be vaccinated and everyone would stay around the area targeted for attack. This is why sending anthrax spores through the mail to indoor destinations in the eastern United States by unknown terrorists during the fall of 2001 was found to be a relatively efficient means of distribution, even though it resulted in only a handful of deaths. It is also hard to imagine that an Iraqi aircraft, presumably some kind of drone, could somehow penetrate the air space of neighboring countries, much less far-off Israel, without being shot down. Most of Iraq's neighbors have sophisticated anti-aircraft capability and Israel has the best regional missile defense system in the world.

As one British scientist put it, "To say they have found enough weapons to kill the world several times over is equivalent to the statement that a man who produces a million sperm a day can thus produce a million babies a day. The problem in both cases is one of delivery systems."[62]

A far more likely scenario for an Iraqi distribution of such biological agents would be through terrorists smuggling them clandestinely into targeted countries. This is what led to some initial speculation, now considered very doubtful, that the Iraqis were behind the anthrax mail attacks. Such a possibility requires aggressive counter-intelligence efforts by the United States and other potentially targeted nations, but they are not the sort of contingency which a bombing campaign is likely to prevent. Indeed, the ongoing sanctions regime and military strikes are more likely to encourage rogue elements of Iraqi intelligence or an allied terrorist group to engage in such an attack as an act of revenge for the heavy Arab casualties resulting from these policies.

U.S. claims that Operation Desert Fox and subsequent bombing campaigns could somehow destroy Iraq's laboratories or storage facilities for biological weapons were quite unrealistic. Unlike chemical or nuclear weapons production, there are no large, visible and stationary processing facilities. An entire operation could take place in a facility the size of a large kitchen and could be packed up and moved at will. Furthermore, if the raw materials are in hand, some biological weapons can be produced as easily as fermenting beer, so any stockpiles destroyed could be replaced in a short period of time.

More seriously, Operation Desert Fox destroyed the ongoing inspection efforts, causing Iraq to go from a 95 percent compliance rate with UNSCOM inspectors to a zero percent compliance rate. This was a major reason why most UNSCOM officials opposed such a military response. Even General Charles Horner, who commanded U.S. air forces in the 1991 Gulf War, correctly predicted in 1998 that "Using force could have negative consequences—and it probably would not solve our major problem: Destroying nuclear, biological and chemical weapons." He added, "Ultimately, neither an air nor a ground invasion would solve the conflict over weapons of mass destruction. We will still need trained inspection teams to look for biological and chemical weapons."[63] Unfortunately, the decision to bomb led to the end of the UNSCOM inspections, something that at the time U.S. officials almost certainly foresaw.

Since the 1991 Gulf War and the subsequent inspections regime destroyed essentially every capability the Iraqi government had to produce or deploy weapons of mass destruction, the only implements remaining are those that could not easily be removed or hidden, such as laboratory samples, scientific instruments and computer ware. As a result, aerial bombing campaigns can hardly be considered an efficient means to destroy them. Good intelligence capability, not firepower, is the most effective means of countering whatever threats such laboratories might harbor. Even during the Gulf War, allied bombers were unable to destroy a single Scud missile on the ground because they did not know where these mobile weapons were at a given time. A 1996 report by the General Accounting Office charged the Pentagon with grossly exaggerating the effectiveness of its most expensive high-tech aircraft, missiles, and "smart bombs."[64] As late as November 1997, a senior intelligence official acknowledged, in reference to anthrax production facilities in Iraq, "If we knew where they were and how much there were, we'd go and get them," but there was no way to do so.[65] The United Nations had the ultimate intelligence network available to them in the form of UNSCOM, but—thanks to Operation Desert Fox— it no longer has access to Iraq.

Iraq's potential for developing WMDs should not be totally discounted. However, Saddam Hussein's lack of full cooperation with the inspections regime prior to the December 1998 bombings and his subsequent outright refusal to cooperate at all is not necessarily an indication that Iraq is hiding anything potentially threatening to neighbors. For example, the motivation for such non-compliance could be simply to provoke a reaction by the United States and thereby capitalize on the widespread Arab resentment over the U.S. obsession with the prospects of Arab countries procuring weapons of mass destruction while tolerating Israel's nuclear arsenal.

Part of the problem is that the United States has not offered any incentive for Iraq to allow inspections to resume. From the outset, the United States made clear that even total cooperation with UNSCOM would not lead to an end to the sanctions. The senior President Bush's National Security Advisor Robert Gates stated, "Iraqis will be made to pay the price while Saddam Hussein is in power. Any easing of sanctions will be considered only when there is a new government."[66] Similarly, Secretary of State Albright noted in 1997, "We do not agree with those nations who argue that if Iraq complies with its obligations concerning weapons of mass destruction, sanctions should be lifted."[67] President Clinton, in reference to Saddam Hussein's continued rule, declared, "Sanctions will be there until the end of time, or as long as he lasts."[68] While testifying before the Senate Foreign Relations committee in March 2002, Secretary of State Powell could say only that if Iraq let weapons inspectors back in, the United States "may look at lifting sanctions."[69] Without the prospect of sanctions being lifted, Saddam Hussein has nothing to lose by continuing to block the return of United Nations inspectors.

Scott Ritter is a retired former U.S. Marine officer who served as a team leader of UNSCOM weapons inspectors in Iraq before resigning in protest of the Clinton Administration's alleged lack of resolve in pushing Iraq to open up its inner sanctums to inspections. Yet even this hard-nosed inspector has challenged alarmist reports from the Bush Administration about Iraq's potential threat. In a 2001 nationally broadcast television talk show, when asked about Saddam Hussein's potential threat to the United States, he replied

> In terms of military threat, absolutely nothing. His military was devastated in 1991 in Operation Desert Storm and hasn't had the ability to reconstitute itself....In terms of weapons of mass destruction...we know that we achieved a 90 percent to 95-percent level of disarmament....We should be trying to get weapons inspectors back into Iraq so that we can ascertain exactly what's transpiring in Iraq today instead of guessing about it.[70]

However, the United States may be more eager to go to war than to resume inspections. Secretary of Defense Donald Rumsfeld has publicly questioned the values of such inspectors.[71] Secretary of State Powell has declared that "U.S. policy is that, regardless of what the inspectors do...the United States reserves its option to do whatever it believes might be appropriate to see if there can be a regime change."[72] Powell's statement is an important indicator of how the U.S. understands its role in the region. In effect, it reflects the belief that the United States can decide not just which countries may possess weapons of mass destruction and which countries cannot, but who rules certain Middle Eastern states and under what circumstances.

Ironically, the real danger of the use of Iraqi chemical or biological weapons getting into the hands of terrorists is not under a strongman like Saddam Hussein, whose primary interest is self-preservation, but in the event of the chaos following a U.S. invasion. (In a further irony, the only nation that has apparently allowed such weaponry to be obtained by terrorists is the United States; U.S. officials have acknowledged that the anthrax mailed to offices around the eastern United States in the fall of 2001 likely came from a U.S. military lab.)[73]

In order to open the way for a large-scale U.S. military assault on Iraq, the United States has launched a campaign to undermine United Nations efforts to address concerns about potential Iraqi acquisition of weapons of mass destruction because to resolve the issue would reduce or eliminate justifications for going to war. One story is particularly illustrative:

One of the most effective instruments for international arms control in recent years has been the Organization for the Prohibition of Chemical Weapons (OPCW), which enforces the chemical weapons convention by inspecting laboratories, factories and arsenals, and oversees the destruction of chemical weapons. The director general, first elected in 1997, was Jose Bustani, a Brazilian diplomat, praised by Britain's *Guardian* newspaper as a "workaholic" who has "done more in the past five years to promote world peace than anyone."[74] Under his strong leadership, the number of signatories grew from 87 to 145 nations, the fastest growth rate of any international organization in recent years and—during this same period—his inspectors oversaw the destruction of two million chemical weapons and two-thirds of the world's chemical weapons facilities. Bustani was re-elected unanimously in May 2000 for a five-year term and was complimented by Secretary of State Powell for his "very impressive" work.

However, by 2002, the United States began raising objections over Bustani's insistence that the OPCW inspect U.S. chemical weapons facilities with the same vigor it does for other signatories. More critically, the United States was concerned about Bustani's efforts to get Iraq to sign the convention and open its facilities to surprise inspections. If Iraq did so, and OPCW inspectors failed to locate evidence of weapons of mass destruction, it would severely weaken American claims that Iraq is developing chemical weapons that needed to be countered by a pre-emptive attack. American efforts to remove Bustani by forcing a recall by the Brazilian government failed, as did a U.S.-sponsored vote of no confidence in March. In April 2002, the United States began putting enormous pressure on weak countries to support its campaign to oust Bustani and threatened to withhold the United States' financial contribution to the organization, more than 20% of its budget.[75] Figuring it was better to get rid of its leader than risk the viability of the whole organization, a majority of nations, brought together in an unprecedented special session called by the United States, voted to remove Bustani.

This apparent preference of the United States to use military rather than diplomatic means to address the risk from the development of weapons of mass destruction is emblematic of the failure to recognize the paradox of this growing militarization of U.S. Middle East policy. Namely, the more the United States has militarized the Middle East, the less secure the United States and its allies have become. As long as the United States fails to recognize that its efforts to militarize the region have backfired, the threat of violence, terrorism and war—even involving weapons of mass destruction—will paradoxically but almost certainly only get worse.

Chapter Three

The Persian Gulf

The triumph by U.S. forces in the 1991 Gulf War was heralded initially as a major advance for American security interests in the Middle East. Yet there is reason to believe that the conduct of the United States before, during and subsequent to the war has contributed greatly to the rise of anti-Americanism in the region, and particularly to the establishment and growth of the Al-Qaeda terrorist network. Indeed, it has been the ongoing U.S. military presence in the Gulf that has been cited as being the primary motivation for Osama bin Laden's dramatic shift from an ally of the United States during the anti-Communist war against the Soviet Union in Afghanistan to its most notorious adversary.

In the years since the Gulf War, the United States has thrown immense military, diplomatic, and economic weight behind the Arab monarchies of the Persian Gulf. Though they make up less than ten percent of the Arab world's total population, these governments control most of its wealth and some of the most strategically important territory on the globe. Prior to the war, it was difficult for the United States to engage in military exercises. Even arranging a port call usually required asking permission months in advance. No more. Throughout the region, while American military personnel often wear civilian clothes so not to offend the local population, they are difficult to miss in the hotels, marketplaces, and restaurants of the Gulf states. When large numbers of U.S. forces were first dispatched to the Gulf in August 1990, they were supposed to be in the area temporarily, pending the ouster of Iraqi occupation forces from Kuwait. Contrary to this expectation, however, the United States' military presence is now effectively permanent. It is based upon a desire to fill in a perceived strategic vacuum, serve as a staging ground for combat training and strengthen military ties with allied Arab states. Underlying this is an assumption that there is a real threat posed by Iraq and Iran, the two largest countries in the region. As a result, then, the United States asserts that it has an obligation to meet the security needs of the six allied Arab monarchies that comprise the Gulf Cooperation Council, or GCC.

In a long-sought triumph for U.S. policy makers seeking to divide the oil-rich monarchies and their allies from the potentially radical nationalists of the poorer Arab countries, the GCC now plays an unprecedented role in Middle East security and diplomacy, backed by the United States. The GCC's power now surpasses the League of Arab States as the leading inter-Arab organization, effectively placing any pretense of pan-Arabism, the long-sought dream of Arab unity—or at least a willingness to share the wealth—to rest. While defenders of U.S. policy see this as a realistic and pragmatic result from the end of the Cold War and the resulting single superpower, many of its critics—particularly from the Middle East—see it as a return to the divide-and-rule tactics of Western imperialism.

The United States maintains between 20,000 to 25,000 American troops in the Gulf, along with highly sophisticated and destructive weapons and delivery systems. This not only has raised the ire of America's primary adversaries—Iraq and Iran—but also large portions of the population within the GCC states the United States is ostensibly trying to protect. Mecca and Medina—the two holiest cities in Islam—are located in Saudi Arabia and the presence of over 5000 troops on Saudi soil from a non-Muslim country that periodically has waged war (either directly or through surrogates) against Muslim peoples is seen by many Muslims as offensive. According to bin Laden, "For its own good, America should leave.... There is no more important duty than pushing the American enemy out of the Holy Land....The presence of the USA Crusader military forces...in the area will provoke the people of the country and push them to take up armed struggle against the invaders occupying the land."[1]

While an emotional flash point for some, the area's religious significance is not really the central concern of most Muslim critics. U.S. forces are primarily in the northeastern part of the country far removed from the holy cities in the west and the boundaries of modern Saudi Arabia bear little resemblance to the tribal areas of control at the time of the Prophet Muhammad. The primary objection to the U.S. military presence from within the Gulf states stems from both the painful reminder of their monarchies' neo-colonial ties with Western interests as well as the very practical concerns over the way this direct military support strengthens the regimes' authoritarian control.[2]

American oil interests, particularly in Saudi Arabia, led to an expanded U.S. role in the region during World War II. This involvement increased still further with the close American relationship with the Shah of Iran after the CIA restored him to the throne in 1953, supplanting Great Britain as the primary outside power in that oil-rich country. Still, Gulf security was seen primarily as a British responsibility until Prime Minister Harold Wilson announced in 1969 that Great Britain would withdraw most of its security commitments from areas east of the Suez Canal. This decision was both a reflection of Britain's declining global power as well as a result of American pressure to take on the lead role in Middle East security.

The Evolving American Strategic Role

In the midst of strong anti-interventionist sentiment among the American public at the height of the Vietnam War, an overt large-scale military presence was not politically feasible. However, the Nixon Administration had had some success in curbing anti-Vietnam War protests through its "Vietnamization" of the war. That is, by increasing the role of South Vietnamese conscripts fighting on the ground and by escalating the American air war, U.S. troop strength could be reduced, resulting in fewer American casualties and smaller draft rolls, even as violence against the Vietnamese was escalated. As a result, in 1971, President Richard Nixon decided to expand this concept through the Nixon Doctrine—also known as the Guam Doctrine (named after the Pacific island where President Nixon first announced the policy)—which institutionalized this "surrogate strategy" of Vietnamization on a global level. According to Nixon, "we shall furnish military and economic assistance when requested...,but we shall look to the nation directly threatened to assume the primary responsibility of providing the manpower for its defense."[3]

The Persian Gulf became the first testing ground for using a regional *gendarme* to promote U.S. interests, essentially an extension of the Vietnamization program of training and arming locals to enforce the U.S. security agenda. The Shah of Iran owed his throne to the United States, had lots of money from the rise in oil prices with which to purchase weapons, and a desire to feed his megalomania—all of which made him a well-suited surrogate. Throughout the 1970s, the United States sold over $20 billion in advanced weaponry to the Shah (with an additional $20 billion on order.) In addition, there were as many as 3,000 American advisors and trainers—mostly working for private defense contractors—in Iran in order to transform the Iranian armed forces into a sophisticated fighting force capable of counter-insurgency operations. This policy was successfully implemented when Iranian troops—with American and British support—intervened in support of the sultan of Oman against a leftist rebellion in the Dhofar province in the mid-1970s. In 1979, however, Iran's Islamic revolution brought this policy crashing down, replacing the compliant Shah with a regime stridently opposed to Western interests.

In response to this shocking recognition of the limits of surrogate strategy, the Carter Doctrine was announced in 1980. The United States would no longer rely on potentially unstable allies and their armed forces, announced President Carter, but would now intervene directly through the Rapid Deployment Force, later integrated into the Central Command. An agreement was reached with the Saudi government whereby, in exchange for the sale of an integrated package of highly sophisticated weaponry, the Saudis would build and pay for an elaborate system of command, naval and air facilities large enough to sustain U.S. forces in intensive regional combat. For example, the controversial 1981 sale of the sophisticated AWACS airborne radar system to Saudi Arabia was to be a linchpin of an elaborate communications system comparable to that of NATO. According to a *Washington Post* report at that time (then denied by the Pentagon), this was to be part of a grand defense strategy for the Middle Eastern oil fields that included an ambitious plan to build bases in Saudi Arabia equipped and waiting for American forces to use.[4]

In the event of war, American forces would be deployed so quickly and with such overwhelming force that the casualty ratio would be highly favorable and the length of the fighting would be short. The result would be that disruptive anti-war protests from the American public would be minimal. This was of particular concern since Congress had recently passed the War Powers Act, whereby the legislative branch could effectively veto a president's decision to send American troops into combat after sixty days. Though the exact scenario in which U.S. forces would be deployed could not have been predicted at the time, the Carter Doctrine made possible the initial American military and political successes in the 1991 Gulf War against Iraq.

During the Iran-Iraq War between 1980 and 1988, the United States armed one side and then the other as a means of insuring that neither of the two countries could become dominant in the region. When the Clinton Administration came to office in 1993, the policy was shifted to that of "dual containment," seeking to isolate both countries, which the

United States saw as potentially dangerous and destabilizing forces in this strategically-important region, labeling them both as "rogue states."

As defined by U.S. national security managers, rogue states are countries that possess substantial military capability, seek the acquisition of weapons of mass destruction and violate what are seen as international "norms." President Clinton's first National Security Advisor Anthony Lake put the matter clearly: "Our policy must face the reality of recalcitrant and outlaw states that not only choose to remain outside the family [of nations] but also assault its basic values...[and] exhibit a chronic inability to engage constructively with the outside world...." Lake argued further that just as the United States took the lead in "containing" the Soviet Union, it must now also bear the "special responsibility" to "neutralize" and "contain" these "outlaw states."[5] In addition to Iraq and Iran, Libya and Sudan were also widely considered as rogue states, with Syria sometimes included on the list by certain foreign policy hawks. (The only countries outside the region given such a label were communist North Korea and Cuba.)

Despite concerns voiced by the U.S. government regarding Iran and Iraq's human rights records and violations of international norms, neither country is unique in the region in such transgressions. For example, due to its powerful armed forces, nuclear arsenal, conquests of neighboring countries, and violations of international legal standards, a case could be made that Israel—America's chief partner in the region and the world's largest recipient of U.S. economic and military support—would also fit this definition. Yet the label of "rogue state" has a clear function in U.S. foreign policy independent of any objective criteria. Iran and Iraq are the only two countries in the Middle East that combine a large population, adequate water resources and oil wealth to be major independent players that have the ability to challenge American hegemony in the region. These two countries have been labeled rogue states ultimately because of their failure to accept the post-Cold War order that requires accepting the American strategic and economic agenda. Prior to the arrival of the current regimes seen as so antithetical to American interests, these countries engaged in large-scale military procurement with the support or acquiescence of the United States as well as engaging in major human rights abuses without American objections. Once their cooperation with the United States ended and their hostility toward American interests emerged, their long ignored human rights abuses and militarization became a focal point for their vilification.

The level of repression these two regimes have demonstrated against their own citizens as well as their histories of aggression and subversion against their neighbors makes such rationalizations for U.S. policy easier to accept. However, a careful analysis of American policy in the Gulf reveals that concerns over the security of allied Gulf monarchies from potential hostile actions by both Iran and Iraq appear to be greatly exaggerated. Both Iran and Iraq are also very dependent on the sale of oil for their own prosperity and would seem to have little incentive to threaten the free flow of this crucial export. Furthermore, the strategic balance in the past decade has swung decisively in favor of the GCC and the West, placing the pro-Western monarchies in a more comfortable strategic position than was even imaginable a little more than a decade ago. Still, U.S. strategy is based upon a fear that Iran and Iraq pose an immediate threat to Gulf security. Only a closer look at U.S. relations with those countries can determine the extent of the security threat, and offer an understanding of the real interests driving U.S. policy.

The United States and Iran: Hostages to Confrontation

Iran—with its strategic location between the Persian Gulf and Caspian Sea, 65 million inhabitants, and control of as much as ten percent of the world's oil reserves—constitutes an important piece of the strategic prize. The United States has been largely hostile towards Iran since the Islamic Revolution ousted the Shah—a close American ally—in 1979.

From 1981 to 1986, the United States clandestinely shipped arms to Iran's Islamic government. By helping to shore up the Iranian military, these shipments were part of the U.S. policy to promote the mutual destruction of Iran and Iraq in their brutal military standoff following Iraq's 1980 invasion. In addition, part of the secret arms transfers was channeled to anti-Soviet Afghan *mujahadin* (resistance fighters) on Iran's eastern border. A factor in some of the later arms transfers was hope for Iranian cooperation in facilitating the release of American hostages held by radical Islamic groups in Lebanon.[6] More significantly, it appears that the primary motivation for the clandestine arms sales was to buy access to the Iranian military in hopes of influencing it. The United States—in recognition of the Islamic authorities' strident anti-Communism—also passed on names of suspected Iranian leftists to government authorities, resulting in the execution of hundreds of dissidents.

Despite this limited cooperation, the United States generally sided with Iraq during the eight-year war that resulted when Saddam Hussein's forces invaded western Iran barely a year after the triumph of the Iranian revolution. While the United States tolerated widespread attacks by Iraq against Iranian oil tankers during the war, the U.S. Navy intervened in 1987 to protect Kuwaiti oil tankers and other Persian Gulf shipping—which included Iraqi oil and other exports and imports by Saddam Hussein's government—from Iranian retaliation. In what became known as the "Tanker War," these Kuwaiti ships were re-flagged as American ships, thereby giving the United States the excuse to attack Iran should these ships be fired upon. This military intervention in support of Iraq and its allies came despite the fact that Iraq had attacked twice as many ships in the Gulf as had Iran, including the 1987 attack on the U.S. Navy frigate *Stark* that resulted in the deaths of 38 American sailors.

This expanded U.S. military role led to a series of armed engagements between the United States and Iran along the country's southern coast. Iraq praised the United States for its "positive efforts" in the war,[7] but the policy was far more controversial within the United States. The consensus of the Senate Foreign Relations Committee in June 1988 was that "there is mounting evidence that shipping in the gulf is less safe now than before the U.S. navy buildup began. Chances for a mishap are high."[8] Indeed, following one military encounter with Iranian forces in July 1988, an American missile fired from a Navy cruiser shot down an Iranian passenger airliner on a regularly scheduled flight over Iranian airspace. All 290 people aboard were killed.[9]

An armistice between Iran and Iraq was signed later that year, ending a brutal war that had resulted in over 400,000 deaths. This human toll reached such staggering proportions in part due to the U.S. policy of arming both sides that had helped prolong the war.

Following the death of revolutionary leader Ayatollah Khomeini in 1989, Iran began making gradual but significant moves toward greater liberalization and political pluralism, substantially reducing its earlier support for radical Islamic movements beyond its borders. Ironically, however, the United States increased its hostility towards the Iranian revolution over the next decade, greatly disappointing Iranian reformers who had hoped for some greater rapprochement with the United States. In May 1995, President Clinton signed an executive order prohibiting all American trade, trade financing, loans, and financial services to the Islamic Republic. This was done without any prior consultation with other countries, many of which simply absorbed the trade to the detriment of American businesses. In an effort to further isolate Iran economically, President Clinton signed into law in August 1996 a bill that imposed a secondary boycott on foreign companies and governments investing more than $40 million in Iran's oil and natural gas industry. This law provides for an array of sanctions, including banning the sale of products of culpable firms in the United States, claiming that Iran was one of "the most dangerous sponsors of terrorism in the world."[10] Clinton dismissed protests from governments and private companies in Europe and elsewhere, saying he could "only hope someday soon that all countries will come to realize you can't do business by day with people who are killing your people by night."[11] He failed to elaborate on his allegation of Iranian nocturnal murders, however. Furthermore, the idea that U.S. sanctions can create sufficient economic pressure on Iran to topple the regime has never been realistic, in part because European and Japanese allies hold most of the country's foreign debt and have refused to cooperate in such a self-defeating policy.

In addition, Congress authorized $18 million to be spent on covert actions to undermine the Iranian regime, raising concerns that the United States—which had overthrown Iran's constitutional government in 1953—was once again making covert action a major facet of its policy.

Recent political trends in Iran—such as the 1997 election of the moderate Islamist Mohamed Khatami as president, sweeps by other moderates in parliamentary elections the following year, and Khatami's landslide re-election in 2001—appear to be going in a direction that should please U.S. policy makers. Despite the dramatic if uneven steps towards liberalization in Iran and some toning down of anti-Iranian rhetoric in the waning months of the Clinton Administration, however, various sanctions and other anti-Iranian measures by the United States were still stricter at the end of Clinton's term than they were during the regime's most repressive and extremist period in the mid-1980s. In addition, the United States still refused to re-establish diplomatic relations with this the largest country in the Middle East.

There was some hope, then, that the new Bush Administration might be willing to pursue less hostile relations than its Democratic predecessor. However, in his 2002 State of the Union address, President Bush linked the increasingly pluralistic Iran with the totalitarian regimes of Iraq and North Korea as part of an "axis of evil, arming to threaten the peace of the world" along with its "terrorist allies."[12] This was seen as a serious blow to Iranian moderates who had been fighting for greater political openness and better relations with the West.

Iranians as a whole, now reflected in key segments of their government, appear willing to support increasing cooperation with the West. However, U.S. policy has so offended nationalist sentiments that it has enhanced the credibility of the very hard-line elements Washington purports to fear. Each escalation of U.S. sanctions, rhetoric, or military presence in the Persian Gulf targeted at an allegedly belligerent Iran becomes a self-fulfilling prophecy as Iranians see themselves increasingly under siege.

Germany, France and most other European countries question the United States' ongoing belligerence towards Iran, particularly in light of recent internal reforms, and cite the fact that efforts to isolate and over-throw the Iranian government are not based on legal grounds. Unlike international sanctions against the former apartheid government of South Africa or the current military junta in Burma, sanctions against Iran are not predicated on significant legal or moral imperatives. The United States has not asked the United Nations to impose sanctions because there is no legal basis for such actions and would thus fail to get any support. As with similar extraterritorial efforts regarding Cuba and Libya, U.S. attempts to pressure other nations to not invest in or trade with Iran have alienated even America's strongest allies. Indeed, EU External Affairs Minister Chris Patten stated categorically that such restrictions "threaten the open international trading system" and that mutual efforts to combat terrorism and the proliferation of weapons of mass destruction "could be damaged by continuing U.S. attempts to promote the goal through unilateral extraterritorial laws."[13] Such American efforts appear to be in violation of World Trade Organization (WTO) guidelines promoting free trade, which the United States has pushed vigorously in disputes with other countries. In 1997, the EU threatened to bring the United States before the WTO's Dispute Settlement Body, but—in a negotiated settlement—the United States agreed to not rigorously enforce the most offensive provisions that would punish European companies.

Similarly, U.S. efforts to subvert the Iranian government are contrary to international legal conventions that recognize sovereign rights and principles of nonintervention. They also run directly counter to the Algiers Declaration of 1981, which led to the release of the American hostages held in Iran, under which the United States unequivocally pledged not to intervene politically or militarily in the internal affairs of Iran.

Throughout the Cold War, the United States sought to place the blame for much of the violence and internal unrest in the Middle East (and in the Third World in general) on the Soviet Union rather than on U.S.

policies or the failures of its own allies to govern fairly. This same pattern soon emerged regarding Iran, with the United States blaming the Islamic Republic for unrest in several Middle Eastern countries. For example, the United States tried to blame Iran for the popular anti-government resistance movement in the Arab island state of Bahrain in the Persian Gulf, where the Shiite Muslim majority began to resist the autocratic rule of the Sunni Muslim monarchy during the 1980s. The United States also sought to link Iran with acts of terrorism throughout the region and beyond, both through its own agents and through local groups, and accused Iran of launching military threats and acts of subversion against Arab monarchies across the Gulf. Even Arab states suspicious of Iran's intentions, however, were concerned about the Americans' tendency to define "Iranian-backed terrorist groups" so broadly as to include, for example, Lebanese guerrillas fighting Israeli occupation forces in their own country.

The Clinton Administration was unable to show any evidence to suggest an upsurge in Iranian-backed terrorism to justify its increased efforts at isolating Iran. Although Iran has trained, funneled arms, and offered financial support to a number of extremist Islamic groups as well as to the repressive military government in Sudan, U.S. charges of direct Iranian responsibility for specific terrorist acts against Israeli or American targets remain dubious.[14] For example, the United States exerted enormous pressure on the Saudi government to implicate Iran in the 1996 terrorist bombing of the Khobar Towers in Dharan that killed nineteen American soldiers, even when Saudi investigators found no such link. Iran has challenged the United States to present evidence in an international judicial forum to prove its allegations, but the United States has refused.[15] Many now believe this terrorist attack may have been one of the first strikes by Osama bin Laden's Al-Qaeda network.

Investigations by the State Department reveal that Iranian support for terrorism has been almost exclusively through the Revolutionary Guards and Intelligence Ministry, both of which are beyond the control of Iran's president and legislature. Furthermore, most acts of international terrorism clearly linked to Iranian authorities have been directed at their own exiled dissidents, not against the United States.[16] Iran's immediate post-revolutionary zeal to export its ideology was short-lived, as internal problems and outside threats deflected the attention of its leadership. In addition, Iranians are culturally and religiously distinct from the Sunni Arabs who dominate most of the Middle East, particularly regarding the hierarchical structure of the Shiite Islam practiced in Iran, thus limiting the revolution's appeal as a model for other Middle Eastern states.

There is little evidence to support American warnings of aggressive Iranian designs in the Gulf, either. Iran has not threatened—nor does it have any reason for provoking—a confrontation over sea lanes as a number of American analysts have feared; the Iranians are at least as concerned as their Arab neighbors are about maintaining unrestricted navigation. By closing the Straits of Hormuz, Iran would be hurting itself: the lack of pipelines from its southern oil fields makes the Iranians far more dependent on tanker shipping than any other country on the Persian Gulf coast.

Iran has been dramatically reducing its military spending due to chronic economic problems. Indeed, Iranian military spending is barely one-third in constant dollars of what it was during the 1980s when the United States was clandestinely sending arms to the Islamic regime.[17] Additionally, despite increased Iranian procurement of sophisticated missiles, the Arab Gulf states have similar missile capabilities, serving along with the U.S. Navy as an effective deterrent force. The United States has cited Iran's occupation of three small islands claimed by the United Arab Emirates as evidence of aggressive Iranian designs in the Gulf.[18] However, Iran originally seized the islands—Abu Musa, Greater Tunbs and Lesser Tunbs—back in 1971 under the Shah with American and British encouragement.[19]

One litmus test of a country's aggressive designs on its neighbors is military procurement. As a country builds up on arms, troops and training, the chance that it may initiate war escalates as the probability that it could succeed rises. On this front, Iran seems *less* of a threat. Iran's military procurement relative to the GCC states is far less than it was during the 1970s under the Shah, when the United States was actually promoting arms sales to Iran. In addition, much of Iran's naval capability was destroyed by the United States in the 1987-88 Tanker War and Iran lost a large amount of its ground weaponry during Iraq's 1988 offensive. As much as half of Iran's inventory of major land-force weapons were destroyed in the course of the war.[20] While Iran's defensive capabilities have improved somewhat, there is little to suggest that they pose any kind of realistic offensive threat to the Gulf. Indeed, their number of tanks and planes is actually less than in 1980.[21]

Regarding potential conflicts on the country's eastern border, Iran came close to going to war against Afghanistan's Taliban regime in 1998 in response to repression against the country's Shiite minority and the killings of nine Iranian diplomats in the northern city of Mazar-e-Sharif. Iran has accepted nearly two million Afghan refugees throughout the more than two decades of war in Afghanistan. Iran also provided military and other support for the Northern Alliance in its fight against the Taliban. Iran has always strongly opposed Al-Qaeda and welcomed their ouster from Afghanistan, a country with which the Iranians have close ethnic and other ties. Al-Qaeda has similarly been antagonistic towards Iran, in part due to its Shia Islam, which bin Laden and his Sunni followers view as heretical.

Despite this, the Bush Administration in January 2002 gave a stern warning to Iran not to interfere in Afghanistan's internal affairs, an ironic admonition given that it came immediately after months of U.S. interference in Afghanistan that including heavy bombing, ground combat, the ouster of one government and the installation of another. The Bush Administration has also claimed that Iran allowed Al-Qaeda members to seek sanctuary in Iran, though it presented no evidence to support this allegation.

U.S. Policy Towards Iraq Through 1991: From Appeasement to War

Modern Iraq was the creation of British colonialists when they established control over the territory following the fall of the Ottoman Empire in 1918, forming the country out of three Ottoman provinces. A nationalist coup in 1958 overthrew the pro-British monarch, limiting Western influence in the country and shifting the ideological orientation towards a left-wing nationalism. The Baath Party, also nationalist and socialist in orientation, first seized power in 1963. Saddam Hussein rose to prominence between 1979 and 1982, imposing what effectively became a totalitarian state under his rule and shifting Iraq's pro-Soviet orientation to one more toward neutrality. France, Great Britain and the United States joined the Soviets in recognizing Iraq's importance in the regional balance of power. All maintained a largely cooperative relationship with Saddam Hussein's exceptionally oppressive regime, much to the chagrin of human rights advocates. While U.S. officials never considered the Iraqi regime an American ally, as some critics have claimed, Iraq was nevertheless seen as a strategic asset with which the United States could cooperate throughout the regime's dramatic military buildup in the 1980s.

For years, Middle East experts, human rights supporters, and many others called on the United States to get tough with Saddam Hussein's regime. Iraq's invasion of Iran, support for international terrorism, and large-scale human rights violations were all valid grounds for sanctions.

Perhaps most significant was Iraq's use of chemical warfare against both Iranian troops and the country's civilian Kurdish population during the 1980s—by far the largest such use of these illegal weapons since World War I. The response of the world's nations was a major test as to whether international law would be upheld through the imposition of stringent sanctions or other measures to challenge this dangerous precedent. The United States, along with much of the world community, failed. U.S. agricultural subsidies and other economic aid flowed into Iraq and American officials looked the other way as much of these funds were laundered into purchasing military equipment. The United States sent an untold amount of indirect aid—largely through Kuwait and other Arab countries—which enabled Iraq to receive weapons and technology to increase its war-making capacity.[22]

When a 1988 Senate Foreign Relations committee staff report brought to light Saddam Hussein's policy of widespread killings of Kurdish civilians in northern Iraq, Senator Claiborne Pell introduced the Prevention of Genocide Act to put pressure on the Iraqi government. However, the Reagan Administration successfully moved to have the measure killed.

This history of appeasement raises serious questions regarding the sincerity of both the strategic and moral concerns subsequently raised by U.S. officials about both the nature of the Iraqi regime and its threat against its neighbors.

In July 1990, with Saddam Hussein making direct threats against Kuwait, the Bush Administration again blocked congressional efforts to place modest sanctions against Iraq. Meanwhile, the U.S. ambassador, April Glaspie, a well-respected career diplomat, told the Iraqi dictator that the United States was neutral regarding the dispute. This stated neutrality, combined with years of appeasement, very likely gave Saddam Hussein the impression that he would be able to get away with an invasion of his southern neighbor.

Iraq invaded Kuwait on August 2, taking over the small emirate within hours. The royal family fled and any resistance to the Iraqi takeover was severely repressed. The United Nations Security Council quickly adopted resolution 660, condemning the invasion and demanding Iraq's immediate withdrawal. No other member of the Arab League supported the invasion and most vehemently opposed it. But most also wanted to keep it as an inter-Arab concern and avoid war if possible. Within days of Iraq's takeover, Arab leaders were apparently very close to convincing Iraq to withdraw. However, the United States decided to send large numbers of American troops into neighboring Saudi Arabia in response to Iraq's takeover, allegedly as a deterrent against further Iraqi aggression. According to then-Crown Prince Hassan of Jordan, the American-Saudi decision to implement what became known as "Operation Desert Shield" scuttled a tentative agreement he had made with Saddam Hussein to withdraw from Kuwait.[23] In return for the Arab-sponsored withdrawal, there may have been some compromises—perhaps on the exact location of the disputed desert border separating Iraq and Kuwait or a referendum on the future of Kuwait's monarchy. However, it appears that Iraq could have been convinced to withdraw from Kuwait within weeks of its invasion had the United States allowed Arab diplomacy to run its course. The Gulf War and the resulting humanitarian catastrophe could probably have been avoided.

Instead, then-Secretary of Defense Dick Cheney flew to Saudi Arabia to try to convince Saudi leaders that a major buildup of Iraqi forces in southern Kuwait indicated an imminent invasion of Saudi Arabia. He argued that the kingdom therefore needed to accept large numbers of American forces on its soil as a deterrent. While such an action by the Iraqis cannot be completely ruled out, it appears extremely unlikely: Iraq has never had territorial claims against Saudi Arabia as they did with Kuwait, their troops had dug into fortified defensive positions immediately upon entering Kuwait, and they chose not to move into Saudi Arabia prior to the arrival of sufficient Western forces to produce a credible deterrent. More significantly, the *St. Petersburg Times* got hold of satellite footage of the area from that critical period soon after the Iraqis seized Kuwait, and, contrary to U.S. government statements, there was no evidence of Iraqi troops massing on the border. The Florida newspaper showed the photos to Peter Zimmerman, formerly of the U.S. Arms Control and Disarmament Agency, and an unidentified Defense Intelligence Agency analyst, who noted, "We didn't see anything to indicate an Iraqi force in Kuwait of even 20% the size the administration claimed."[24] The newspaper asked the Pentagon to present evidence that would support its contention that Iraq was preparing to invade Saudi Arabia. It refused. Furthermore, Iraq apparently only had sent enough troops to suppress the Kuwaiti population initially, dramatically increasing the number of its troops only *after* U.S. forces arrived in the region. In any case, the decision to bring in American troops enabled Saddam Hussein to project himself not as the aggressor who had just invaded a small neighboring country, but as the defender of the

Arab world against an army of Western imperialists.

In an interesting historical footnote, bin Laden—then back in Saudi Arabia after fighting against the Soviets in Afghanistan—had been strongly denouncing Saddam Hussein for months and even warned the Saudi government that Iraq could be on the verge of invading Kuwait. The Saudis sought to silence him, but he persisted in his warnings. When Iraq did invade, bin Laden sent an "I told you so" letter to King Fahd, but promised that he could organize a massive international force of *mujahadin* to repel the Iraqi invaders. In what bin Laden would later call "the most shocking moment of his life," Fahd rejected this offer of pan-Islamic solidarity against the Iraqi invasion and instead accepted the American plan.[25]

Even after U.S. troops entered the region, there were possibilities for a negotiated settlement. However, there was no American attempt to negotiate. The only direct contact between the two nations prior to the outbreak of the war was one meeting in Geneva at the foreign ministry level a week before hostilities broke out. There, Secretary of State James Baker presented a letter written by President Bush informing Saddam Hussein that his only choice was to capitulate without negotiation or be crushed by force. In the letter, which was rejected by Iraqi Foreign Minister Tariq Aziz for its undiplomatic language, Bush stated, "There can be no reward for aggression. Nor will there be any negotiation. Principle cannot be compromised."[26] Specialists on the negotiation process were very critical of U.S. conduct prior to the war, primarily noting how the United States never gave the Iraqis any opportunity to save face. Says Harvard Law School professor Roger Fisher, Director of the Harvard Negotiation Project, from the Iraqi perspective

> The choice of staying in Kuwait outweighed the choice of withdrawal because there was no reason to believe that the U.S. would remove its forces from Saudi Arabia after Iraq left Kuwait, that UN sanctions against Iraq would be lifted after withdrawal, that Palestinian interests would be linked to withdrawal, that Iraqi access to the sea would be ensured, etc. Thus, Hussein's position on this issue becomes understandable. Knowing this, something could have been done to reduce his uncertainty about the consequences of the decision to withdraw. [27]

There were certainly a number of ways the United States may have been able to negotiate an Iraqi withdrawal from Kuwait and other legitimate security concerns short of war, but these were not pursued. Indeed, it is commonly assumed in the Arab Middle East that the Bush

Administration wanted to go to war.[28]

The United Nations Security Council imposed comprehensive military and economic sanctions on Iraq in the aftermath of its invasion of Kuwait, but they were unsuccessful in convincing the Iraqis to withdraw. These pre-war sanctions would have probably worked with time, however. The CIA estimated that UN sanctions blocked 90 percent of Iraqi imports and 97 percent of Iraqi exports;[29] no country so heavily dependent on trade can survive very long under those conditions. This was a much higher rate of compliance than what has existed in the far more controversial post-war sanctions regime. In Iraq during this period, there were long gas lines in a country that had been a major exporter of oil; there were chronic shortages of basic foodstuffs, such as rice, bread, and sugar, which are staples in the Iraqi diet; there were breakdowns from lavatories to automobiles because of a lack of spare parts; in a country with a largely planned economy that had controlled prices, hyper-inflation was ignited.[30]

The sanctions were working materially, in severely limiting imports and exports and thereby causing great economic hardship, but they were not working politically. The reasons were two-fold: first, the United States insisted that sanctions would continue even if Iraq withdrew from Kuwait. Viewed from Iraq's perspective, why withdraw if sanctions were to continue anyway? Secondly, the Iraqis were faced with a simultaneous military threat. When a country is faced with an external threat to its security—in this case, a half million troops in the largest multi-national force ever assembled poised to attack across their southern border—people are willing to tolerate more economic deprivation than they might otherwise as they rally around the flag.

Had sanctions been imposed some years earlier, as a response to Saddam Hussein's previous crimes—when he invaded Iran in 1980 or when he first used chemical weapons soon thereafter—it is likely he would not have invaded Kuwait because he would have known there would be severe economic consequences as a result. Or, had the sanctions been applied following his invasion of Kuwait but with an offer to lift them upon withdrawal and without a simultaneous military threat, he likely would have withdrawn prior to the outbreak of hostilities. War was not the only option.

However, the United States systematically rejected a series of peace overtures by the French, the Soviets, and the Yemenis, instead favoring a massive military response. Indeed, in the weeks before the launch of the bombing on January 16, the talk in Washington of a "nightmare scenario" was in reference to an Iraqi withdrawal from Kuwait without having to go to war.[31] The U.S. position was that, without a war, Saddam Hussein's regime would remain with its military assets intact, free to sell its oil, popular among some segments of the Arab world's population and still able to threaten its neighbors. This was considered unacceptable. However, Saddam Hussein could only have become the threat he did with the help of the United States and various European countries during the previous years. As a result, the need to destroy Iraq's potential for future aggression through war was unnecessary, since preventing the regime's future development as a threat required only that the United States and others in the international community cut off Iraq's acquisition of weapons.

As a result, just as the United States had downplayed Iraq's potential threat previously when the regime was seen as a potential asset, the United States then began to exaggerate Iraq's potential threat, as exemplified by the senior President Bush's characterization of Saddam Hussein as "another Hitler." The Hitler bogeyman has been used repeatedly to justify attacks by Western nations against the Third World. Prior to their invasion of Egypt in 1956, the British and French insisted that Egyptian leader Gamal Abdul-Nasser was comparable to Hitler. In the 1960s, the United States argued that without a major war in Vietnam, the Communists would then try to take over the rest of Southeast Asia as the Nazis did in Europe, as part of an effort to take over the world.[32] In the 1980s, Secretary of State George Schultz claimed the Sandinista government of Nicaragua was like the Nazis in that they were going to invade the rest of Central America if they were not overthrown. Such terminology was used again in order to frighten a skeptical American public into supporting a war against Iraq. As an example of the extent of this manipulation, a photograph of Saddam Hussein on the cover of the influential New Republic magazine was airbrushed in such way that his long moustache was significantly shortened so he would look more like Adolf Hitler.[33]

The fact is, however, that Iraq never had the industrial capacity, the self-sustaining economy, the domestic arms industry, the population base, the coherent ideology or political mobilization, the powerful allies, or any of the necessary components for large-scale military conquest as did the German, Italian, and Japanese fascists of the 1930s and 1940s. Though better off than most of the non-Western world, Iraq was still a Third World country. While the regime certainly could do damage to its own population and territories on its immediate border, it never had the capability of seizing or holding on to large amounts of territory. Furthermore, Hitler's conquering armies could never have been defeated in less than six weeks, as were the forces of Saddam Hussein.

The use of such hyperbole by the Bush Administration was successful not just in getting a reluctant Congress and public to support the decision to go to war. It also served to discredit domestic anti-war critics who incorrectly predicted high American casualties. Historically, armed forces have exaggerated their own strength and minimized their opponents' strengths in order to convince their enemies not to engage in an act of aggression. This has been one of the foundations of the theory of deterrence. However, recent decades have witnessed the reversal of this. The U.S. government consistently has exaggerated the military force of its opponents—be they Soviet, Nicaraguan, or Iraqi—and downplayed the ability of the United States and its allies to resist or overcome it. From the perspective of deterrence, this would be totally foolish, since to exaggerate your enemy's strength while understating your own ability to resist it would be to invite attack. However, if a country's national security is not really at stake and the primary goal of the government is to convince the public that it is worth diverting a large amount of the nation's resources to military production and/or to engage in a war, making such claims then makes sense. In addition, after the Bush Administration deliberately exaggerated the strength of the enemy and U.S. forces ended up defeating Iraq soundly with minimal American casualties, it came across as an incredible victory. As a result, the popularity of the U.S. military and President Bush soared. In any case, this one-sided military victory led the American public—who initially had been very skeptical, with only 47% of the public favoring going to war at the end of 1990—to support it overwhelmingly, with over 80% expressing their approval three months later.

There was impressive unity in the international community in opposing Iraq's aggression against Kuwait and the pre-war sanctions were almost universally respected. However, there was not as much international support for the U.S.-led war effort as claimed at the time. Within the Arab world, only the unpopular Gulf monarchs, Syrian dictator Hafez Assad (a bitter rival of Saddam Hussein despite sharing his Baathist roots), and the autocratic rulers of the economically dependent North African regimes of Egypt, Tunisia and Morocco supported the war. No other Arab leader supported the U.S.-led military campaign against Iraq.[34] The primary support for the American military operation came from Western Europe.

Even the United Nations Security Council resolution authorizing the use of force, passed on November 29, was not as clear an indication of international support as it was made out to be by the United States. In return for the Chinese not vetoing the resolution, the U.S. dropped trade sanctions imposed following the brutal suppression of the pro-democracy movement in 1989 and approved new loans. In return for the Soviet Union's support, the United States agreed not to discuss the Soviet repression in the Baltic republics in the upcoming Paris Peace Conference. Colombia and Zaire, non-permanent members, were promised increased aid and extensions of loans. When Yemen, also a non-permanent member, refused to buckle under to similar pressure, the U.S. yanked $70 million in aid scheduled to go to that impoverished country.[35] Even among the many Arabs and other Muslims who opposed Iraq's conquest of Kuwait and wanted it reversed, the U.S.-led war was seen as avoidable, unnecessary, and more of an excuse for a major U.S.-led military operation than a genuine American desire to support international law and stop aggression.

The Gulf War: The Storm and its Residue

In a military campaign dubbed "Operation Desert Storm," the United States and its allies began bombing Iraq on January 16, 1991, one day after the United Nations-imposed deadline for Iraqi withdrawal from Kuwait. It was almost exclusively an air war until American ground troops entered the fighting in late February, liberating Kuwait and occupying a large swath of southern Iraq in slightly more than four days.

In mid-February, after four weeks of bombing and prior to the launch of the allied ground assault, Iraq accepted a Soviet peace proposal in full and agreed to withdraw from Kuwait in compliance with UN Security Council resolution 660. The United States, however, rejected the deal and pledged to continue prosecuting the war. Even as Iraqi forces finally began withdrawing from Kuwait, the United States continued its assault in violation of provisions of the Fourth Geneva Convention that outlaw the killing of soldiers who are out of combat.[36] Rather than the one-sided victory in the ground war being exclusively the result of American military prowess, it appears that most of the Iraqis were evacuating or already had evacuated their positions when the U.S. ground forces arrived. The *Washington Post* confirmed that tens of thousands of Iraqi troops had withdrawn a full 36 hours before the first allied forces reached Kuwait City. These forces, too, were pursued relentlessly by the American assault. Thousands of retreating soldiers as well as some civilian refugees and hostages were slaughtered as they fled northward on what became known as "the highway of death." American pilots referred to it as a "turkey shoot."[37]

Though the United Nations had only authorized member states to do what was necessary to rid Iraqi forces from Kuwait, the United States was determined to inflict a devastating blow to Iraq's infrastructure through what became, in a period of just six weeks, the heaviest bombing campaign in the history of war. Even Saddam Hussein's most strident critics in the Gulf were offended at the level of overkill, particularly what was inflicted upon Iraq's civilian population, unwilling conscripts, and the country's non-military infrastructure.[38] By attacking roads, bridges, factories, irrigation systems, power stations, water works, and government offices, the U.S.-led military offensive against Iraq went well beyond what was necessary to rid Iraqi occupation forces from Kuwait.

According to a *Washington Post* report soon after the war,

> Many of the targets were chosen only secondarily to contribute to the military defeat of Iraq....Military planners hoped the bombing would amplify the economic and psychological impact of international sanctions on Iraqi society....Because of these goals, damage to civilian structures and interests, invariably described by briefers during the war as "collateral" and unintended, were sometimes neither.....They deliberately did great harm to Iraq's ability to support itself as an industrial society.[39]

Most of Saddam Hussein's forces were conscripts. Many were opponents of Saddam Hussein, who may have opposed the invasion of Kuwait and been as unwilling as many American draftees were in Vietnam. In fact, the Iraqi dictator deliberately placed a disproportionate number of Kurds, Assyrian Christians, Shiites, and other groups traditionally opposed to his rule on the front lines, hoping that they would bear the brunt of the casualties. The United States obliged, killing tens of thousands of them, even as they retreated. The result is that more opponents of the Iraqi government were killed by six weeks of U.S. attacks than in the previous twenty years of Saddam Hussein's repression. There are many stories by American troops of how desperate Iraqi soldiers were to surrender. While many were able to do so, the majority were never given that chance. Large numbers were buried alive by high-speed U.S. Army bulldozers.

Most estimates put the Iraqi death toll in the Gulf War in the range of 100,000. Due to the increased accuracy of aerial warfare, the proportion of Iraqi civilians killed was much less than it had been in previous air campaigns. At the same time, because the bombing was the heaviest in world history—consisting of tens of thousands of sorties—the absolute numbers were quite high. Most estimates of the civilian death toll are approximately 15,000.[40] It should be noted that even the so-called "smart bombs" had at most a 60 percent accuracy rate—Americans did not see any footage of the 40 percent that missed their targets, sometimes by miles. It should also be noted that only 9% of the bombs dropped were these laser-guided weapons.[41] The degree of destruction wrought by U.S. forces during the Gulf War is well-known throughout the Islamic world, however, and is yet another source of anger at the United States, even among those who supported the liberation of Kuwait by force.

Meanwhile, the long-suppressed Kurds in the north and Shiites in the south launched a rebellion against Saddam Hussein's regime at the end of the war. They initially made major advances, only to be crushed in a counter-attack by Iraqi government forces. Despite President Bush calling on the people of Iraq to rise up against the dictatorship, U.S. forces—which at that time occupied the southern fifth of the country—did nothing to support the post-war rebellion and stood by while thousands of Iraqi Kurds, Shiites, and others were killed. In the cease-fire agreement at the end of the war, the United States made a conscious decision to exclude Iraqi helicopter gunships from the ban on Iraqi military air traffic. These were the very weapons that proved so decisive in crushing the rebellions. It appeared to be a repeat of what happened only fifteen years earlier: After goading the Kurds into an armed uprising with the promise of military support, the United States abandoned them precipitously as part of an agreement with the Baghdad government for a territorial compromise favorable to Iran regarding the Shatt al-Arab waterway.[42] Thousands were slaughtered.

The reason that the United States allowed the Iraqi regime to crush the post-war rebellions was another triumph of political interest over principle. The Bush Administration feared that a victory by Iraqi Kurds might encourage the ongoing Kurdish uprising in Turkey, a NATO ally.[43] Similarly, the United States feared that a radical Shiite Arab entity might emerge in southern Iraq, which could have serious implications for American allies in the Gulf with restive Shiite populations.

Saddam Hussein's regime, then as now, is extraordinarily brutal. Yet this has never been what bothered the United States, given that the U.S. has provided large-scale military support to regimes that have been responsible for even more civilian deaths, such as that of Suharto in Indonesia. Still, Saddam Hussein was admired throughout the Islamic world for the fact that, despite corruption and the enormous amount of resources diverted to the military, pre-war Iraq ranked among the highest countries in the Third World in terms of health care, nutrition, education and other social and economic statistics. Part of what has always bothered the United States about Saddam Hussein has been his ability to articulate the frustrations of the Arab masses on the Palestinian question, on control of their natural resources, and on resistance to foreign domination. He was certainly opportunistic and manipulative in doing so, but he was effective. Most Arabs strongly opposed Iraq's takeover of Kuwait and were keenly aware of the nature of Saddam Hussein's regime and of its brutality. Yet Kuwait was not the issue to them; it became much more than that. With the launch of the allied attacks, it became a conflict between the West and one of the most forceful spokesmen for Arab nationalism. There was real concern in the region and beyond that the United States used Iraq's invasion of Kuwait as an excuse to advance its long-desired military, political, and economic hegemony in the region. As a result, the U.S. prosecution of the war inflamed and created new hatreds of the United States throughout the Muslim world.

Indeed, the U.S.-led military response to Iraq's invasion of Kuwait turned Saddam Hussein from aggressor to defender and from bully to hero in the eyes of much of the Arab world. As a result, there were many Arabs, like the majority of Jordanians and Palestinians, who had never particularly liked Saddam Hussein but came to his side. This is a perspective that spread throughout the Islamic world and beyond, based upon a very deep-seated feeling of a people who have repeatedly been subjected to foreign domination and who found a symbol of resistance in Saddam Hussein, who came to represent Arab frustrations. Though tarnished by the decisiveness of the dictator's defeat, his use as a symbol of resistance has not boded well for the development of more responsible leadership in the Middle East.

In this respect, the United States won the battle, but lost the war. The United States defeated Saddam Hussein's army, but is now faced with tens of millions of Arabs, both inside and outside of Iraq, who are more hostile to the United States than they had been previously and with whom the United States will have to contend for many years to come. It is from such people that Osama bin Laden has found his recruits and other supporters. Had war actually been the only viable option and the goal really was to deter Iraqi aggression against Kuwait and potential aggression against Saudi Arabia, upholding international law and other important principles, the United States would have had far more support for its actions. However, the senior President Bush, in a moment of candor, acknowledged what he saw as the real lesson of the Gulf War for dictators who challenge the United States: "What we say goes."[44]

The Ongoing Bombing of Iraq

Though Iraq was forced out of Kuwait more than a decade ago, the United States has continued periodic bombing campaigns against the severely war-damaged nation. In April 1993, the Kuwaiti government revealed that it had evidence that Iraqi operatives had infiltrated Kuwait as part of an effort to assassinate former President George Bush during a visit to the emirate and convicted several men in the alleged plot. Though the evidence was never made public and the fairness of the Kuwaiti judicial system frequently has been questioned, President Clinton ordered the bombing of Baghdad in retaliation. The U.S. raids destroyed a number of government buildings and struck a residential neighborhood as well, killing Leila al-Attar, the country's leading female artist, and several others. In September 1996, following an Iraqi incursion into the northern part of the country at the request of a Kurdish faction battling a rival Iranian-backed Kurdish faction, the United States launched another series of major bombing raids against Iraq. This rush to the defense of the Kurds may have been just a pretext, however: while the incursion took place in the north, most of the U.S. air strikes took place in the central and southern parts of Iraq.

The United States, Great Britain and France unilaterally initiated "no-fly zones" in northern and southern Iraq in March 1991 in response to widespread international concern over the humanitarian crisis following the aborted uprisings by Kurds and Shiites against the government. These no-fly zones have no precedent in international law and no authorization from the United Nations; France subsequently dropped out of the enforcement efforts. Despite their dubious legality, however, the no-fly zones initially received widespread support as a means of curbing the Iraqi government's savage repression of its Kurdish and Shiite communities. The "no-fly zones" initially were designed to protect these areas from Iraqi air strikes by banning Iraqi military flights.

According to two State Department reports in 1994 and 1996, however, the creation and military enforcement of "no-fly zones" in fact do not protect the Iraqi Kurdish and Shiite populations from potential assaults by Iraqi forces. The straight latitudinal demarcations of the no-fly zones do not correspond with the areas of predominant Kurdish and Shiite populations and the targets of the American and British air strikes have no relation to preventing Iraqi attacks against vulnerable minorities. That the United States has allowed the Turkish Air Force to conduct bombing raids and large-scale incursions within the northern Iraq "no-fly zone" against Kurdish targets is but one indication of the lack of concern about actually protecting the Kurdish population. What began as an apparent humanitarian effort has turned into another excuse for continuing a low-level war against Iraq.

Hopes that the new Bush Administration might reverse the Clinton Administration's policies were shattered within weeks of assuming office when the United States bombed a series of targets in suburban Baghdad. Despite Bush Administration claims that the United States was simply enforcing the no-fly zones in northern and southern Iraq, the targets of the March 2001 attacks were well outside both no-fly zones and had no apparent defensive rationale. Marine Lieutenant General Gregory Newbold, director of operations for the Joint Chiefs of Staff, justified the air strikes as a necessary response to Iraqi "aggression," namely its locking its radar on American warplanes. While the Iraqi government certainly has engaged in acts of aggression in the recent past, this may be the first time in history that the use of radar to track foreign military aircraft encroaching within a country's internationally-recognized airspace has been declared an act of aggression.

Initially, the American use of force was justified as a challenge to Iraqi encroachments into the proscribed airspace. Then, it was escalated to include assaults on anti-aircraft batteries that fired at allied aircraft enforcing the zone. It escalated still further when anti-aircraft batteries were attacked simply for locking on their radar toward allied aircraft, even without firing. Then, the Clinton Administration began attacking radar installations and other military targets within the no-fly zone, even when they were unrelated to an alleged Iraqi threat against a U.S. aircraft. With the March 2001 air strikes, the Bush Administration has expanded the targeting still further, attacking radar and command-and-control installations well beyond the no-fly zones. Since early 1999, U.S. and British warplanes have been bombing Iraq an average of once a week.

The actual extent of the threat posed by Iraq may be understood by looking at the actions of its neighbors who would suffer from potential Iraqi aggression. Throughout all the U.S. air strikes since the end of the Gulf War, none of the GCC states that the United States purportedly is defending has ever requested such military action from the United States on their behalf. During the September 1996 air strikes following Iraqi incursions into Kurdish areas, Operation Desert Fox in December 1998, as well as subsequent air strikes, the Saudis have refused to allow U.S. air force jets stationed in their territory to participate. This has forced the United States to rely primarily on Navy jets based on aircraft carriers or Air Force jets at NATO facilities in Turkey. In short, there is little strategic rationale for the ongoing U.S. attacks against Iraq. Given that these attacks are creating widespread resentment throughout the Arab and Islamic world, it raises serious questions as to whether such military activity does more harm than good to American security interests.

The administrations of both parties, echoed by media pundits, portray the ongoing low-level air war as putting pressure on Iraqi dictator Saddam Hussein, yet—as in the Gulf War—the Iraqi dictator has not been harmed. However, hundreds of Iraqi civilians and Iraqi conscripts have been killed in these air attacks. This creeping escalation of the enforcement of the no-fly zones adds to the considerable belief that the United States actually has been looking for excuses to bomb Iraq, increasing still further the growing anti-American sentiment in the Arab and Islamic world.

Although American political leaders often dismiss those resentful of U.S. power projection in the region as irrational, opponents of the ongoing air strikes against Iraq do have a strong case regarding international law. The United States initially rationalized Operation Desert Fox—the four-day bombing campaign in December 1998—on the grounds that Iraq was in violation of United Nations Security Council Resolution 687. As described in Chapter Two, under the imposed cease-fire agreement at the close of the 1991 Gulf War, Iraq is required to allow unimpeded access by UNSCOM inspectors to insure that Iraq has disarmed to the degree required under that resolution.

However, the conflict regarding access for UN inspectors has always been between the Iraqi government and the United Nations, not between Iraq and the United States. Though UN Security Council resolution 687 was the most detailed in the world body's history, no enforcement mechanisms were specified. Enforcement is a matter for the UN Security Council as a whole, as is normally done when governments violate all or parts of such resolutions. According to articles 41 and 42 of the United Nations Charter, no member state has the right to enforce any resolution militarily unless the UN Security Council determines there has been a material breach of its resolution and that all non-military means of enforcement have been exhausted and then specifically authorizes the use of military force. This is what the Security Council did in November 1990 with resolution 678 in response to Iraq's ongoing occupation of Kuwait. Therefore, every U.S. attack against Iraq since the Iraqi withdrawal from Kuwait in 1991 has been illegal. Indeed, they create a very dangerous precedent. Following the U.S. example, Russia could claim the right to attack Israel,

France could claim the right to attack Turkey and Great Britain could claim the right to attack Morocco simply because those governments, no less so than Iraq, are in violation of UN Security Council resolutions. The U.S. insistence on the right to attack unilaterally has effectively undermined the principle of collective security and the very authority of the United Nations.

International law is quite clear as to when military force is allowed. In addition to the aforementioned case of UN Security Council authorization, the only other time any member state is allowed to use armed force is described in Article 51, which states it is permissible for "individual or collective self-defense" against "armed attack...until the Security Council has taken the measures necessary to maintain international peace and security."[45] If any of Iraq's neighbors or the United States had felt threatened by Saddam Hussein's armed forces, any one of these countries could have approached the Security Council and made their case as to why their security was threatened. Iraq's neighbors have not done so subsequent to 1991, apparently because they have not felt threatened. The United States has not done so because such a claim would be seen as ludicrous, and, as a result, would have virtually no support on the Security Council. Despite the fact that the UN Charter was ratified by the United States and thus, according to the U.S. Constitution, has force of law, the Clinton and Bush Administrations and the leaders of both major political parties have supported the ongoing bombing. As Secretary of State, Madeleine Albright callously dismissed the lack of international support by saying that the United States would act against Iraq "multilaterally if we can and unilaterally if we must" because "We recognize this area as vital to U.S. national interests." [46]

When the UN Security Council unanimously endorsed Secretary General Annan's agreement with Iraq in March 1998 to open the so-called "presidential sites" to inspections, it rejected American insistence that they authorize the use of force in the case of future non-compliance. While warning Iraq of "severest consequences," the Security Council, in the resolution's final paragraph, declared that it alone had the authority to "ensure implementation of this resolution and peace and security in the area."[47] This point was reiterated by a number of ambassadors as well as in most analyses by the media that followed. Despite this, U.S. Ambassador to the United Nations Bill Richardson declared that the agreement "did not preclude the unilateral use of force."[48] Similarly, State Department spokesman James Rubin insisted "we've made clear that we don't see the need to return to the Security Council if there is a violation of the agreement."[49] President Clinton claimed, despite the wording of the final paragraph, that the resolution "provides authority to act" if the United States was not satisfied with the level of Iraqi compliance.[50] Nine months later, the United States launched major air strikes against Iraq and periodic bombing raids have continued ever since.

Given the strong legal tradition to which the United States professes, this open contempt for international law has resulted in enormous anger among Arabs and other Muslims, particularly in light of Islam's own strong historical commitment to legal principles. This has made it possible for radical elements in the Middle East to discount international law and even the United Nations itself as simply tools of U.S. imperialism and excuses for American militarism.

Post-War Sanctions Against Iraq: Fuel to the Fire?

The international sanctions were originally imposed on Iraq in August 1990 in response to its refusal to abide by UN Security Council resolution 660, requiring its withdrawal from Kuwait. Despite Iraq's forced compliance with the resolution seven months later, the sanctions have continued, this time on the grounds that Iraq has not fully complied with the provisions of UN Security Council resolution 687.

While the repressive nature of Baathist rule under Saddam Hussein during the 1980s is well documented, the Iraqi regime also maintained a comprehensive and generous welfare state. The nutritional and health care needs of the population were mostly fulfilled and Iraqis enjoyed the highest per capita caloric intake in the Arab Middle East. Most of the population had direct access to safe water and modern sanitation facilities; there was a wide network of well-functioning and well-supplied hospitals and health care centers. The overall economy was strong, with Iraq considered a "middle income" country, importing large numbers of foreign guest workers to fill empty spots in its growing economy. Now, it ranks as one of the most impoverished countries in the world.

The limited media coverage in the United States regarding the hardships inflicted by the sanctions has focussed primarily upon the once-prosperous Iraqi middle class, and has featured professors selling their valuable books, families selling their beloved pets and women selling their family jewelry in order to buy basic necessities. Yet it is Iraq's poor, particularly the children, who have suffered most.

Ongoing United Nations sanctions—most vigorously supported by the United States—have in Iraq's case killed many times more civilians than did the war itself. An August 1999 UNICEF report noted that the mortality rate for children under five has more than doubled since sanctions were imposed.[51] Estimates of the total number of Iraqis killed as a result of malnutrition and preventable diseases as a direct consequence of the combination of war damage and sanctions have ranged from a quarter million to over one million, the majority of whom have been children.[52] Though the sanctions have been justified as a means of preventing Iraq from developing weapons of mass destruction, they have already killed more civilians that all the chemical, biological and nuclear weapons ever used. Perhaps there has been no other time in history when so many people have been condemned to death from malnutrition and preventable diseases due to political decisions made overseas.

In an interview on the CBS news show 60 Minutes when she was Secretary of State, Albright was asked about the devastating impact sanctions were having on the children of Iraq, with host Lesley Stahl quoting the figure of half a million killed. Albright replied that "we think the price...is worth it."[53]

These deaths are a result of inadequate medical supplies, impure water and nutritional deficiencies. During the Gulf War, the United States destroyed eighteen out of twenty electrical power stations, disabling water pumping and sanitation systems, some of which were also hit directly. The result has been untreated sewage flowing into rivers used for drinking water. Since the embargo prohibited the importation of many of the spare parts, allegedly because they could also be used as components in military systems, the Iraqis have been unable to repair these facilities. As a result, there has been a dramatic increase in typhoid, cholera and other illnesses that largely had been eliminated in Iraq prior to the 1991 Gulf War. Importation of ambulances and other emergency vehicles, and even their spare parts, were also among the items banned under the sanctions. Similarly, hospitals were unable to acquire spare parts for incubators, kidney dialysis machines and other equipment. Even materials such as food and medicines not covered by the ban have become difficult to purchase due to the lack of capital. Electricity is irregular and conditions at hospitals are becoming increasingly unsanitary. A full quarter of the school-aged population is no longer in school in a country that previously had near-universal primary education. For those who can attend school, books and other educational resources are in extremely short supply. Severe malnutrition has led to stunted physical and mental development of hundreds of thousands of Iraqi children.

According to the UN Food and Agricultural Organization (FAO), "Four million people, one-fifth of the population, are currently starving to death in Iraq. Twenty-three percent of all children in Iraq have stunted growth, approximately twice the percentage before the war....Alarming food shortages are causing irreparable damage to an entire generation of children."[54]

There was little controversy within the international community in 1990 when sanctions were originally imposed by the United Nations immediately following Iraq's invasion, occupation and annexation of Kuwait. But these post-war sanctions have far less international support. Unlike some other countries subjected to heavy air strikes, such as largely rural societies like Vietnam in the 1960s and Afghanistan in the 1980s, the heavily urbanized Iraqis suffered far greater with the collapse of their civilian infrastructure. In addition to the sudden absence of clean drinking water, there was a breakdown of the normal distribution systems for basic commodities due to damaged roads, railways and bridges. Furthermore, due in part to the fact that it is a largely arid country dependent on irrigation systems that were severely damaged (and apparently deliberately targeted) by the bombing, there have been severe food shortages as well.

U.S. officials blame the suffering on the Iraqi regime for its failure to cooperate more fully with the United Nations and for delaying for six years the implementation of the oil-for-food program. According to former Secretary of State Albright, "Saddam Hussein is the one who has the fate of his country in his hands, and he is the one who is responsible for starving children, not the United States of America."[55] The far better health situation in the Kurdish areas not controlled by the Iraqi government has also led to claims that the Iraqi regime could be doing a better job. However, these northern areas are subjected to less stringent sanctions regarding local cash and procurement and the northern part of the country suffered less damage from the war, gets more rainfall and receives proportionally more aid. Another criticism is in regard to the Iraqi government's decision to use scarce resources for the construction of opulent mosques and additional palaces for Saddam Hussein, his family and associates. The Iraqis claim that these function as public works projects using indigenous materials and are paid for in Iraqi *dinars*, currency that is worthless outside Iraq.

Albright insisted that the Iraqi government's response to the sanctions was a test to prove if Saddam Hussein really cared about his people. Most knowledgeable observers of Iraq recognize that no such test is necessary: the Iraqi dictator's primary concern has always been his own power. While Saddam Hussein is indeed ultimately responsible for his people's suffering from the sanctions, it has long become apparent that such suffering is not altering Iraqi policy, therefore raising the question as to whether the United States shares some of the moral culpability for this humanitarian disaster. Most of the Islamic world seems to think it does.

Oil exports, Iraq's primary source for foreign exchange, were also subject to the embargo until December 1996, when the United Nations and the Iraqi government agreed to establish an oil-for-food program, where a limited amount of petroleum could be sold for food under strict UN monitoring. Initially, Iraq was allowed to sell only $2 billion in oil for food. A full 25% of the oil sales go to Kuwait—one of the wealthiest countries in the world—for war damage from the seven-month Iraqi occupation in 1990-91, a reduction from the initial 30%. Another 13% goes to Kurdish areas in the north through a UN-controlled program. An addition 3% goes to cover UN administration costs, leaving only 59% going to the rest of Iraq. Though the FAO and the WHO have given Iraq high marks for their distribution of food and medicine, the UN estimates that about $4 billion is the minimum needed to meet basic needs for food and medicines. Over initial U.S. objections, the UN raised the amount of oil that could be sold to $5.2 billion (or $3.5 billion which actually could go to Iraq) in the spring of 1997 and removed the cap altogether in December 1999. However, the inability of Iraq to import spare parts for its oil industry has made it difficult for Iraq to pump enough oil to meet the minimum needed. There is also the risk of serious environmental consequences as the Iraqis pump as much as they can using aging equipment.

The oil-for-food program was crippled by allowing any member of the Security Council, through the 661 Committee, to block indefinitely any Iraqi imports outside of food and medicine, resulting in more than $5.3 billion worth of contracts being held up by 2002, largely as a result of U.S. objections. UN Secretary General Annan accused the United States of "disrupting the Oil-For-Food program upon which millions of people depend for their survival." [56]

The United States tacitly acknowledged this failure through Secretary of State Powell's advocacy, soon after he came to office in early 2001, for what he termed "smart sanctions." On May 14, 2002, the UN Security Council unanimously endorsed a U.S.-sponsored overhaul of sanctions that makes it somewhat easier for Iraq to import civilian goods. Most Security Council members wanted the economic sanctions lifted altogether, so it took more than a year of negotiations to come to this compromise. According to this new sanctions regime, the 661 Committee has been abolished. Humanitarian goods are now able to go through unencumbered. Military items are still banned and a new committee now reviews potential dual use items.

This reform has allowed additional food, medical supplies and other humanitarian goods into the country, but will do virtually nothing to rebuild Iraq's badly damaged public infrastructure, including its public health facilities. The problem has always been less what Iraq can or cannot import as much as its inability to use the oil money to pay wages, finance public works projects, run hospitals or provide social services. The lack of cash allows the regime to monopolize access to essential goods and services. For example, Iraqi children are dying not as much from lack of food as they are from bad water resulting from the lack of funds or parts to rebuild the country's water treatment system. The conservative British magazine *The Economist* referred to smart sanctions as "stringent and intrusive controls on trade and finance, keeping Iraq a soup kitchen, albeit a more efficient one."[57] Furthermore, the magazine noted,

> Although the country would be able to import more, it would still be denied the free movement of labor and capital that it desperately needs if it is at last to start picking itself up. Iraq needs massive investment to rebuild its industry, its power grids and its schools, and needs cash in hand to pay its engineers, doctors and teachers. None of this looks likely to happen under "smart sanctions."[58]

In short, while the revised sanctions regime may marginally ease some of the worst aspects of the humanitarian crisis, there is no way it will meet most of the basic needs of the Iraqi people. Only an end of the economic sanctions will stimulate the economy to a degree that will make it possible to rebuild the country's infrastructure so badly damaged in the war and to allow any semblance of civil society to return. As one anonymous U.S. official told the *Financial Times*, despite all the media attention given to the new sanctions regime, "In reality, this is a change of perceptions."[59]

The sanctions have not only led to enormous human suffering, they have been counter-productive to the broader U.S. goal of bringing down the Iraqi dictator. As with other Arab countries, the forces capable of successfully challenging Saddam's regime would likely have arisen out of Iraq's middle class. Unfortunately, having been reduced to penury and struggling simply to survive, they no longer serve as an effective political opposition. Thousands have emigrated. Meanwhile, as more and more families become dependent on government rations for their very survival, they are forced to cooperate even more with the government and the already-high risks of challenging Saddam Hussein's rule has become too great for most. In addition, a new and powerful elite has emerged from the resulting black market economy that has a strong stake in maintaining the status quo. Lifting non-military sanctions would allow for the country to be deluged with businesspeople and other outsiders, creating an environment far more likely to result in a political opening than the current sanctions regime which places this country of 22 million in impoverished isolation under Saddam Hussein's grip.

One litmus test for the effectiveness of any sanctions regime is the willingness of leaders of the pro-democracy movement to have their people endure the hardships imposed. Calls by opposition groups for sanctions are a strong indication that they can indeed be useful. However, in the case of Iraq, virtually every recognized Iraqi opposition group has come out against the sanctions. This is in sharp contrast to apartheid South Africa, where representatives of its black majority lobbied for sanctions by the international community, sanctions that ultimately had a very positive and perhaps decisive impact in the struggle for majority rule. (Ironically, in this case, the United States opposed sanctions against South Africa until a growing anti-apartheid movement in the United States forced a change of policy in 1986.)

Part of the ineffectiveness of the sanctions comes from the nature of Saddam Hussein's regime. It is more than simply another authoritarian Middle Eastern government; next to North Korea, it is probably the most totalitarian regime in the world. Therefore, the ability of the population to organize effectively against the government or its policies, particularly under such dire economic conditions as those created by the sanctions, is severely limited.

The morality of a particular foreign policy is tempered by its results. If human suffering from economic sanctions can advance a policy goal that would lead to less suffering in the long term, one could make the case that it is morally justified. Yet the apparent failure of the sanctions to move Iraq's level of compliance with the international community forward raises serious doubts. Former UN Secretary General Boutros Boutros-Ghali challenged the international community to confront "the ethical question of whether suffering inflicted on vulnerable groups in the target country is a legitimate means of exerting pressure on political leaders whose behavior is unlikely to be affected by the plight of their subjects." [60] Indeed, there is little indication that Saddam Hussein, his inner circle or key elements of the military leadership are suffering any shortages of food, drinking water or medical supplies. The suffering of the civilian population has become a powerful propaganda tool to stir up anti-American sentiment, but it does not seem to have had any impact towards altering Iraqi policy in ways consistent with U.S. interests. If there is any political impact from the sanctions that could be construed as positive by American officials, it may simply be that it has made Iraq an example for other countries as to what could happen if they dare challenge U.S. prerogatives.

Current U.S. policy on Iraq has failed and has largely lost credibility. It is widely viewed internationally as reflecting U.S. (and to a lesser degree British) insistence on maintaining a punitive sanctions-based approach regardless of the humanitarian impact, and increasingly is recognized as having failed to bring about either democratic changes in Iraq or security for the Gulf region. Numerous countries are challenging, if not directly violating, the sanctions regime and international support has largely eroded. Several prominent United Nations personnel in Iraq have resigned in protest. At the Beirut summit of the Arab League in March 2002, the Arab nations unanimously endorsed a resolution calling for a total lifting of economic sanctions. Foreign Minister Sheik Sabah al-Ahmad al-Sabah of Kuwait, whose country's occupation by Iraq initially prompted the sanctions, has stated categorically "Kuwait has no objection to the launching of a call to lift the economic sanctions from Iraq."[61] Even Richard Butler observed that the sanctions "simply aren't working other than to harm the ordinary Iraqi people"[62] and that they have been "utterly counterproductive for this disarmament purpose."[63]

The United States is the driving force behind UN policy, with the United States holding effective veto power over any proposed changes. The United States is becoming increasingly isolated in the world body, with only Great Britain remaining in support of the American position. There is little question that the UN Security Council as a whole would quickly accept a change to a more humane and practical policy if advocated by the United States.

The U.S.-led sanctions against Iraq—in terms of human costs, the greatest ongoing tragedy in the Middle East—has resulted in widespread anger throughout the Islamic world, particularly at the street level and increasingly at the governmental level as well. Despite their longstanding opposition to Saddam's secular regime, the humanitarian impact of the sanctions has been mentioned frequently by Osama bin Laden and other Islamic radicals, as the Al-Qaeda leader has repeatedly raised the tragedy of "innocent children being killed every day in Iraq"[64] in his public statements.

In the United States, neither the former sanctions regime nor the "smart sanctions" have had much support, but there has not been strong opposition to ending the sanctions outside of grassroots religious and humanitarian groups, as politicians fear being accused of being "soft on Saddam Hussein." The result is a largely politically driven inertia, with the cost-benefit assessment limited to whether changing the policy carries a higher domestic political price than maintaining the current policy.

The Threat of a U.S. Invasion of Iraq

In the decade following the Gulf War, the coalition built by the senior Bush Administration is in tatters. U.S. credibility has been further compromised in the international community in general and in the Arab world in particular. The standing of Saddam Hussein has been enhanced in Iraq and throughout the Middle East. Meanwhile, problems that threaten the stability of the region far more than the Iraqi dictator—the breakdown in the Israeli-Palestinian peace process, uneven economic development, and the militarization of the region—continue to grow, in part due to U.S. policies.

Rather than reconsider the failed punitive approach, there has been some pressure by hawks within the Bush Administration for a dramatic escalation in the ongoing air strikes against Iraq and perhaps even a full-scale invasion to topple the government of Saddam Hussein. In the months following the September 11 terrorist attacks, there were leaks to the media about alleged evidence of a meeting in Prague between an Iraqi intelligence officer and one of the hijackers of the doomed airplanes that crashed into the World Trade Center. Subsequently, however, the FBI, CIA, and Czech Intelligence have declared that no such meeting occurred.[65] It is unlikely that the decidedly secular Baathist regime—which has savagely suppressed Islamists within Iraq—would be able to maintain close links with bin Laden and his followers. Saudi Prince Turki bin Faisal, his country's former intelligence chief, noted how bin Laden views Saddam Hussein "as an apostate, an infidel or someone who is not worthy of being a fellow Muslim."[66] Much of the money trail for Al-Qaeda comes from U.S. ally Saudi Arabia; none has been traced to Iraq. Fifteen of the nineteen hijackers were Saudi; none were Iraqi. Admitting that there was no evidence of direct links between Iraq and Al-Qaeda, the best CIA director George Tenet could come up with in testimony before Congress was that the "mutual antipathy" the two have for the United States "suggests that tactical cooperation between the two is possible,"[67] an extraordinarily weak justification for war.

Iraq's past terrorist links have largely been limited to such secular groups as Abu Nidal, a now largely defunct Palestinian organization. Abu Nidal himself was apparently murdered by Iraqi security in his Baghdad apartment in August, 2002. At the height of Iraq's support of Abu Nidal, in the early 1980s, the United States dropped Iraq from its list of countries that supported terrorism in order to support Iraq's war effort against Iran. (They were added back on only after the Iraqi invasion of Kuwait, despite a lack of evidence of increased ties to terrorism.) A recent CIA report indicates that the Iraqis have actually been consciously avoiding any actions against the United States or its facilities abroad.[68] Further, the State Department on state-sponsored terrorism failed to note any active support for international terrorism.[69]

The United States would be mistaken to think that defeating Iraq would be as easy as the defeat of the ragtag band of tribesman that constituted the Taliban. Though Iraq's offensive capabilities have been severely weakened by the bombings, sanctions and UNSCOM-sponsored decommissioning, their defensive military capabilities are still strong. A military victory would not be as easy as during the Gulf War, either. Prior to the launching of Operation Desert Storm, when the Iraqis figured out the extent of the forces being deployed against them, they decided not to put up a fight for Kuwait, relying mostly on young conscripts from minority communities, many of whom were literally chained to their positions. Only two of the eight divisions of the elite Republican Guard were ever in Kuwait, and they pulled back before the war began in mid-January. The vast majority of Iraq's strongest forces were withdrawn to areas around Baghdad to prepare for a possible fight for the survival of the regime itself, which did not happen at that time. These divisions are still intact.

In the event of war, defections from these units are not likely. There are close to one million Iraqi elites who have a vested interest in the regime's survival. These include the Baath Party leadership and its supporters, security and intelligence personnel, core elements of the armed forces as well as their extended families.

Nor is there an equivalent to Afghanistan's Northern Alliance, which did the bulk of the fighting on the ground against the Taliban. The Kurds, having been abandoned twice by the United States, are unlikely to fight any more beyond Kurdish-populated areas. The armed Shiite opposition has largely been eliminated and they too would be unlikely to fight beyond the majority Shiite sections of southern Iraq. The United States would be reluctant to support either, given the result could mean a breakup of the country that could incite the Kurds in southeastern Turkey and the Shiites in northeastern Saudi Arabia. U.S. forces would have to march on Baghdad, a city of over five million, virtually alone. Unlike the Gulf War, which was conventional open combat in a flat desert area where U.S. forces could excel and take full advantage of their firepower and technological superiority, American soldiers would have to fight their way through heavily populated agricultural and urban lands. Invading U.S. forces would be faced with bitter, house-to-house fighting in a country larger than South Vietnam. Iraqis who may have had little stomach to fight to maintain their country's conquest of Kuwait would be far more willing to sacrifice themselves to resist a foreign Western invader in the heart of their country. Even after toppling the regime, American occupation troops could be subjected to constant hit-and-run guerrilla attacks in Baghdad's narrow alleyways, forcing the U.S. troops into a bloody counterinsurgency war.

During the Gulf War, the United States was able to repel even greater criticism than it might have otherwise received because it had support of important segments of the international community, including a number of Arab states. This would not be the case in the event of a new war against Iraq, which would not be seen as a justifiable response to an attack on the United States or an act of aggression against an ally. This would be seen as an unprovoked invasion. Unlike 1991, when most of Iraq's neighbors supported—and even contributed to—the U.S.-led war effort, or were at least neutral, the opposition today is strong. Mustapha Alani, a Middle East specialist with the Royal United Services Institute in London noted, "This is a very sensitive issue for them. Liberating Kuwait is a legitimate objective, but toppling regimes is completely different."[70] Saudi Crown Prince Abdullah has warned that the United States, "should not strike Iraq because such an attack would only raise animosity in the region against the United States."[71] When Vice-President Dick Cheney visited the Middle East in March 2002, every Arab leader he visited made clear their opposition. At the Beirut summit of the Arab League at the end of that month, the Arab nations unanimously endorsed a resolution categorically opposing an attack against Iraq.

Even Kuwait has reconciled with Iraq. In March 2002, Iraq and Kuwait signed an agreement written by Kuwaiti Foreign Minister Sheik al-Sabah in which Iraq, for the first time, formally agreed to respect the sovereignty of Kuwait. Sabah declared that his country was 100% satisfied with the agreement.[72] Saudi Arabia's Crown Prince Abdullah called it a "very positive achievement" and expressed confidence that Iraq would uphold the agreement.[73] However, rather than welcoming this breakthrough that could make it more difficult to justify going to war with Iraq, State Department spokesman

Richard Boucher declared that the United States was "profoundly skeptical" of the agreement.[74] Kuwait also reiterated its opposition to a U.S. invasion of Iraq.

The lack of Arab support for American war aims does not have just political implications. Without a land base from which to launch its aerial attacks, the United States would have to rely exclusively on Navy jets launched from aircraft carriers. Without permission to launch aerial refueling craft, even long-range bombers from U.S. air bases would have trouble being deployed. It is hard to imagine being able to provide the necessary reconnaissance and surveillance aircraft under such circumstances as well. The deployment of tens of thousands of troops from such a distance could also be problematic. Still, the United States seems determined to press ahead with or without allies. According to Secretary of Defense Rumsfeld, "In this war, the mission will define the coalition—not the other way around."[75]

There is also the question of what happens if the United States is successful in overthrowing Saddam Hussein's regime. As is becoming apparent in Afghanistan, throwing a government out is easier than putting one together. America's Arab allies still press their concerns that an Iraq without a strong central government could disintegrate into a Shia Arab state, a Sunni Arab state and a Kurdish state.[76]

A number of scenarios for such an invasion have been leaked to the press. There was some indication in the late spring of 2002 that should a full-scale invasion be seen as too problematic, the United States might engage in a series of bombing attacks and commando raids in an attempt to kill Saddam Hussein and top Iraqi leaders. There were also leaks regarding an attempt to assassinate the Iraqi leader through clandestine operations. The latter scenario may have been floated to undermine UN negotiations with Iraq going on at that time to resume United Nations inspections of Iraqi weapons facilities. It is their potential abuse for such purposes that has been the major stumbling block in the talks.

This is part of the Bush Administration's explicit rejection of the doctrine that has guided U.S. foreign policy for the better part of a century to strike out militarily only in self-defense based on international law. In a number of cases, successive administrations have interpreted this so broadly as to be almost meaningless, yet this new strategy of "pre-emption," calling for early unilateral action against perceived enemies that may pose even a *potential* threat to American interests is unprecedented. It basically undermines the very laws, norms and international institutions the United States has helped build for nearly a century, essentially becoming a law into itself by setting its own rules for engagement. This profoundly destabilizing strategy was once the province of the far right, but has now been endorsed by the president and the leaders of both parties in Congress. There has been only limited opposition from the Democrats regarding President Bush's calls for a dramatic escalation of military operations against Iraq, for example.

The European Union's external affairs chief Chris Patten, expressing his concerns about the apparent American desire to go to war against Iraq, warned "The Afghan war perhaps reinforced some dangerous instincts: that the projection of military power is the only basis of true security; that the U.S. can rely on no one but itself; and that allies may be useful as optional extras."[77]

Motivations for U.S. Policy in the Gulf

There are a number of domestic political forces in the United States pushing U.S. policy in the direction of hostility towards Iran and Iraq.

There is the time-honored tradition for political leaders to maintain their popularity at home by striking out at a perceived external threat from which the public needs protection. Witness President Clinton ordering a series of air strikes against Iraq just two months prior to his re-election in 1996 and again on the eve of his impeachment in 1998. Given that so very few Americans have much sympathy for these regimes, Iraq and Iran are among the few nation-states left against which a politician can build a reputation for toughness.

Another factor comes from mainstream-to-conservative Zionist groups and their supporters, long an influential lobbying force in Congress, that have used the alleged threats against Israel from these countries as a major argument for continuing large-scale military and economic aid to the Israeli government. There are several problems with this rationalization, however. First of all, Israel is separated from Iraq and Iran by distances of hundreds of miles and the land in between consists of countries that are formally at peace with Israel and openly hostile to these regimes. In addition, the Israeli air force is more than capable of protecting Israel's border against any combination of these opponents and the country has a strong defense system against medium-range missiles. Furthermore, there are serious questions as to whether—despite the frequently bellicose rhetoric these countries have directed towards Israel—they really have such hostile intentions even if they were capable. Saddam Hussein, whose war-making capability was largely destroyed in the Gulf War, will likely not be a threat to anyone (besides his own people) for a long time to come. Finally, it is high-ly unlikely that Israel would have clandestinely armed the Ayatollah Khomeini's government throughout the 1980s if the Islamic Republic actu-ally was considered such a threat, particularly since hard-line anti-Israel elements were more prominent in the Iranian government during that peri-od than they are now. With Egypt and Jordan formally at peace with Israel, with the weak Palestinian regime struggling for survival under Israeli sieges, with Syria reducing its military and absent a great power sponsor, with Lebanon as weak as ever, and with the Gulf states focused on Iraq and Iran, Israel is in a far stronger position militarily than it ever has been. Similarly, with the demise of the Soviet Union, Israel is no longer of use as a Cold War asset. As a result, having Israel portrayed as both a potential victim of and potential bulwark against Iraq and Iran provides justification for ongo-ing high levels of U.S. aid to Israel, most of which comes back to the United States to military contractors for their weapons and to banks as interest on previous military loans.

Ultimately, the United States may be motivated by what has moti-vated other great powers that have tried to exert their influence in the Gulf: the desire to control the world's greatest concentration of oil. About two-thirds of the world's oil wealth exists along the Persian Gulf, with par-ticularly large reserves in Saudi Arabia, Kuwait and the United Arab Emirates. About one-quarter of U.S. oil imports come from the Persian Gulf region. The imposition of higher fuel efficiency standards and other conservation measures, along with the increased use of renewable energy resources for which technologies are already available, could eliminate U.S. dependence on Middle Eastern oil in a relatively short period of time. This could be accomplished with far less cost than maintaining the U.S. military presence in the region. For a number of reasons, however, the United States has chosen its current far more dangerous path. It is perhaps significant that the Gulf supplies European states and Japan with an even higher percentage of those countries' energy needs, leading some to specu-late that this forces these countries ultimately to rely on the United States for their energy security. Maintaining such a presence in the Gulf, there-fore, does not mean controlling the source of much of the world's oil for American consumers as much as it does exercising a degree of control over other industrialized countries as well. As long as tensions remain with the Iraqi and Iranian regimes, the United States can maintain its base and pre-positioning rights in Saudi Arabia and other Gulf states, keeping a major military presence in this strategically and economically important region.

Ultimately, it may simply be about control. Air Force Brigadier General William Looney, head of the U.S. Central Command's Airborne Expeditionary Force, bluntly stated what he saw as positive about American policy towards Iraq: "They know we own their country. We own their airspace...We dictate the way they live and talk. And that's what's great about America right now. It's a good thing, especially when there is a lot of oil out there we need."[78] Keeping Iraq united but weak is seen as advantageous. As one RAND Corporation analyst puts it, "An impasse over [weapons] inspections is actually the best realistic outcome for the United States.....[The] most dangerous scenario is the possibility that Hussein will co-operate...which could...spell the end of sanctions."[79] In short, if the United States cannot yet overthrow Saddam Hussein, the U.S. wants to keep his country as weak and impoverished as possible.

In the post-Cold War world, the United States has demonstrated little tolerance for any regime that is both antagonistic to U.S. goals and has the potential of establishing a credible deterrent against the United States and its allies by possessing or attempting to possess weapons of mass destruction. The destruction of such regimes—either slowly through sanctions or more quickly through an invasion—serves as a warning that any other state that would even consider challenging American hegemony would suffer serious consequences.

The Illusion of Security

In diplomacy, as in military confrontations, it is important to be engaged with the enemy. Not only has the United States refused to engage in serious dialogue with Iran and Iraq, it has actively discouraged its Gulf allies from engaging in such dialogue as well. Stability requires the integration of all major parties into a structure that can sustain peace and security, yet the United States has made this virtually impossible.

There is a dangerous tendency in Washington to discount the importance of public opinion in Middle Eastern countries. And U.S. policy is breeding enormous dissent even among the West's closest Arab allies. The ongoing U.S.-led militarization of the region rationalized to counter these "rogue states" severely retards economic development and political liberalization. Most GCC countries are more threatened by potential internal instability than external attack.[80] The highly visible military role of the United States in the region and the U.S.-promoted militarization and its deleterious economic impact encourages dissent, often by radical and destabilizing elements. In effect, adherence to an American-defined security doctrine may actually threaten the security of these regimes, which are squandering their nations' wealth on weapons to the detriment of education, health care, housing and employment for their rapidly growing populations. One need only look at Iran under the Shah to see what could happen.

The irony of U.S. policy in the Persian Gulf is that it has little strategic justification given the costs. And the costs are more than financial. They also come in the form of the increasingly violent reaction to the ongoing American military presence, most evident in the September 2001 terrorist attacks against the United States, but in other ways as well. Indeed, this and other manifestations of current U.S. policy in the Gulf actually endangers the security of both the United States and its Gulf allies.

This is only one part of the arrogance of power that fuels this anti-American backlash. Quite a number of diplomats in the Gulf have complained about the way U.S. officials have lectured their officials—at times in public—about their policies in the region and have "overstepped the boundaries of diplomacy" and demonstrated an "arrogance and disdain for others."[81] One classic example is when the senior George Bush, when he was vice-president, responded to the international outrage over the destruction of an Iranian airliner by an American missile by saying, "I will never apologize for the United States of America—I don't care what the facts are!"[82]

Another example of this arrogance comes from the ongoing deadly but futile U.S. military actions against Iraq: The United States gives an ultimatum to Saddam Hussein, naively expecting him to capitulate. When he does not, the United States feels obliged to follow through with some kind of military action to preserve its credibility, even though U.S. officials realize that the response will not have the desired effect.[83]

Indeed, American military actions in the Gulf seem almost to be a kind of foreign policy by catharsis rather than based on any rational strategic calculation. There is a palpable frustration by American policy makers at not getting their way against upstart regimes in a post-Cold War New World Order in which they assume they have accomplished a level of authority that should be respected. Such bellicosity may help a president's standing in public opinion polls, but actually accomplishes little in terms of protecting the United States.

It is becoming increasingly apparent that the most serious offenses by Iran and Iraq in the eyes of U.S. policy makers are not in the area of human rights, terrorism, nuclear ambitions, subversion or conquest, but in daring to challenge American power in the Middle East. It is these two governments that are preventing the United States from exercising its political dominance over this crucial region. Having these regimes overthrown or under control, American policy makers hope, will create the kind of environment that would give the United States unprecedented leverage in shaping the future direction of the Middle East. Thus, the final irony: Serving as an impediment to such American ambitions gives these regimes credibility and legitimacy they would not otherwise receive from large numbers of Middle Eastern peoples resentful of such foreign domination, thereby strengthening these regimes' rule at home as well as their influence throughout the Middle East and beyond.

It is the American role in the Gulf that makes the United States the enemy in the eyes of millions of Muslims, some of whom are willing to join the ranks of Al-Qaeda and other terrorist organizations. A less visible and less militarized role would likely mean improved relations and provide greater security. Current policy, however, appears to do little to enhance peace and security for the Gulf, for the rest of the Middle East or for the United States.

Chapter Four

The Israeli-Palestinian Conflict

For many years, the role of the United States as the primary military, economic and diplomatic supporter of Israel in its conflict with the Palestinians and other Arabs has been one of the most contentious issues in the Islamic world. There have always been hostile feelings among most Muslims towards Zionism—the Jewish nationalist movement that arose a century ago advocating an ingathering of Jews from their worldwide Diaspora to Palestine, site of the ancient Jewish kingdoms. This comes not out of any innate hostility towards Jews, but out of an awareness that Zionism conflicted with the nationalist aspirations of Palestinian Arabs, who had lived on the land for many centuries prior to the arrival of the Zionists. The Palestinians' expectation during the British mandate period for an Arab state in all of historic Palestine was shattered when the United Nations partitioned the territory in 1947, granting 55% of Palestine to the Zionist immigrants, who then owned only a small percentage of the land. The ongoing inter-communal fighting escalated dramatically upon Israel's declaration of independence in May 1948 as armies from neighboring Arab countries attacked the new Jewish state. In the resulting war, the Israelis seized approximately 78% of Palestine. Most of the Palestinian population went into exile, in some cases in what they assumed to be a temporary escape from the fighting and in other cases through forcible removal as part of an Israeli policy of what is now known as ethnic cleansing.[1] Neighboring Jordan and Egypt took control over the remaining 22% of Palestine, which then become known, respectively, as the West Bank and the Gaza Strip. Following a series of threats and provocations from Egypt and other Arab neighbors, Israel conquered these remaining Arab parts of Palestine, along with other Arab lands, in June 1967.

The Palestinian-populated West Bank and Gaza Strip is recognized by the United Nations and virtually the entire international community as occupied territories. There are currently three million Palestinians under direct or indirect Israeli military occupation and four million Palestinians living as refugees from their homeland. Palestinians make up both the largest refugee population in the world as well as the world's largest population living under a foreign military occupation. Israel, meanwhile, in violation of international law, has been colonizing parts of the occupied West Bank and Gaza Strip with upwards to 400,000 Jewish settlers.

Over the decades, despite ongoing opposition to Israeli policies towards the Palestinians, many of Israel's most intractable foes in the Islamic world have belatedly come to the realization that Israel exists as a permanent Jewish state in the Middle East and are willing to live with that. Egypt and Jordan—Israel's most important neighbors—have formally recognized Israel and the remainder have promised to do so in return for a total Israeli withdrawal from the occupied territories. There are extremist Islamic groups, however, like the Al-Qaeda terrorist network, that do not simply oppose Israel's occupation of the West Bank and Gaza Strip but oppose Israel altogether. They do not just oppose Jews settling on confiscated Palestinian land in the occupied West Bank, but Jews everywhere. At the same time, it is the occupation and U.S. support for it that fuels much of the anger and frustration that has driven thousands of Muslims to support terrorism and extremist ideologies. It raises the question as to whether policies pursued by the United States—along with Israel—that are purportedly designed to curb the threat of terrorism targeted at both nations, actually are helping to foment terrorism. The evidence seems to indicate that U.S. policy has been not just deleterious for its most immediate victims—the Palestinians—but ultimately for Israel and the United States as well.

There is a widespread assumption in the United States that resolution of the conflict between the Israelis and Palestinians is an extremely complex issue and that the United States is an "honest broker" that has been and is the best hope for peace. The reality, however, may be just the opposite.

For nearly thirty years, the international consensus for peace in the Middle East has involved the withdrawal of Israeli forces to within Israel's internationally-recognized (pre-June 1967) boundaries in return for security guarantees from Israel's neighbors, the establishment of a Palestinian state in the West Bank and Gaza Strip, a shared Jerusalem as the co-capital of both states, and a just resolution for the Palestinian refugees. During the same thirty-year period, the Palestine Liberation Organization (PLO), which served for many years as the Palestinians' de facto government-in-exile under the leadership of Yasir Arafat, has evolved from openly calling for Israel's destruction to supporting this international consensus for a two-state solution. The PLO had hinted at a willingness to accept a small Palestinian state living in peace alongside Israel as far back as the mid-

1970s, made it official in 1988, and formally repealed sections in its charter calling for Israel's dissolution in 1996.[2]

The United States, however, rejected the international consensus for
the establishment of an independent Palestinian state alongside Israel. A
UN Security Council resolution reflecting this international consensus,
which had the support of virtually the entire international community—
including most Arab states and the Palestinians—was put up for a vote as
far back as 1976, but was opposed by Israel and was vetoed by the United
States. This strident opposition to Palestinian statehood finally shifted
when President Clinton, toward the end of his presidency, and President
Bush, in a more direct way in the fall of 2001, declared that the United
States would support a Palestinian state in parts of the West Bank and Gaza
Strip. However, both administrations made clear that the United States
would not support anything beyond the very limited sovereignty and
severely circumscribed boundaries that the nation's Israeli occupiers were
willing to offer, restrictions that would make Palestine an independent
state largely in name only. Furthermore, the United States supports a
Jerusalem primarily under Israeli sovereignty, only partial Israeli withdrawal from occupied Palestinian territories and no right for Palestinian refugees
to return. Nor is the United States willing to demand an end to Israel's illegal policies of confiscating Palestinian land and constructing Jewish-only
settlements and roads within the occupied territories.

The Palestinians, through the PLO, effectively recognized Israeli control of over 78% of historic Palestine—the territory within Israel's internationally recognized borders—in the Declaration of Principles agreed to in
Oslo, Norway in 1993. Israel redeployed its forces from parts of the remaining 22% of Palestine (the West Bank and Gaza Strip, which they seized in
the 1967 War) in a phased withdrawal between 1993 and 1997. At that
point, about forty percent of the West Bank and Gaza Strip, including most
of its towns and cities, was placed under the rule of the newly-established
Palestine National Authority and divided into dozens of non-contiguous
zones wherein the Palestinians could exercise some limited autonomy.
Since the start of the Palestinian uprising in September 2000, there have
been frequent armed clashes between Israeli occupation forces and
Palestinian militiamen, which have also led to the deaths of many hundreds of Palestinian civilians. Meanwhile, heavily armed Jewish settlers in
the occupied territories have attacked nearby Palestinian civilian areas and
Palestinian forces have attacked both armed and unarmed Jewish settlers.
In addition, underground Palestinian groups—primarily affiliated with rad-

ical Islamic organizations—have launched terrorist attacks inside Israel itself. The Israelis have re-occupied much of the area handed over to Palestinian control during the 1990s and have subjected what is left to periodic military incursions, shelling, sniper fire and air strikes.

Since the late 1960s, the United States has been the primary international supporter of the Israeli government and its occupation forces while at the same time playing the role of mediator in the Arab-Israeli conflict. Maintaining these contradictory roles is in large part responsible for the ongoing Israeli-Palestinian violence, which has brought neither justice for the Palestinians nor security for Israel. Indeed, as will be shown below, having an anti-Palestinian bias does not mean that U.S. policy necessarily helps Israel. It has also contributed to the dramatic rise of anti-American sentiment, not just among Palestinians, but by Arabs and Muslims in lands well beyond Palestine.

The Nature of U.S. Aid to Israel

The United States aid relationship with Israel is unlike any other in the world, or indeed, like any in history. In sheer volume, it is the most generous foreign aid program ever between any two countries, totaling over $100 billion.[3] No country has ever received as much Congressionally mandated aid as has Israel. What is perhaps even more unusual is that Israel, like its benefactor, is an advanced, industrialized, technologically sophisticated country, as well as a major arms exporter.

Some U.S. aid to Israel began in the early 1950s but shifted after the 1967 War, when the United States greatly expanded military loans. These were replaced exclusively by grants in 1985. U.S. economic aid increased greatly in subsequent years as grants replaced loans for economic assistance in 1981. In recent years, the annual U.S. subsidy for Israel has remained at approximately $3 billion in military and economic grants, in addition to assistance from other parts of the budget or off-budget, which have totaled up to an additional $500 million in recent years.[4] Most U.S. recipients of economic aid are required to use the bulk of the money for specific projects, such as buying certain U.S. agricultural surpluses or finished goods. Normally, among countries receiving U.S. foreign aid, officials of the U.S. Agency for International Development (AID) oversee the actual programs, either administered directly through non-governmental organizations or under co-sponsorship with a government agency. The exception is Israel, where most U.S. aid goes directly into the government's treasury to use at its discretion. The U.S. government sets the funding level and these become simply cash transfers to the Israeli government.[5]

In addition, Congressional researchers have disclosed that between 1974 and 1989, $16.4 billion in U.S. military loans were converted to grants and that this was the understanding from the beginning. Indeed, Congress eventually has forgiven all past American loans to Israel. As a result, while other countries struggle under onerous debt loads and repayment programs, Israel can maintain its often-touted claim that it has never defaulted on a U.S. government loan for the simple reason that it has never been forced to repay them. U.S. policy since 1984 has been that economic assistance to Israel must equal or exceed Israel's annual debt repayment to the United States. Direct economic aid to Israel is six times all U.S. foreign aid to the impoverished countries of sub-Saharan Africa and ten times what the United States has planned to give to war-torn Afghanistan after months of bombing. In addition to the more than $3 billion in annual grants, between 1992 and 1996, the United States also provided loan guarantees for Israel totaling an additional $10 billion.

Furthermore, unlike other countries, which receive aid in quarterly installments, aid to Israel since 1982 has been given in a lump sum at the beginning of the fiscal year, leaving the U.S. government to borrow from future revenues. Israel even lends some of this money back through U.S. treasury bills and collects the additional interest. This special arrangement costs the U.S. government approximately $50-60 million each year.[6] In addition, there is the more than $1.5 billion in private U.S. funds that go to Israel annually in the form of $1 billion in private tax deductible donations and $500 million in Israeli bonds.[7] This ability of Americans to make what amounts to tax-deductible contributions to a foreign government, through a number of Jewish charities, does not exist with any other country. Nor do these figures include short and long-term commercial loans from U.S. banks, which have been as high as $1 billion annually in recent years.[8]

For a country that consists of just one-tenth of one percent of the world's population, total U.S. aid to Israel as a proportion of the foreign aid budget is enormous: approximately one out of every four dollars for foreign aid goes to Israel. Israel does not receive this kind of support because it is poor—Israel's GNP is higher than the combined GNP of its immediate neighbors Egypt, Lebanon, Syria, Jordan, the West Bank and Gaza Strip. With a per capita income of about $18,000, Israeli Jews enjoy the sixteenth highest per capita income in the world, better off than oil-rich Saudi

Arabia and only slightly less well-off than most Western European countries. Given Israel's relative prosperity, U.S. aid to Israel is becoming increasingly controversial. As Yossi Beilen, former deputy foreign minister of Israel and a Knesset member, told the Women's International Zionist organization in 1994, "If our economic situation is better than in many of your countries, how can we go on asking for your charity?"[9]

Aid to Israel, particularly in recent years, has been justified as necessary to support the peace process. However, U.S. aid to Israel has increased as the peace process stagnated and then collapsed. With repeated public pronouncements by U.S. officials that aid to Israel is unconditional, Israel has no incentive to make concessions necessary for peace, or even to end its human rights abuses and violations of international law and UN Security Council resolutions. As former Secretary of State Henry Kissinger once told a colleague, in reference to the Israeli prime minister then in office, "I ask Rabin to make concessions, and he says he can't because Israel is weak. So I give him more arms, and he says he doesn't need to make concessions because Israel is strong."[10]

The United States and the Peace Process

Despite the widespread portrayal of the United States as an honest broker in the Middle East, American opposition to a comprehensive peace settlement between Israel and its Arab neighbors goes back for at least a quarter century. Officially, the United States has backed UN Security Council resolutions 242 and 338—that call for Israel's withdrawal from the territories seized in the 1967 War in return for security guarantees from Israel's neighbors—as the basis for peace. However, as far back as 1969, then-National Security Advisor Kissinger passed on to the Israelis the advice that they ignore the Rogers Plan—crafted by U.S. Secretary of State William Rogers—that would have required Israel to return, with some minor alterations, to its 1967 borders in return for peace with the Arabs. The Nixon Administration did not even encourage the far more modest Allon Plan, proposed by Israel's foreign minister soon after the war, which would have led to an Israeli withdrawal from most of the occupied territories outside of the Jordan Valley. Instead, Kissinger encouraged the Israeli government to hold on to its captured Arab lands. When Egyptian President Anwar Sadat made peace overtures towards Israel in 1971, Kissinger successfully advised the Israelis to ignore it. As a result, Egypt—along with Syria—attacked Israeli forces in October 1973, advancing into Israeli-occupied territories in the Sinai Peninsula and Golan Heights before a massive U.S. re-supply operation enabled Israel to mount a successful counter-attack. Only after the war did the United States support disengagement talks, and then only under American auspices. The United States has never pursued peace plans brought forth by the Europeans, the United Nations or even the Arab states, including such Saudi initiatives as the 1981 Fahd Plan and the very similar 2002 Abdullah Plan that essentially reiterated the principle of land for peace. In the common lexicon in the United States, the "peace process" refers only to efforts initiated by the U.S. government.

The United States has consistently rejected an international peace conference that would lead to a comprehensive all-parties peace settlement. Instead the United States has pushed for a succession of bilateral arrangements that could maximize American influence in the region, such as the 1978 Camp David agreement between Israel and Egypt and the 1994 peace treaty between Israel and Jordan. Neither of these, however, effectively addressed the underlying source of the Arab-Israeli conflict: the fate of the Palestinians. Furthermore, by neutralizing Egypt—by far Israel's biggest military rival—in the Camp David agreement, Israel was emboldened to invade its northern neighbor Lebanon in 1982 and redouble its colonization and repression in the occupied Palestinian territories.

The PLO, like most Arab governments, initially ruled out any negotiations with Israel. By the mid-1970s, however, the Palestinians began expressing their desire to be included in the peace process. Both Israel and the United States refused to include them, however. The United States insisted that the Kingdom of Jordan—a U.S. ally that had controlled the West Bank between 1948 and 1967 and was host to a sizable population of Palestinian refugees—would serve as the Palestinians' representative. Given the traditional hostility between Jordan and the PLO, however, that led to a civil war in Jordan during the early 1970s in which thousands of Palestinian civilians were killed, few Palestinians felt the Hashemite monarchy could fairly represent their interests. The U.S. position was that the PLO could participate in the peace process only on three conditions: 1) they recognized Israel's right to exist; 2) they recognized UN Security Council resolutions 242 and 338 as the basis of the peace talks; and, 3) they renounced terrorism. While most observers believed these conditions were in themselves reasonable, what seemed to be unreasonable was that the United States refused to insist that Israel reciprocate: Israel at this time was refusing to recognize Palestine's right to exist and also rejected 242 and 338. Furthermore, only the PLO was asked to renounce terrorism, even though Israel's armed forces were responsible for far more civilian deaths than were the various Palestinian militias.

For more than a decade, the PLO unsuccessfully tried to convince the United States to call for reciprocal declarations in support of the UN resolutions and against violence directed at civilians. Most crucially, the PLO called for mutual and simultaneous recognition of Palestine and Israel,. This was rejected by both the Carter and Reagan Administrations. In 1988, the PLO finally relented and agreed to those three provisions without any reciprocity by Israel.

However, the United States still refused to allow the PLO in the peace process, limiting official contact with the PLO to no higher than the U.S. ambassador to Tunisia, where the PLO had relocated its offices following its ouster from Lebanon by invading Israeli forces in 1982. These talks were broken off within two years when the United States determined that the PLO had not sufficiently criticized an attempted terrorist attack against Israel by a small Palestinian splinter group.

Continuing to reject calls for an international conference under UN auspices, the United States set up a major peace conference in Madrid in 1991. While some meetings were to take place on a multilateral basis, the United States determined that the real negotiations were to take place bilaterally with a strong American presence. While most Arab nations were invited to participate, the United States explicitly excluded the PLO from taking part. The United States allowed for Palestinian participation only if they came as part of the Jordanian delegation and their delegates were neither from the Palestinian diaspora nor Israeli-occupied East Jerusalem and they had no affiliation with the PLO. This may have been the first time that the convenor of a peace conference granted itself the right to choose the delegation from one of the participants.[11] Real progress was made on the Israeli-Palestinian track only when the Israelis did an end-run around the restrictive U.S. formula and met in direct talks with the PLO secretly in Norway in 1993. These were the talks that resulted in the Declaration of Principles, also known as the Oslo Accords, that—while failing to recognize the Palestinians' right to statehood and imposing other limitations—did provide a framework where more substantive progress towards Israeli-Palestinian peace might result.

During that summer, unaware of the secret Israeli-PLO talks in Norway, the United States put forward what it called a "compromise" proposal for Palestinian autonomy. However, the Israeli negotiating proposal being put forth at the same time, that was largely incorporated in the

Declaration of Principles, was actually more favorable to the Palestinians than the U.S. version. Palestinian officials described the U.S. proposals as "closer to the Israeli Likud position," referring to the Rabin government's right-wing predecessors. This was one of more than a half dozen occasions during the 1990s where the United States actually took a harder line towards Israel's Arab adversaries than did the ruling Israeli Labor Party and/or Israeli public opinion. Indeed, while Israel was secretly meeting with the PLO that summer, the Clinton Administration, Congress and both major American political parties were on record opposing the inclusion of the PLO in the peace process.

Peace talks resumed in Washington in the fall of 1993 within the Oslo framework. Under the more moderate Labor Party, elected to office in 1992, Israeli negotiators recognized that—in terms of domestic Israeli politics—the peace movement did not have as much political clout as the right wing. As a result, it was difficult politically for the Israeli government to take the necessary steps for achieving peace, such as bringing Israel into compliance with UN Security Council resolutions and granting Palestinians their independence within viable borders. As a result, members of the Israeli negotiating team in Washington privately asked U.S. officials to openly push the Israeli government to compromise further so to give the prime minister sufficient political cover to make the needed concessions.[12] The Clinton Administration, however, refused.

Over the next seven years, the United States brokered a series of Israeli-Palestinian agreements that led to the withdrawal of Israeli forces from most of the Gaza Strip and parts of the West Bank. Some of the areas came under control of the PLO-led Palestinian Authority, giving the Palestinians a degree of self-governance in their own country for the first time. The majority of the West Bank and about 20% of the Gaza Strip remained under Israeli military occupation or some kind of joint administration. During this period, the Israeli government severely limited the mobility of Palestinians within and between the West Bank and Gaza Strip and dramatically expanded its expropriation of land in the occupied territories for colonization by Jewish settlers. In addition, the Israelis refused to withdraw from as much territory as promised in the U.S.-brokered disengagement agreements. Meanwhile, the increasingly corrupt, inept and autocratic Palestinian Authority—under the leadership of PLO Chairman Arafat—had alienated much of the Palestinian population and proved itself unable to suppress the growth of radical Islamic groups, which saw the Palestinian Authority as an entity designed to suppress resistance against the ongoing Israeli occupation. On more than two dozen occasions between 1994 and 2000, Islamic extremists engaged in terrorist attacks against civilian targets inside Israel.

From the beginning of the talks following the signing of the Declaration of Principles negotiated in Norway, it became apparent that the two sides saw the process very differently. The Palestinians saw the Oslo process as a means to end the occupation and establish a Palestinian state on the lands seized by Israel in June 1967—the West Bank (including Arab East Jerusalem) and the Gaza Strip. By contrast, the United States and Israel apparently saw it more as a way of maintaining an Israeli occupation of major sections of these territories. In this scenario, the Palestinian Authority would be in charge of administering most major Palestinian population centers and cooperating with Israel in protecting Israel and its settlements in the occupied territories.

The Palestinians, in signing the Declaration of Principles, worked on the assumption that the agreement would result in concrete improvements in the lives of those in the occupied territories, that the interim period would be no more than five years, and that the permanent settlement would be based on UN Security Council resolutions 242 and 338. They trusted that the United States, as guarantor of the agreement—signed on the White House lawn on September 13, 1993—would be able to pressure Israel, upon which it had considerable influence, to insure cooperation. However, none of these came to pass.

Countering the Threat from the United Nations

As with Morocco's occupation of Western Sahara, the United States has consistently blocked the United Nations from enforcing international law regarding its ally. U.S. opposition to the Palestinians has run so strong that the United States has withdrawn or has threatened to withdraw badly needed financial support from UN agencies that have supported Palestinian rights.[13] There have also been scores of occasions where the United States was the only country besides Israel (sometimes joined by one or two small Third World states dependent on U.S. aid) to vote against otherwise unanimous resolutions in the UN General Assembly.[14] More critically, between1972 and 2001, the United States used its veto power in the Security Council thirty-nine times to block resolutions critical of Israeli policies in the occupied territories, more than all other countries have used their veto on all other issues during this period combined. This is in addition to the scores of times when the threat of a U.S. veto has led to a weakening of a resolution's language or the withdrawal of the proposed resolution prior to the vote. For example, in March 2001, the United States scuttled a series of proposed resolutions by European nations by threatening to veto any resolution that used the term "siege" in reference to Israeli occupation forces surrounding and shelling Palestinian towns, or said anything in relation to Israel's illegal settlements, the Geneva Conventions, international law or the principle of land-for-peace.

Having renounced armed struggle and unilaterally recognized Israeli control of most of Palestine in the 1993 Oslo Accords, the strongest tool left at the Palestinians' disposal was a series of UN Security Council resolutions reconfirming principles of international law that applied to their conflict with Israel. The Palestinians assumed that, as guarantor of the Declaration of Principles, the United States would pressure Israel to make needed compromises later, based upon UN Security Council resolutions that the United States, as a Security Council member, was obliged to uphold. However, both the Clinton Administration and the subsequent Bush Administration have claimed that the United Nations no longer has any standing in the Israeli-Palestinian conflict, arguing that the UN resolutions have been superseded by the Oslo Accords. According to Madeleine Albright, when she served as Clinton's ambassador to the United Nations, "resolution language referring to 'final status' issues should be dropped, since these issues are now under negotiations by the parties themselves. These include refugees, settlements, territorial sovereignty and the status of Jerusalem."[15]

This attempt to unilaterally negate the authority of the United Nations, however, is not shared by the international community. No UN resolution can be rescinded without a vote of the body in question. Neither the UN Secretary General nor any other member of the Security Council agrees with the U.S. assessment discounting the relevance of the resolutions. Furthermore, no bilateral agreement between two parties can supersede the authority of the United Nations Security Council. This is especially true when one of the two parties (in this case, the Palestinians) has made it clear that such resolutions are still very relevant.

The United States barred the PLO from participating in the U.S.-sponsored peace process for nearly twenty years in part because the PLO refused to accept UN Security Council resolutions 242 and 338 as the basis of negotiation. The resolutions call on Israel to withdraw from the occupied territories in return for security guarantees. Since the resolutions did not recognize Palestinian national rights, however, the PLO initially rejected them. When the Palestinians formally accepted the resolutions as the basis for peace talks in 1988 anyway and were finally allowed into the peace process five years later, the U.S. essentially dropped these resolutions as the basis of the peace talks.[16] This follows a pattern seen in recent years by successive U.S. administrations: following a concession made by the Palestinians or another Arab party, the United States, in effect, then moves the goal posts. In this case, however, the Bush Administration appears to have moderated the Clinton Administration's decision to jettison these resolutions and has returned to the policy that existed in prior administrations, that is to give lip service to 242 and 338 while providing Israel with the means to ignore them.

U.S. diplomatic opposition to Palestinian rights has even extended to attempts to block open debate at the United Nations, where the PLO has had observer status since 1974. In 1988, Congress passed a law banning the PLO from operating its UN Mission, an effort later voided by rulings from both the International Court of Justice and a U.S. Federal Court, citing U.S. commitments to the UN Charter. Undeterred, the United States, which is also required by the Charter to allow invited guests of the world body access to UN facilities, successfully violated the Charter soon thereafter by preventing Arafat, the PLO leader, from addressing the 43rd General Assembly. The rationale for the U.S. action was that Arafat's trip to the United Nations would somehow threaten U.S. security, given the PLO's history of terrorism. However, such attacks by the PLO had been suspended some years earlier and there was no evidence to suggest that Arafat could somehow organize an attack during his brief visit to New York. The entire General Assembly had to move its session to UN facilities in Geneva, Switzerland in order to hear his address. Ironically, Arafat's speech was far more conciliatory regarding the legitimate rights of both Israelis and Palestinians than those of representatives from Israel, the United States, and some of America's Arab allies.

The U.S. government does not take these positions because the public demands it. Public opinion polls have shown that more than two-thirds of Americans believe that the United Nations should take the lead in resolving the conflict; a similar percentage believe that the UN Security Council should decide the territorial boundaries between Israel and a Palestinian state.[17] Despite this, a cornerstone of the U.S.-led peace process has been to keep the United Nations out. A 1991 Memorandum of Understanding between the United States and Israel explicitly stated that the UN would not have a meaningful role. Sometimes the United States has to go to some lengths to justify such a position. For example, in October 2000, then-U.S. Ambassador to the UN Richard Holbrooke claimed that a UN Security Council resolution (to which the U.S. abstained) criticizing the excessive use of force by Israeli occupation forces demonstrated a bias that put the UN "out of the running" in terms of any contributions to the peace process. The Palestinians noted, however, that an even more strongly worded Congressional resolution criticizing the Palestinians that was passed that same month did not similarly disqualify the United States from its leadership role.

According to UN Security Council resolutions 242 and 338, the only caveat for Israel's complete withdrawal from the territories occupied in the 1967 War is security guarantees from Israel's Arab neighbors.[18] This was generally interpreted to mean promises of non-aggression by neighboring states, presumably enforced through arms control, demilitarized zones, early warning systems and international peacekeeping forces. The United States has dramatically expanded this interpretation, however, now insisting that the resolution essentially requires that the physical safety of every Israeli citizen must be somehow guaranteed. In effect, the United States argues that Israel is under no obligation to withdraw from the occupied territories unless there is a total halt of attacks by suicide bombers or other terrorists. Since most of these come from underground terrorist groups that are beyond the effective control of any government, particularly a disempowered Palestinian Authority under siege by Israeli occupation forces, this effectively means that the Israelis need not be obliged to withdraw.

With the U.S. government ruling out enforcement of UN Security Council resolutions, virtually the only significant diplomatic weapon left for the Palestinians has been the Arab boycott of Israel, which has severely restricted trade between Israel and most of its Arab neighbors and has pressured some American companies not to invest in Israel. As a result, immediately after the Oslo Accords were signed, the United States greatly escalated its pressure against Arab states for an end to the boycott of Israel. Most Arab governments expressed their willingness to end the boycott, but only after Israel recognized Palestinian self-determination and came into compliance with UN Security Council resolutions and international law. The United States, which has successfully pushed for international sanctions against Arab states such as Libya, Sudan, and Iraq for their violations of UN Security Council resolutions, strenuously objected to any such similar sanctions against its ally Israel. In statements about the future of the

Middle East, U.S. officials repeatedly have emphasized the need to end economic pressure against Israel for its occupation and to integrate the region economically under American and Israeli leadership prior to a peace settlement.[19] In 1993, Arab states offered to end the boycott of Israel simply in return for an Israeli freeze on building new settlements. Israeli Prime Minister Yitzhak Rabin refused. In response, U.S. Secretary of State Warren Christopher insisted that the Arabs end the boycott anyway, arguing "It is certainly illogical for Arab nations to continue their boycott of Israel.... The boycott is a relic of the past. It should be relegated to history right now."[20]

With the United States having successfully blocked most diplomatic options available to the Palestinians, it is not surprising that many, out of desperation and hopelessness, have become susceptible to those who argue that armed resistance, and even terrorism, is necessary to pursue their objectives. Incidents such as these belie the myth that the United States is trying to bring the sides together. According to the late Knesset member and Major General Matti Peled, U.S. policy has done little beyond pushing Israel "toward a posture of calloused intransigence."[21] It is not surprising, then, that the peace process collapsed.

The U.S. Role in the Collapse of the Peace Process

Throughout the peace process, the Clinton Administration seemed to coordinate the pace and agenda of the talks closely with Israel, ignoring Palestinian concerns. In an episode that revealed the partisanship of the U.S. role behind the façade of even-handed peace broker, a top Israeli negotiator admitted that, throughout the peace process, Israel and the United States worked closely with each other on their respective proposals prior to presenting them to the Palestinians. For all intents and purposes, these were largely joint efforts,[22] hardly the stance of an impartial mediator that the U.S. projects itself to be.

In a similar vein, the United States appeared to be treating Israeli security as the primary focus of the negotiations, not equally legitimate Palestinian concerns as well. The U.S. assumption has always seemed to be that only Israel has a security problem. While there is no question that Israel has legitimate security concerns that need to be addressed, the United States has never seemed to recognize that the Palestinians might also have security concerns at least as pressing. It is the Palestinians whose territory is under foreign military occupation, whose cities have repeatedly been attacked and placed under siege, whose political institutions have been overrun and ransacked, and who have suffered far more casualties.

During the summer of 2000, the Clinton Administration unsuccessfully attempted to forge a final peace agreement between the two sides at a summit conference in Camp David, Maryland, site of the historic Israeli-Egyptian peace talks hosted by President Carter in 1978. President Clinton's summit failed in large part because neither side was ready for a final agreement. He naively thought that he could pressure Arafat to accept Israeli terms even though negotiations up to that time indicated the two sides were still far apart on some key issues.

In the spring of that year, a series of missteps by both the Israelis and the Palestinians, and by President Clinton as well, appear to have doomed the Camp David summit. For example, Clinton relayed to Arafat that Israeli Prime Minister Ehud Barak would transfer three occupied Palestinian villages on the outskirts of Jerusalem to Palestinian control, which Arafat then announced to the Palestinian public. When Barak reneged on the promise, Clinton refused to push the Israeli prime minister to honor his pledge.[23]

This was part of a growing distrust Palestinians developed toward the United States and Israel in the peace process. Barak, throughout his tenure, was extremely reluctant to even meet with Arafat. He also refused to withdraw from certain Palestinian lands as part of the third phase of withdrawals previously agreed upon by his rightist predecessor, Benyamin Netanyahu of the Likud Bloc. Nor did the prime minister free many of the Palestinian prisoners he had pledged to release or open the promised four safe passages between Palestinian areas that would have allowed for Palestinians to move more freely from one point to another within their occupied lands. Instead, Barak increased the number of closures, where Palestinians were unable to travel to jobs in Israel, leave the country, or even travel to many areas within Palestinian Authority control. Barak also moved forward with the construction of illegal Jewish settlements at an even faster pace than did his right-wing predecessor. Indeed, during Barak's eighteen months in office, the number of settlers grew by an astounding twelve percent.[24] The Clinton Administration neither challenged the dramatic upsurge in construction of new settlements, the closures, the expropriation of land nor the continued incarceration of Palestinian prisoners.

President Clinton's insistence to then jump to final status negotiations without prior confidence-building measures, such as a freeze on new settlements or the fulfillment of previous pledges to withdraw, led the

Palestinians to question the sincerity of both Israel and the United States. Arafat and other Palestinian officials repeatedly warned both Israeli and American officials of the growing resentment among ordinary Palestinians resulting from the rapid growth of settlements and other Israeli policies. Furthermore, they argued that the previously agreed upon withdrawals needed to take place before the more difficult issues of the rights of refugees and the status of Jerusalem be addressed. The Palestinian side certainly contributed to some of the misunderstandings during this period as well through the lack of effective communication between Arafat and some of his negotiators. However, both the United States and Israel insisted on moving directly to a summit on the final status issues, even though they had only begun to be addressed in earnest during the previous eight weeks of what had been a more than seven-year process.[25]

A series of meetings in Sweden and in Jerusalem during the spring of 2000 produced some substantial progress, but news leaks in mid-May about compromises made by the two sides created political problems for both Barak and Arafat. As a result, the talks stalled. Had they continued, there might have been enough groundwork for the Camp David summit to have been successful. However, despite strong Palestinian objections, President Clinton insisted that the two parties come to Maryland anyway to try to hammer out a final agreement. Arafat pleaded that they needed more time, but Clinton pushed Arafat to come and try anyway, promising "If it fails, I will not blame you."[26]

However, Clinton did not do as he promised. Not only did he put enormous pressure on Arafat to accept the Israeli proposals, he did blame Arafat for the collapse of the talks when the Palestinian leader rejected Barak's peace proposals on the grounds that they fell way short of Israel's obligations under international law. At the news conference at the close of the talks, Clinton declared that "Prime Minister Ehud Barak showed particular courage, vision and an understanding of the historical importance of the moment"[27] while insisting that it was Arafat who had been unwilling to compromise.[28]

American media pundits and both Democrats and Republicans on Capitol Hill claim to this day that Barak made an extremely generous offer to the Palestinians at Camp David. An actual examination of the proposal reveals otherwise.

Barak's proposal presented at Camp David did not include an Israeli withdrawal from all of the occupied Palestinian territories. In the 1993 Oslo agreement, the Palestinians essentially recognized Israeli control over

78% of Palestine, the part generally recognized as being within the international boundaries of Israel. This was a major concession from the long-standing Palestinian demand for all of Palestine or even the 43% of Palestine set aside for them in the 1947 UN partition plan. The negotiations since 1993 have been on the fate of this remaining 22%, which the Palestinians assumed—rightly, by virtually every international legal standard—should go to them. However, the United States and Israel have steadfastly insisted that the Palestinian demand for that remaining 22% is too much and that the Palestinians should be willing to give up even more. This is understandably difficult for even Palestinian moderates to accept, since Palestinian Arabs—whose families have lived on the land for centuries prior to the advent of Zionism—were the majority throughout all of Palestine as recently as 1948. Counting refugees, Palestinians today outnumber the Israelis by at least a 3:2 ratio. More fundamentally, Israel took over this remaining 22% of Palestine by military force in 1967. Throughout the U.S.-managed peace process, the United States worked on the assumption that Israel would not need to give up any of its internationally recognized territory or sovereign rights for peace but that the Palestinians would.

The United Nations, in Security Council resolution 242—long considered the basis for Arab-Israeli peace—underscored the longstanding principle of international law, reiterated in the UN Charter, of "the inadmissibility of the acquisition of territory by war." Both Israel and the United States are signatories to the UN Charter and are thereby legally bound to abide by its provisions. The resolution also calls on Israel to withdraw "from territories occupied in the recent conflict" in return for security guarantees.[29] Palestinian demands for implementation of UN Security Council resolution 242, related resolutions and other longstanding canons of international law were dismissed by President Clinton, who insisted that the talks be based instead on what he termed "creative ideas." The so-called creative ideas ended up being a U.S. position paper designed to undercut these longstanding legal principles.

Robert Malley, special assistant to President Clinton for Arab-Israeli affairs and director of Near East and South Asian Affairs for the National Security Council, acknowledged in March 2001 that Israel stuck to positions clearly unacceptable to the Palestinians in the full knowledge of U.S. support. Furthermore, he noted, there was a clear bias towards the Israeli negotiating position. The U.S. position substantially departed from UN resolutions 242 and 338, which the Palestinians had been promised would be the basis of the negotiations. Malley further charged that instead of judging the Israeli proposals on these terms, the Israeli government was instead rewarded for taking extreme positions initially as a tactical maneuver then partially backing off from them. When Barak had inched away from the hard line of his predecessors on some issues, Clinton gave these so-called "concessions" undue significance. Progress was based on relative movement from previously held positions, not on substance; missing from the negotiations were international legal requirements and simple notions of reasonableness and equity.[30]

Initial reports, encouraged by U.S. officials and repeated in the American media, indicated that Barak was willing to hand over a full 95% or more of the West Bank back to the Palestinians. Yet Israel presented no maps to show precisely what lands they were including in the offer. It now appears that this widely quoted percentage did not include greater East Jerusalem, which includes not just the Palestinian-populated eastern half of the city, but also encompasses a series of Palestinian villages and rural areas well to the north and east. (Israel effectively annexed the area in 1967 and no longer considers it as part of the West Bank, though the United Nations and virtually the entire international community insists that it is indeed part of the occupied territories.) Nor did this figure include much of the Jordan Valley, the Dead Sea coast and parts of the Judean Desert, which Barak insisted be leased to the Israeli military for exclusive use for an indefinite period. Taking these additional areas into account, this offer totaled not the 95% claimed but only slightly more than 80% of the West Bank, forcing the Palestinians to relinquish land needed for their development and absorption of refugees.

Barak also insisted on holding on to 69 Jewish settlements in the West Bank, where 85% of the settlers live. Therefore, even though Israel is legally required—under the Fourth Geneva Convention and two UN Security Council resolutions—to completely evacuate the settlements, Barak offered to remove only 15% of the settlers. Furthermore, under Barak's U.S.-backed plan, the West Bank would have been split up by a series of settlement blocs, bypass roads and Israeli roadblocks, by some interpretations dividing the new Palestinian "state" into four non-contiguous cantons. This would require Palestinians to go through Israeli checkpoints to go from one part of their state to another and allow the Israelis to restrict the movement of both people and goods. In addition, Israel would have supervision of border crossings between the new Palestinian state and neighboring Arab states. Israel would also control Palestinian airspace, its seacoast and its water resources. Altogether, these restrictions would make a viable independent Palestinian state impossible.

The Israelis also rejected the right of Palestinian refugees expelled from what is now Israel in the 1948 war to return to their homes, despite international treaty obligations concerning the right of refugees to return.

According to Barak's plan, the Palestinians would have only very limited administrative authority over Arab neighborhoods and Muslim holy sites in occupied East Jerusalem, which would be cut off from the rest of the Palestinian state. In response to Palestinian demands that they be allowed to establish their capital in East Jerusalem, the Israelis agreed only to allow them to set up their new government in Abu Dis, a West Bank village not far from the city's outskirts that could be annexed into greater Jerusalem, thereby allowing the Palestinian Authority to also claim Jerusalem as their capital. In return, the Palestinians would be required to recognize Israel's annexation of virtually the entire remainder of the city.

It is not surprising, therefore, that Arafat rejected the offer. Indeed, it is hard to imagine any national leader accepting peace under conditions that would have effectively put an end to their aspirations for self-determination. The claims by Clinton's team of negotiators that the parties were "so close" at Camp David failed to acknowledge the substantial gap between the two parties and seemed more designed to discredit the Palestinian side than to be an adequate reflection of what actually transpired at the negotiations. Even if Clinton had forced Arafat to capitulate, lack of support among Palestinians would have prevented the agreement from being viable. An unsustainable peace would have been even worse than no peace.

Despite this, President Clinton declared on Israeli television that the Israeli prime minister "was more creative and more courageous"[31] than Arafat and the White House leaked a series of accusations blaming the Palestinian leader for the breakdown of talks. This decision to criticize Arafat's alleged lack of flexibility while praising Barak made the ramifications of this failed summit far worse than it otherwise might have been. According to Palestinian negotiator Nabil Shaath, "I personally pleaded with President Clinton: 'Please do not put on a sad face and tell the world it failed. Please say we broke down taboos, dealt with the heart of the matter and will continue.' But then the president started the blame game, and he backed Arafat into a corner."[32]

Such disappointment over Clinton's role was shared by Israeli negotiator Shlomo Ben-Ami, who noted, "At the end of Camp David, we had the feeling that the package as such contained ingredients and needed to go on. But Clinton left us to our own devices after he started the blame game."[33]

While Barak's offers did go further than any previous Israeli government, they fell well short of what Israel was required to do under international legal standards and a series of UN Security Council resolutions. This is significant, since the Palestinian refusal to give into these demands was therefore completely within their prerogative, given Israel's obligations under international law. Furthermore, as Malley noted, from the Palestinian perspective, "The notion that Israel was 'offering' land, being 'generous,' or 'making concessions' seemed to them doubly wrong—in a single stroke both affirming Israel's right and denying the Palestinians'. For the Palestinians, land was not given but given back."[34]

Since the outstanding Palestinian demands were solidly grounded in international law and human rights covenants, American calls for greater compromises from the Palestinians are tantamount to calling for the denial of these basic rights and for the abrogation of international law. While the United States has been largely successful in forcing the Palestinians to scale back their long-held nationalist aspirations, the Palestinians have been unwilling to give up on these fundamental rights. As a result, the Palestinians have been roundly condemned by American political leaders and in the U.S. media for their failure to compromise more.

In October of that year, the U.S. House of Representatives, with only 30 dissenting votes, adopted a bipartisan resolution that claimed that Israel had "expressed its readiness to take wide-ranging and painful steps in order to bring an end to the conflict, but these proposals were rejected by Chairman Arafat."[35] To this day, members of Congress and media pundits distort what was really offered at Camp David. Typical are remarks of House Minority Leader Nancy Pelosi, who insisted—at the height of Israel's April 2002 military offensive in the West Bank—that Barak had made "a generous and historic proposal."[36] Senator Diane Feinstein, in an editorial column in the *San Francisco Chronicle* that same month claimed that Arafat had been offered "97 percent of the territory of the West Bank [and] a Palestinian capital in East Jerusalem...[but that] Arafat rejected everything that was asked of him."[37] Even President Bush claimed that Arafat "had a chance to secure the peace as a result of the hard work of President Clinton, and he didn't."[38]

Such statements and resolutions are designed to make Americans and Israelis believe that the Palestinians had actually turned down a valid peace offer and are therefore not really interested in peace. For example, near the first anniversary of the summit, influential California Democrat Howard Berman of the House International Relations Committee claimed that Arafat's turning down Barak's proposal was indicative of the Palestinians' determination "to destroy Israel."[39] Such efforts stir up deep-seated and widely-held fears of Jews in Israel, the United States and elsewhere—as a result of both Arafat's history and the enormous mistrust internalized as a result of centuries of anti-Semitism—that the actual Palestinian goal is simply to destroy Israel and kill the Jews. The United States has reasons for encouraging this suspicion. In recent years, Israelis, as well as American Jews and other supporters of Israel in the United States, had finally begun to show an openness to making peace with the Palestinians, which—if successful—could reduce Israel's dependence on the United States and its level of military cooperation. However, by going on record assuming the worst intentions by the Palestinians, American political leaders could help reverse this dovish trend and re-enforce Israeli hard liners who believe that repression, not negotiation, is the answer.[40] This could then help build support for U.S. backing of Israel's right-wing government dedicated to destroying any possibility of Palestinian self-determination, even on a bare-fifth of their country, and thereby insure a close and profitable strategic relationship between the United States and Israel for years to come.

The argument that the breakdown of the talks at Camp David was solely the Palestinians' responsibility is buttressed by the equally inaccurate assumption that their failure meant the end of substantive negotiations or an end of the Palestinians' desire for a negotiated settlement. In fact, negotiations continued, with more than fifty meetings in Jerusalem in the subsequent two months, where significant headway was made.

When Arafat learned in late September that right-wing opposition leader Ariel Sharon was planning a deliberately provocative visit to what Muslims refer to as the Haram al-Sharif, or the Noble Sanctuary (and which Jews call the Temple Mount), he pleaded with Barak to block Sharon's plans. Even though this was in East Jerusalem, which is Israeli-occupied Palestinian territory, Barak insisted it was an internal Israeli matter. To support Sharon's move, Barak brought in hundreds of Israeli troops to accompany the rightist opposition leader, resulting in violent demonstrations by Palestinians over the following days. These were brutally suppressed by Israeli occupation forces, using American-supplied attack helicopters and heavy weapons, killing over two dozen Palestinians, mostly teenagers. The U.S. government made no public objection. Despite subsequent investigations reporting to the contrary, leading members of Congress in both parties insist that these spontaneous demonstrations were actually pre-planned by Arafat and other Palestinian leaders to destroy the peace process. This seems highly unlikely, however, since the Palestinian demonstrators in the first days and weeks of the uprising were primarily Islamists and young people, the two groups most alienated from Arafat's leadership and least likely to obey his requests.

Despite these huge obstacles, Israeli and Palestinian negotiators pressed on. In late December 2000, in a major address, President Clinton presented for the first time an American proposal for a permanent Israeli-Palestinian peace. It was only a marginal improvement over Barak's proposal in July, however. The Palestinians formally rejected the Clinton proposal in early January and hopes that the United States would convene a new summit did not materialize. At this point, the United States ended its active involvement. However, both the Israelis and Palestinians recognized they were closer than they had been at Camp David and resumed talks in Taba—an Egyptian town on the north end of the Gulf of Aqaba—and the nearby Israeli town of Eilat. There, Israel presented new proposals and the Palestinians responded favorably. Despite Barak's claims after Camp David that Israel could go no further, these Israeli proposals six months later were found by the Palestinians to be a distinct improvement. Israeli negotiators significantly modified longstanding territorial-based security demands and its settlement-related requirements, effectively disaggregating Israeli security issues from the territorial and settlements issues. For example, the Israelis would limit their security posts in the Jordan Valley to more discreet and limited outposts that no longer required control of large stretches of Palestinian territory. These late Israeli offers were more generous than the supposed "compromise" proposal offered by President Clinton the previous month.

Meanwhile, the Palestinians made a number of concessions, agreeing to allow Israel to annex large settlement blocs in the West Bank in return for some Israeli territory in the Negev Desert south of the Gaza Strip. The Palestinians further agreed to Israeli sovereignty over eleven Jewish settlements in and around greater East Jerusalem that surrounded historically Arab-populated areas, as well as the Western Wall and the Jewish Quarter in the Old City. This was the first time the Palestinians presented a map that acceded to Israeli annexation of West Bank territories. Both sides discussed and appeared to be getting close to an agreement on the difficult refugee issue that would meet both the Palestinian demand for justice and the Israeli concerns regarding the demographic implications of repatriating large numbers of returning Palestinians. The idea was based upon an Israeli acknowledgement of the right of return combined with financial incentives that would entice most of the refugees to settle in the new Palestinian state and a quota on the number of refugees actually allowed to resettle within Israel.

However, as the February 7 Israeli election got close, the new Israeli proposal was abruptly withdrawn, and hopes for a follow-up summit in Stockholm in which a final peace agreement could be signed never materialized. Barak lost the election to right-wing leader Ariel Sharon and the new Israeli government refused to return to the bargaining table. The fact is, however, that peace did come tantalizingly close. Yet this near-breakthrough was not at Camp David in July with strong U.S. pressure on the Palestinians, but in Taba in January without an American presence and nearly five months after the Palestinian uprising began. In fact, top U.S. officials apparently had never seen the Taba maps that—despite some remaining obstacles—had the two sides within striking distance of a final peace agreement.

Most international observers have recognized that the Palestinian participation in negotiations after the failed Camp David summit and their willingness to offer some major concessions on their part was demonstrative of their interest in peace. Despite this, American political leaders still insist that the Palestinians were not interested in a negotiated settlement and are only interested in pursuing their demands through violence. U.S. officials have roundly criticized Arafat for refusing to sign a peace agreement when the two sides were still far apart at Camp David, but have never criticized Barak from backing away from a peace agreement when the two sides were quite close at Taba. This seems to still be the American position to this day, angering even moderate Muslims who believe the Palestinians had negotiated in good faith.

The U.S. Role in the Settlements

There is little question that the chief obstacle to Israeli-Palestinian peace, at least since the 1980s, has been the Israeli settlements, established by the Israeli government for Jews only in the occupied Gaza Strip, East Jerusalem and the rest of the West Bank. It is illegal under the Fourth Geneva Convention for any country to transfer its civilian population onto lands seized by military force. Under UN Security Council resolutions 446 and 465, Israel is explicitly required to withdraw from these settlements.

The United States initially supported these resolutions, but has since blocked the United Nations from enforcing them. Former Israeli Defense Minister Moshe Dayan acknowledged that while the settlements did not help Israel's security situation they were still needed since, "Without them the IDF would be a foreign army ruling a foreign population."[41] Sharon, who served as housing minister and in other cabinet posts in previous right-wing governments, played a major role in the expansion of these illegal settlements. He bragged back in 1995 about how these settlements were "the only factor" that had prevented then-Prime Minister Rabin from agreeing to withdraw from the occupied territories entirely and was proud of the fact that this had "created difficulties" in the negotiations with the Palestinians.[42] Indeed, had Israel's Labor governments not had to worry about the domestic political consequences from such a withdrawal as a result of the settlements, there would probably have been peace years ago.

President Clinton's insistence that the settlement blocs be incorporated into Israel in his peace plan essentially vindicated the Israeli right's plan to create a demographic transformation in the West Bank that could then become the basis for later territorial claims. This U.S. policy, unchanged under the Bush Administration, has implications for the future. Sharon and his successors can assume that future settlements will likewise become the basis for further U.S.-approved annexations of Palestinian land. Ironically, as settlement expansion has covered ever-wider swaths of Palestinian territory, making a viable Palestinian state alongside Israel increasingly difficult, growing numbers of Palestinians who once supported a two-state solution now argue that such a partition is no longer possible. Instead, they believe that it may actually be more realistic to work for the abolition of Israel as a Jewish state and have it replaced by a democratic secular state where Palestinians and Jews would have equal rights.

This trend towards greater American acceptance of the settlements has mirrored their growth. The United States acknowledged the illegality of the settlements through the Carter Administration. By the senior Bush Administration, they were labeled only as an "obstacle to peace." Under Clinton, they were simply considered "unhelpful." The Clinton Administration even began referring to the more established settlements around occupied East Jerusalem simply as "Jewish neighborhoods."

Former President Carter thought he had a promise of a five-year settlement freeze from Israeli Prime Minister Menachem Begin as part of an annex in the 1978 Camp David Agreement with Egypt.[43] When the prime minister resumed construction after only three months, Carter refused to act, however, even though the United States was a guarantor of the peace treaty. Thirteen years later, the senior President Bush insisted on a settlement freeze as a condition to granting a controversial $10 billion loan guarantee to Israel. However, pressure from Democrats in Congress and 1992 Democratic presidential nominee Bill Clinton led him to capitulate and approve the loan guarantee with Israel, getting Rabin's agreement only to limit construction to the "natural growth" of existing settlements. It soon became apparent that Israel, with the acquiescence of the new Clinton Administration, interpreted this restriction so liberally that the number of new Israeli colonists in the occupied territories grew faster than ever.

When the Oslo Accords were signed the following year, the Palestinians pressed to address the settlements issue immediately. The United States, however, insisted that such discussions be delayed. By putting off such a fundamental issue as the settlements as a "final status issue," the United States gave the Israelis a full eight years to create facts on the ground through a dramatic growth in settlements. The Clinton Administration knew this would make a final peace agreement all the more difficult, yet at no point did they insist that Israel stop the expansion of Jewish settlements and confiscation of land destined to be part of a Palestinian state. It is only because of these settlements that the boundaries for a future Palestinian state envisioned by Clinton and Barak in 2000 took their unviable geographic dimensions, which could have been avoided had the United States used its considerable leverage to halt their expansion early in the process. Top Clinton Administration officials like Robert Malley have acknowledged that the United States had not been tough enough on Israel for its settlement drive and this failure to do so was a major factor in the collapse of the peace process.[44]

A somewhat revealing episode demonstrating Clinton's support of Israel's colonization drive came during the 1992 debate over the proposed $10 billion loan guarantee to Israel. During the presidential campaign that year, Clinton attacked President Bush from the right, criticizing his initial insistence that the loan guarantee be linked to curbing the Israeli settlements in the occupied territories. (Clinton also criticized Bush's strategy of withholding a decision until after the Israeli election in order to help Labor Party challenger Yitzhak Rabin, a position that many Israelis interpreted as an effective endorsement by Clinton of the incumbent Likud Prime Minister Yitzhak Shamir.) Though Clinton claimed that the loans would be used as housing for Jewish immigrants from the former Soviet Union (whom he referred to as "refugees"), none of the money was actually earmarked for such purposes. In fact, Israel had thousands of unoccupied housing units then available, even in the city of Beersheva, where most refugees were initially settled.[45] The Israeli government later acknowledged that the loans were more of a cushion than anything vital to the economy and were instrumental in the dramatic expansion of Israeli settlements in the coming years.[46]

Under pressure from peace and human rights groups, Congress attached a provision requiring the president to deduct the costs of additional settlement activity from the $2 billion annual installment of the loan. In October 1993, the U.S. officially announced to Israel that there would be a $437 million deduction in the next year's loan guarantee due to settlement construction during the 1993 fiscal year. However, State Department Middle East peace talks coordinator Dennis Ross immediately let the Israeli government know that the United States would find a way to restore the full funding. Within a month, Clinton authorized Israel to draw an additional $500 million in U.S. military supplies from NATO warehouses in Europe. A similar scenario unfolded the following year: after deducting $311.8 million spent on settlements from the 1995 loans, Clinton authorized $95.8 for help in redeploying troops from parts of the Gaza Strip and an additional $240 million to facilitate withdrawal from some West Bank cities, based on the rather dubious assertion that it costs more to withdraw troops than to maintain them in hostile urban areas. Clinton explicitly promised the Israelis that aid would remain constant regardless of Israeli settlement policies. What resulted, then, was that the United States began effectively subsidizing the settlements, since the Israelis knew that for every dollar that they contributed to maintaining and expanding their presence in the occupied territories, the United States would convert a loan guarantee into a grant.

Between sixty and one hundred settlements lie outside what most observers consider could realistically be annexed to Israel under a mutually acceptable peace plan. Sharon created most of these outlying settlements during his previous cabinet positions quite explicitly to prevent the creation of a territorially viable Palestinian entity. Between the Oslo II accord in September 1995 and the start of final status talks in March 2000, successive Israeli governments were envisioning maintaining all but the most isolated of these settlements and dividing the new Palestinian state into a series of non-contiguous cantons. What the Israelis presented in Taba in January 2001 largely abandoned this strategy, reducing them to a small number of settlement blocs. But the progress represented by the amended Israeli position on the settlements presented at Taba is gone. Under Sharon, they have reverted back to the old strategy with no apparent American objections.

Israel has never defined where its borders are, which gives Israeli leaders an enormous amount of leeway as to what they consider to be occupied territories. Sharon has even claimed "there is no occupation."[47] This attitude has exacerbated Arab fears that Israel is an expansionist power. In a discussion on the future of the Palestinians during his visit to Washington in February 2001, Sharon reportedly told Secretary of State Powell, "We learn a lot from you Americans. We saw how you moved West using this method."[48]

A particular sore point for Palestinians over the settlements arose from the Oslo accords, which refer to the West Bank and Gaza Strip as a "single territorial unit, the integrity and status of which will be preserved during the interim period."[49] This was essentially a prohibition against either side taking steps that could prejudice the permanent status negotiations. As a result, the Palestinians—when they signed the agreement—assumed that this would prevent the Israelis from building more settlements. Furthermore, as the principal guarantor of the Oslo Agreement, the United States was arguably obliged to force Israel to cease its construction if they tried to do so. However, Israel and the United States have refused to live up to their obligations and—since the signing of the Oslo Accords—the total number of settlers in the occupied territories has grown from approximately 250,000 to close to 400,000. They are moving onto land that the Palestinians assumed would be returned to the three million Palestinians that already live there and the large numbers of refugees who would presumably be resettling to the new Palestinian state. Since the Oslo Accords were signed, the numbers of Israeli settlers on areas in the West Bank outside of greater East Jerusalem have increased by 70% to more than 200,000, some within thirty new settlements and the rest in expansions of existing settlements. Settlers within greater East Jerusalem have increased by at least one-third. It is very difficult for Palestinians and many others to appreciate the sincerity of Israel and the United States in reaching a negotiated peace while Israel's settlement drive continues unabated.

The Israelis are also in the process of building a massive highway system of 29 roads totaling nearly 300 miles, designed to perpetuate effective Israeli control of most of the West Bank. These highways—designed to connect the settlements with each other and with Israel proper—will create a series of borders and barriers, effectively isolating Palestinian areas into islands. In addition, since Israel has defined these highways as "security roads," they reach a width of 350 yards (50 yards of road plus 150 yards of "sanitized" margins on each side), the equivalent of three and a half football fields. This has resulted—and, assuming the Israelis will continue the project as planned, will result still further—in the destruction of some of the area's richest farmland, including olive groves and vineyards, that have been owned and farmed by Palestinian families for generations. The impact of such a massive road system in an area the size of Delaware is staggering, and has serious political, economic and environmental implications. Once filled with enormous hope with the signing of the Oslo Accords in 1993, the Palestinians have since seen more and more of their land confiscated and more and more Jewish-only settlements and highways constructed, all under the cover of a U.S.-sponsored "peace process."

As part of what President Clinton referred to as "implementation funding" of the 1998 Wye River Agreement, in which Israel agreed to withdraw from an additional 14% of the West Bank, the United States offered $1.2 billion in supplementary foreign aid to the Israeli government. Most of the funding was reserved for armaments. Much of the non-military funding was apparently earmarked to build these "bypass roads" for Israeli settlers in the occupied territories, placing the United States in violation of Article 7 of UN Security Council resolution 465, which prohibits member states from assisting Israel in its colonization drive. So, not only has the United States allowed Israel to violate UN Security Council resolutions in continuing to maintain and expand its illegal settlements, the United States has placed itself in violation of a UN Security Council resolution as well.

Meanwhile, growing numbers of Israeli soldiers are expressing their resentment at having to risk their lives protecting these settlers. Many have also expressed moral opposition to providing support for their country's illegal colonization drive and hundreds have risked jail for refusing to serve in the armed forces outside of Israel's internationally-recognized borders. Particularly problematic for the IDF soldiers is being ordered to protect settlements in isolated areas populated by right-wing Jewish fundamentalists who deliberately provoke nearby Palestinian villagers through violent attacks against persons and property only to then hide behind the young Israeli conscripts, expecting protection from Palestinian retaliation.

These Jewish extremists are much like their Islamic Palestinian counterparts in their zealotry, intolerance, and propensity towards violence. The difference is that the extremist Jewish groups are legally sanctioned, issued arms by the Israeli government, and are often directly supported by elements of the Israeli military. General Peled accused his government of connivance as the settlers' "openly declared war against the peace process. Not only are they allowed to carry out with impunity pogroms against Palestinian cities and villages, they are also given free time on the state-owned media."[50] Dozens of Israeli soldiers from different units have written to the Israeli press, to Knesset members, and to government ministers, complaining that they had been ordered to stand aside as rampaging settlers dragged Palestinian motorists out of their cars, beat them up, and torched their vehicles.[51]

The relationship between the Israeli military and these far right wing extremists bears a striking resemblance to those between the established armed forces and the paramilitary death squads that terrorized such Central American countries as El Salvador, Guatemala and Honduras during the 1980s. And, as was the case then, the United States is providing financial support, both through foreign aid to the Israeli government as well as through tax-deductible private donations to the settler groups directly.

Adding to the bad feelings among the largely native-born Israeli soldiers forced to defend the settlers is that as many as half of the colonists in the right-wing settlements are American émigrés. In addition, much of the direct funding for Gush Emunim, Kach, and other far right Israeli groups comes from private contributions from the United States. Through an executive order by President Clinton, two of these extremist Jewish organizations were labeled as terrorist groups and had their assets seized, but they were apparently tipped off beforehand and withdrew most of their investments from American banks just prior to the seizure. Despite a long criminal record in both the United States and Israel and his links to Israeli terrorists, Kach founder Meir Kahane was routinely granted a U.S. visa during the 1970s and 1980s to recruit American Jews to join his far-right movement. Among his American recruits was Baruch Goldstein, who massacred 29 Palestinians in a Hebron mosque in 1994. By contrast, the U.S. government during that same period was consistently denying visas to PLO officials, including moderate elements advocating peace with Israel. (Egyptian Islamist El Sayyid Nosair, a follower of Sheik Omar Abdel Rahman's "Islamic Group" that later developed ties with the Al-Qaeda network, assassinated Kahane during one of his visits to New York in 1990.)

While the current Bush Administration has termed Israeli settlement expansion "provocative," they have not repudiated the Clinton Administration's support for "natural growth" of the settlements. Given the history of "natural growth" allowing for unabated expansion, the Bush Administration position is essentially an endorsement of Sharon's colonization drive. Much of Israel's violence against Palestinians has been justified in protecting settlers who have no legal right to be in the occupied territories. The Bush Administration's position is that even talking about the Israeli settlements in the occupied territories is premature. According to Secretary of Defense Rumsfeld, who fails to acknowledge that there may ever be a Palestinian state on the West Bank and Gaza Strip, "it's hard to know whether there are settlements in portions of the real estate that will end up with the entity that you make an arrangement with or Israel. So it seems to me focusing on settlements at the present time misses the point."[52]

Rather than ally itself with Israelis supporting peace and reconciliation, the United States has tended to side with the Israeli settlers and other hard line elements. Even with the recent swing of Israeli public opinion to the right, a great majority of Israelis support a total freeze on the settlements in return for a cease-fire. However, Sharon has refused and the U.S. appears to be backing him.

The Peace Process and Occupation Under Bush and Sharon

Upon assuming office in February 2001, the newly elected Prime Minister Ariel Sharon rejected the previous Israeli government's premise that it is important to make territorial sacrifices to end the conflict with the Palestinians. Sharon made clear that any Palestinian entity would have to be limited to the areas that had been handed over to the Palestinians in previous negotiations—totaling at most 42% of the West Bank and 80% of the Gaza Strip—that would be divided into dozens of small non-contiguous segments. Meanwhile, the Bush Administration, which came into office a few weeks earlier, dismissed Clinton's peace proposal from the previous December that would have returned more than twice that much of the occupied territories to the Palestinians.

The Palestinian leadership still called for a resumption of negotiations, but the Israeli government refused. The Israelis insisted—with American support—that there be a total end of Palestinian violence for an extended period before talks could resume. This, however, gave Palestinian extremists beyond the control of the Palestinian Authority who opposed the peace process altogether an incentive to launch terrorist attacks and other acts of violence to make sure that the talks would not resume. The motivation to suspend armed resistance in order for negotiations to reconvene was further hampered by Prime Minister Sharon's insistence that his government would take an even more uncompromising position than the already-rejected proposals of the previous Barak government.

During its first year in office, the Bush Administration made a number of contradictory statements regarding the conflict. Secretary of State Powell criticized certain Israeli policies on several occasions only to have his statements soft-pedaled by the White House and then openly challenged by both Republican and Democratic congressional leaders. The overall Bush Administration position was based on the premise that the two parties needed to work things out among themselves, which had little chance of success given the Israeli refusal to negotiate. Furthermore, the Bush Administration insisted that both sides needed to compromise, thereby implying that the territorial demands of an occupying power were equally legitimate to those whose lands were under occupation. Furthermore, bilateral negotiations between a government representing the strongest economic and military power in the region with a weakened and corrupt leadership of an occupied people can hardly be considered fair. Ignoring the gross asymmetry in power between the Palestinians and their Israeli occupiers simply favors the status quo, namely continued occupation, repression, and colonization from the Israeli side and rioting, guerrilla warfare and terrorism from the Palestinian side.

Sharon became prime minister largely as a result of events that grew out of his deliberately provocative visit to the Noble Sanctuary in September 2000. The strong U.S. support for his government, despite occasional mild rebukes, is widely seen in Israel as rewarding him for the action that lit the spark to the widespread killing and suffering that followed.

Sharon's political history is revealing. The Likud leader opposed the U.S.-brokered peace treaty with Egypt in 1978, the 1993 Oslo Accords and the 1996 agreement on Israeli redeployment from parts of the West Bank city of Hebron. He also opposed the partial Israeli withdrawal from Lebanon in 1985 and the total withdrawal in 2000. Sharon even refused to support the U.S.-brokered peace treaty with Jordan in 1994. The right-wing prime minister has refused to negotiate with Arafat and his political party is on record opposing Palestinian statehood. As an army officer and

Defense Minister, he has been implicated in a number of mass killings of Palestinian civilians that are widely recognized as war crimes. These include his command of a unit that massacred scores of civilians in the West Bank village of Qibya in 1953, his leadership in the 1972 "pacification" campaign in refugee camps in Gaza that killed hundreds of non-combatants, his 1982 order for Israeli forces to bombard Lebanese population centers that killed thousands, and his facilitation of the massacre of over one thousand Palestinian refugees by Lebanese Phalangist militiamen that same year.

Nevertheless, the Bush Administration and Congressional leaders have insisted he is sincerely interested in pursuing peace with the Palestinians. At the height of Israel's devastating military offensive in the West Bank during the spring of 2002, President Bush lauded Sharon as "a man of peace," adding, "I'm confident he wants Israel to be able to exist at peace with its neighbor."[53] While President Bush has welcomed the rightist prime minister to Washington on several occasions, he has refused to meet with President Arafat, yet another indication of U.S. support for Sharon's negotiating position.

In the fall of 2000, the United Nations General Assembly created a commission charged with investigating the causes and possible solutions to the ongoing conflict. As a means of short-circuiting the commission, President Clinton appointed a U.S.-led team to put forward its own report. To head the commission, Clinton named former Senate Majority Leader George Mitchell, who had attacked the senior Bush Administration from the right on its policy toward Israel and Palestine, particularly when then-Secretary of State James Baker accurately declared that Israeli settlements ringing eastern Jerusalem were in the occupied territories. The United States determined that the commission would operate primarily out of Washington and would limit its investigations on the ground. Israeli journalist Meron Benvenisti, after witnessing Mitchell's team in their interviews with Israeli officials predicted, "The committee will become one more instrument for stifling any initiative for examining the actions of Israeli security forces and for uncovering the truth lurking behind the propaganda smokescreen."[54]

The commission's report, released at the end of April 2001, refused to hold either side solely responsible for the breakdown of the peace process or the ongoing violence. The report called for a cease-fire, in particular for the Palestinian Authority to "make clear through concrete action to Palestinians and Israelis alike that terrorism is reprehensible and unacceptable, and that the PA will make a 100 percent effort to prevent terrorist operations and to punish perpetrators" and for the Israelis to "ensure that the IDF adopt and enforce policies and procedures encouraging non-lethal responses to unarmed demonstrators, with a view to minimizing casualties and friction between the two communities."[55] The report correctly recognized that the violence was not solely a result of Sharon's provocative visit to the Islamic holy site in occupied East Jerusalem the previous autumn nor was it part of a preconceived plan by the Palestinians to launch a violent struggle. It recognized that the root of the uprising was in Palestinian frustrations in the peace process to get their land back, fueled by unnecessarily violent responses by both sides in the early hours and days of the fighting. Yet the report's failure to call for an international protection force underscored the commission's unwillingness to support the decisive steps necessary to effectively curb further bloodshed. More seriously, the report refused to call for Israel's withdrawal from the occupied territories, even in return for security guarantees, which Israel is required to do under UN Security Council resolutions 242 and 338.

The Mitchell Commission Report also failed to call for Israel to withdraw from its illegal settlements as required under UN Security Council resolutions 446 and 465. However, it did call on Israel to "freeze all settlement activity, including the 'natural growth' of existing settlements," emphasizing that "A cessation of Palestinian-Israeli violence will be particularly hard to sustain unless the Government of Israel freezes all settlement activity."[56]

However, in June, the United States—spearheaded by CIA director George Tenet—followed up on the Mitchell Commission Report by pushing for a cease-fire agreement from the Palestinians even as the Sharon government pledged to continue building more settlements. The Bush Administration and Congress essentially put forward the Mitchell Commission Report only in terms of getting a cease-fire, conveniently dropping the report's insistence on a settlement freeze and other Israeli responsibilities. Tenet's plan called on a complete cessation of violence for one week followed by a six-week cooling off period where Israeli forces would withdraw to where they were prior to the outbreak of violence in September 2000. In effect, the report was used to put the pressure on the Palestinians to cease their resistance to Israeli occupation forces without anything in return from Israel other than redeploying their forces to the demarcation lines to which they were already obliged to withdraw according to previous treaties.

The U.S.-brokered cease-fire, which technically went into effect that June but never fully materialized, left the situation on the ground with no changes that might have provided the Palestinians with any incentive to end the uprising. Not only did Tenet's proposal not insist that Israel stop building more settlements, no international monitors or verifiers for a cease-fire were included and no buffer zones were established to separate the two sides. Instead, the United States essentially permitted Israel to serve as the monitor and verifier as well as the decision-maker regarding its implementation and subsequent steps. Within days of the agreement, Israel launched its assassination squads into Palestinian Authority areas, killing several Palestinian leaders, claiming that these killings were not cease-fire violations but self-defense against terrorists.

For Arafat to attempt to stop Palestinians fighting against the occupation with nothing in return would make him appear to be a collaborator, and few would heed such a decree. It might even lead to a Palestinian civil war if he attempted to crack down with full force. From the perspective of the Palestinians, the seven years of U.S.-managed peace negotiations since the signing of the Declaration of Principles agreed to in Oslo had simply resulted in ever-increasing poverty, loss of land, humiliation and harassment at Israeli checkpoints, and still no state of their own. As a result, frustration mounted until extraordinary violence erupted in September 2000 in the Israeli-occupied territories.

International law sees terrorism as a war crime but recognizes the right of people under foreign military occupation to armed resistance against the occupying forces. Unfortunately, both sides have muddied the issue. Some Palestinians claim that suicide bombings against Israeli civilians—which increased dramatically in 2001 and 2002—constitute legitimate resistance. On the other side, the American and Israeli governments condemn Palestinian attacks against uniformed Israeli occupation forces as "terrorism." The Bush Administration has spoken only of stopping "the cycle of violence," as if the violence was some kind of ethnic conflict or border dispute, not one of an occupied population fighting for its right of self-determination. Ironically, leading Congressional Democrats—such as Gary Ackerman, the ranking Democrat on the House International Relations Subcommittee on the Middle East—have criticized the administration from the right, claiming, "It is not a cycle of violence. It is Palestinian violence and Israeli response."[57]

The Palestinians are probably seriously mistaken, however, to believe that violence will lead Israel to end the occupation or the United States to end its support of the occupation. The violence has simply hardened Israeli and American attitudes. In short, not only is such violence—particularly when directed towards civilians—morally wrong, but it is politically counter-productive as well.

At the same time, it is totally unrealistic to believe that the Palestinians would unilaterally halt their uprising without anything concrete in return from the Israelis, such as a settlement freeze. Yet this is precisely the policy demanded by the Bush Administration and Congress. Furthermore, the United States has failed to recognize that Palestinian terrorism and other violence is a direct consequence of the occupation and the U.S. refusal to uphold international law.

By the end of 2001, Israeli occupation forces erected more than 100 new military posts surrounding Palestinian population centers in a series of multiple sieges, dividing Palestinian-controlled areas into 220 tiny enclaves, where the civilian population began experiencing severe food shortages, lack of medical care and unemployment of over 70%. Once one of the more prosperous regions of the Arab world, more than 60% of the Palestinian population in the West Bank and Gaza Strip found themselves living in abject poverty. In November of that year, Amnesty International condemned both terrorist violence by Palestinians as well as human rights abuses by Israeli occupation forces, which—the report noted—included extrajudicial killings, detention without charge, collective punishment, the use of torture, the demolition of homes and other abuses

After a particularly destructive and deadly wave of Israeli attacks into civilian areas of the West Bank in early March 2002, Vice-President Dick Cheney visited the region. He met with Prime Minister Sharon but refused to meet with Arafat until the Palestinian leader "renounced once and for all the use of violence."[58] At this time, Arafat was under siege inside his offices in the West Bank city of Ramallah and his security forces were scattered to avoid being killed by Israeli forces that were bombing their facilities. Apparently, at no point in his meetings with the Israeli prime minister did the American vice-president bring up the possibility of a freeze of settlements, a resumption of peace negotiations, a withdrawal of Israeli troops to the areas of control promised under U.S.-brokered disengagement agreements, or an end to Israeli violence.

To follow up on the Tenet Plan, President Bush dispatched retired Marine Commandant Anthony Zinni in November 2001 as his special Middle East envoy. Zinni, former head of the U.S. Central Command, had only limited experience in diplomacy. His mission was solely to establish a cease-fire, not to restart negotiations or address any of the other elements of the Mitchell report. Zinni presented his plan on March 26, 2002. In it, he used unconditional language in reference to the Palestinians, requiring them to "cease" violent activities, while only asking the Israelis to "commit to cease." This new U.S. proposal also dropped the Tenet Plan's requirement that Israel should stop its attacks on "innocent civilian targets" and its other restrictions against "proactive" Israeli military operations. Instead, Zinni's proposal would permit Israeli attacks on Palestinian Authority buildings, including prisons, "in self-defense to an imminent terrorist attack," a situation that the Israelis had defined quite liberally. The Palestinians rejected such revisions, arguing "It is impossible to imagine a scenario in which bombing a prison or the president's compound would be 'self-defense'...this, in effect, justifies all the so-called 'retaliatory' attacks the Israelis have conducted so far."[59]

Throughout this period, it was becoming increasingly clear within the international community that the Palestinians had international law and UN Security Council resolutions firmly on their side and that the ongoing Israeli occupation and colonization of the West Bank and Gaza Strip was the central issue. As a result, U.S. policy makers had to find a way to bolster their position backing Israel and its rightist prime minister. The Bush Administration and Congressional leaders of both parties then zeroed in on the Palestinians' most vulnerable area: Palestinian Authority president Yasir Arafat.

Even many of their strongest supporters acknowledge that the Palestinians have been saddled with what may be the worst leadership of virtually any national liberation movement in recent decades. The rule of Arafat and his Fatah organization—originally organized as a guerrilla group during exile—has alienated broad segments of Palestinian society, making it difficult to control much of his population. Similarly, the Palestinian Authority failed to create a socio-political base necessary to promote a viable sovereign entity. Furthermore, Arafat did not sufficiently prepare the population for the likelihood that the vast majority of refugees would not be able to return home and that even getting back most of Arab East Jerusalem would be a protracted struggle. Arafat refused to disarm Fatah's Tanzim militia, which had grown largely beyond his control as the uprising had pushed younger more militant leaders to the forefront, attacking both Israeli occupation forces and civilian settlers in the occupied territories. Segments of the Palestinian Authority, including some of its own media, had even encouraged such violence. The most serious charges against Arafat, however, involved terrorism.

Palestinian Terrorism Against Israelis and the U.S. Response

For the first fifteen years after Arafat's Fatah organization took control over the Palestine Liberation Organization in 1968, they launched a series of terrorist attacks against Israel and Israeli targets elsewhere in the world, killing scores of Israelis, mostly civilians. These included cross-border raids into Israel where Palestinian commandos would seize and often murder hostages or plant bombs in public places. In addition, Israeli embassies abroad became targets of violent assaults and hostage taking. Some of the more radical PLO factions, such as the Popular Front for the Liberation of Palestine and other Marxist-Leninist groups, engaged in airline hijackings. Fatah largely ceased its terrorist activities by the early 1980s, though some smaller PLO factions continued such attacks for a few more years. Some anti-PLO Palestinian factions—such as Abu Nidal—continued terrorist attacks against Israelis and others into the early 1990s, including the assassination of moderate PLO officials advocating peace with Israel. Largely as part of an effort to be incorporated into the peace process, the PLO formally renounced terrorism in 1988.

Since the mid-1990s, there have been a series of terrorist attacks by Palestinian Islamic groups, targeting both civilian Israeli settlers in the West Bank and Gaza Strip as well as Israeli civilians inside Israel. These escalated dramatically in 2001 and 2002 in response to increased Israeli repression in the occupied territories. Most of the attacks have been organized by the Izzedine al-Qassam Brigades, the armed wing of Hamas, a large multifaceted Palestinian Islamic organization based in the occupied territories. A smaller and even more radical group, Islamic Jihad, has been responsible for a number of terrorist attacks as well. Both groups oppose Yasir Arafat and his secular Fatah movement and vehemently oppose the peace process with Israel, seeking the establishment of an Arab Islamic state in all of Palestine through armed revolution. These attacks have killed hundreds of Israeli civilians and have been particularly traumatic for a country that has suffered from terrorism for decades and for a people who have experienced systematic violent persecution for centuries.

Arafat and the Palestinian Authority have repeatedly condemned such acts of terrorism, though there are serious questions regarding the sincerity and consistency of their opposition. While Palestinian police have arrested hundreds of Islamic militants, there has been some infiltration by radical Islamist sympathizers within the ranks of Palestinian police.

Combined with corruption, incompetence and popular pressure, some terrorists have been released from prison and major suspects remain free.

However, while it would be wrong to assume Arafat and his government are blameless for the terrorist attacks, it would also be wrong to assume that they are directly responsible for most of them, as Israeli officials and U.S. Congressional leaders have alleged. For example, a large number of the terrorists implicated in attacks inside Israel have come from areas under Israeli security control. Secondly, Israeli attacks on the Palestinian Authority's offices and jails have severely crippled their anti-terrorism efforts by destroying records and killing investigators. In some cases, in the midst of an Israeli attack or believing an attack was imminent, suspected terrorists were hurriedly released in order to spare their lives. In addition, Israel's multiple sieges of Palestinian towns and cities have oftentimes made it impossible for Palestinian police and investigators to get from one town to another to follow through on their tips and arrest suspects.

Many Arabs and Muslims have pointed out that Israeli forces firing missiles into inhabited homes, shelling civilian areas, utilizing death squads, and using live ammunition against protesting children are also acts of terror. Similarly, they argue that is wrong for the United States to demand that the Palestinians punish terrorists who murder Israeli civilians but not demand that Israel punish its soldiers who murder Palestinian civilians.

However, in November 2001, 88 out of 100 U.S. senators signed a letter addressed to President Bush intending to prevent Secretary of State Powell from including direct or indirect criticism of Israel in a speech he was planning to give at the University of Louisville. The senators insisted that President Bush not restrain Sharon from retaliating fully against Palestinian violence and to give the Israeli military assaults his full support, declaring "The American people would never excuse us for not going after the terrorists with all our strength and might. Yet that is what some have demanded of the Israeli government after every terrorist incident they suffer. No matter what the provocation, they urge restraint." The senators also voiced opposition to the United States offering any inducements to the Palestinians.[60]

In mid-December 2001, bowing to Israeli and American pressure, Arafat turned his crippled security forces on Hamas and Islamic Jihad, arresting scores of militants, closing offices and even shooting into crowds of Islamist protestors. As a result, Arafat was able to force nearly four weeks of calm in late December and early January. However, Israel then engaged in a series of assassinations of local Palestinian leaders. Immediately afterwards, Palestinian violence resumed.[61] As the *Washington Post* noted, in a review of the ongoing conflict, "Each period of Palestinian restraint was greeted with Israeli assassinations, home demolitions or incursions into Palestinian territory. Each terrorist attack launched by Arafat's extremist rivals was answered by devastating Israeli assaults on Arafat's own security forces."[62] Strategic analyst Zbigniew Brzezinski, who served as National Security Advisor in the Carter Administration, provided an observation crucial to understanding apparent Israeli intentions, criticizing the "deliberate overreactions by Mr. Sharon designed not to repress terrorism, but to destabilize the Palestinian Authority and to uproot the Oslo Agreement—which he has always denounced."[63]

In the subsequent months, despite State Department and CIA analysts noting Sharon's ongoing provocations and over-reactions, President Bush continued to focus virtually exclusively on Palestinian terrorism as the cause of the crisis, using the same basic rhetoric of Sharon.[64] In part this was a reflection of President Bush's decision to give Defense Department officials unprecedented clout in the formulation of U.S. policy towards the conflict, which had previously been largely under the purview of the State Department. One result was that the hard line Pentagon officials who view the conflict strictly in security terms—Secretary of Defense Rumsfeld, Deputy Secretary of Defense Paul Wolfowitz and Undersecretary of Defense Douglas Feith—have marginalized the more pragmatic conservatives, such as Secretary of State Powell, who see the conflict more in political terms. For example, Feith—prior to joining the administration—contributed to a 1996 paper that advised Israeli Prime Minister Netanyahu to make "a clean break from the peace process."[65] Similarly, Feith wrote a widely read 1997 article that called on Israel to re-occupy "the areas under Palestinian Authority control" even though "the price in blood would be high."[66] These hawkish voices have been augmented significantly by a coalition of Democrats and right-wing Republicans in Congress.[67] For the struggle in the occupied territories, in the eyes of the Bush Administration and both parties in Congress, was not a matter of a military occupation of one country against another, but simply a part of the U.S.-led war on terrorism.

As a result, the Israelis refused to ease off on their siege of Palestinian towns and cities or end the closures. Not surprisingly, then, the violence continued. Despite this, it appeared that the majority of Palestinians were still interested in peace, with a majority polled showing that they supported neither Hamas nor Arafat.[68]

Israeli commentator Gideon Samet, in his analysis of American support for Sharon, complained,

> With favors like that from our friends, we don't need enemies. Bush should have learned from the superpower's blitz against the Taliban that force is not enough. The trouble is that both the American administration and Sharon's regime have mixed up cause and effect...In the current Bush-Sharon lexicon, the source of evil is terrorism. But terror has its reasons, historical and immediate, which must be dealt with wisely.[69]

However, Secretary of State Powell declared that the Israeli-Palestinian conflict was not a result of "the absence of a political way forward" but from "terrorism...in its rawest form." Furthermore, he accused Iraq, Iran and Syria of "using the Middle East conflict as an excuse for those terrorist organizations" operating in the region."[70]

Part of the dilemma for U.S. policy makers comes as a result of President Bush's insistence, in the aftermath of the September 2001 terrorist attacks on the United States, that those who harbor terrorists or have any other links to terrorists will be treated as terrorists themselves, thereby being subjected to military action and excluded from negotiations. In the case of Israel and Palestine, this would essentially require the United States to support Sharon's attacks against Palestinian institutions and his refusal to engage in peace talks. The Bush Doctrine, however, not only fails to address the problem of the far greater civilian casualties inflicted by government forces—such as the Israeli occupation troops—but it ignores the structural violence—like the U.S.-backed military occupation—that results in the terrorist backlash. American officials are therefore in a weak position to condemn Palestinian terrorism as long as the United States supplies much of weaponry used in carrying out the even greater Israeli acts of violence. While the United States has little direct control over Palestinian violence, the United States could stop the Israeli violence by turning off the spigot of military and economic aid to the Israeli government. This, in turn, could force Israel to return to the negotiating table, bringing hope for a peace settlement and thereby reduce or even eliminate the Palestinian violence. The Bush Administration has chosen not to do so.

In the early weeks of 2002, Arafat convinced Hamas to join Palestinian Authority militias in focusing their armed resistance exclusively in the occupied territories and to cease terrorist attacks inside Israel. After a series of successful strikes against Israeli occupation forces, Israel launched some devastating incursions into Palestinian cities in retaliation, along with a series of assassinations, leading the Islamic groups to return to their attacks against Israeli civilians inside Israel. This new round of Israeli incursions and assassinations accelerated a trend whereby the Palestinian public, which had largely opposed such terrorism, began to shift noticeably in support of suicide bombing as their situation worsened and they lost any hope that the United States would pressure Israel to end its attacks and its 35-year occupation.

At this point, there are some indications that Arafat and his senior commanders made a major shift in strategy: Perhaps aware that they were losing popular support in favor of Hamas and wanting to demonstrate to Sharon that the increased repression was not working, they apparently authorized a Fatah faction known as the Al-Aqsa Martyrs Brigade to begin a series of terrorist attacks inside Israel as well. If indeed this was the decision, they must have known this would likely harden American and Israeli attitudes still further, but perhaps they felt there was little to lose, since the Israeli and American governments were accusing them of being responsible for the terrorist attacks anyway.

On March 20, the Israeli newspaper *Yediot Ahronoth* quoted IDF intelligence reports that the U.S.-backed IDF actions in the occupied territories had made matters worse by preventing the Palestinian Authority from taking actions against terrorists. Furthermore, according to the reports, the IDF assassinations and bombings had motivated subsequent suicide bombings against Israelis, leading senior Palestinian Authority leaders to start cooperating with terrorist groups. In short, a bloody stalemate had come to the fore because the Israeli attacks made it politically impossible for Arafat to crack down on the terrorists while the terrorist attacks gave Sharon the excuse to put off peace negotiations and continue his assaults on Palestinian population centers.

In early March, Israeli forces re-occupied large areas of the West Bank that Israel had handed over to the Palestinian Authority in previous disengagement agreements. The United States initially supported the incursions, again blaming Arafat and calling for a cease-fire without anything in return from the Israelis. As international criticism of the Israeli assaults on the Palestinian infrastructure grew, the Bush Administration—in one of a series of public rebukes against the Sharon government—finally insisted that Israel withdraw and Sharon ordered the troops to pull back.

At the end of the month, however, a particularly devastating series of terrorist attacks in Israel by both Hamas and Fatah suicide bombers prompted Israel to launch its largest military incursion yet.

U.S. Support for Israel's Spring 2002 Offensive

Israel began its offensive on March 30, occupying most major towns, cities and refugee camps in the West Bank. The Israeli military operation had been planned for months, though the unusually vicious acts of Palestinian terrorism during the last week in March—including a blast at a Passover seder in Netanya that killed 28 people—gave the Israeli government the excuse it was looking for. On March 28, Zinni told Arafat that he could stop the planned attack if Arafat accepted his implementation proposal, but Arafat reiterated that it was unrealistic to impose a cease-fire under such conditions.[71]

Meanwhile, Saudi Crown Prince Abdullah announced a peace proposal that called on Arab states to not only provide security guarantees for Israel, but establish full normal diplomatic relations, in return for a full Israeli withdrawal from the occupied territories. At the Beirut summit of the League of Arab states in late March, every Arab government, including the Palestinian Authority, endorsed the Saudi proposal. Just as with Sharon's 1982 invasion of Lebanon, the 2002 invasion of the West Bank—probably not coincidentally—took place just when the Palestinians were making diplomatic headway through a peace initiative.

It soon became apparent that the goal of Sharon's offensive was to destroy political life in the occupied territories in pursuit of the Israeli right's dream of a "Greater Israel." Uri Avnery, writing in the Israeli newspaper *Maariv*, confirmed reports of most foreign observers that "the real aim" of the offensive was to "break the backbone of the Palestinian people" and "crush their governmental institutions" resulting in "the destruction of organized Palestinian society."[72] Serge Schmemann, writing in the *New York Times*, observed how there was "a systematic effort by the Israeli Army to strip institutions of the Palestinian Authority of as much data as possible,"[73] with the Cultural Ministry and Education Ministry ransacked and records destroyed. Scores of civil agencies, commercial establishments and non-governmental organizations were looted, damaged or destroyed, mostly after the military had established firm control of the given area. In addition, a large number of historic buildings, particularly in the casbah of Nablus, were reduced to rubble.[74] Independent Israeli analysts observed that Sharon's strategy was to totally destroy any kind of central Palestinian government of any kind, in the hopes that it might lead to an effective reoccupation by Israel or the establishment of a kind of Vichy-style collaborationist authority.[75]

On the day Sharon launched the offensive, Bush endorsed the Israeli action by declaring "I fully understand Israel's need to defend herself."[76] The UN Security Council, in emergency special session, voted in support of a cease-fire and for an Israeli withdrawal from the recently re-occupied cities. The U.S. voted in the affirmative, but only after successfully demanding that there be no call for an immediate withdrawal or a set timetable and that the Security Council call for the implementation of Zinni's interpretation of the Tenet Plan.[77] Two days later, Secretary of Defense Rumsfeld ruled out sending U.S. forces to enforce a cease-fire and focused his remarks on Iran, Iraq and Syria for allegedly "inspiring and financing a culture of political murder and suicide bombing in Israel."[78] As reports of widespread civilian casualties intensified protests against Israel's incursions, Bush made a speech which, while condemning Palestinian terrorism and claiming the violence was Arafat's fault, did call on Israel to "halt the incursions and begin withdrawal." He did not, however, say how soon Israeli forces should pull back. Two days later, with the global outrage growing, Bush clarified that he meant "without delay." He did nothing to pressure the Israelis to actually do so, however, leading Israeli Defense Minister Benjamin Ben-Eliezer to publicly dismiss Bush's request, telling American reporters, "I don't think that he meant that."[79]

Israel's attacks continued with increasing reports of widespread civilian casualties. On April 15, the White House sent Deputy Secretary of Defense Wolfowitz to speak at a right-wing rally in Washington in support of Israel's military offensive. Two days later, Bush claimed that Israel had finally heeded his call, though the Israeli pullback was limited to only a few specific locations while the offensive continued and even expanded elsewhere. Bush added that he "understood" Israel's continued siege of Ramallah.[80] On April 19, the United States supported another UN Security Council resolution that largely emphasized the humanitarian concerns but did not condemn the Israeli assaults.[81]

Meanwhile, to give the world the appearance that the United States was concerned about the violence, the Bush Administration announced on April 2 that Secretary of State Powell would be dispatched to Israel on an "urgent" mission. However, Powell took almost a week before arriving in Israel. En route, he visited Morocco (where he met with both Moroccan and Saudi officials), Spain, Egypt, and Jordan, a reflection of the administration's position that it was the Arabs, not the Israelis, who required pressure to change their policies. When Powell finally arrived in Jerusalem, he refused to see Arafat until the Palestinian president issued a strong statement in Arabic condemning attacks against civilians; Arafat complied, reiterating similar statements he had made previously. Powell did not, however, make a similar demand of Sharon. As Arafat remained besieged in two rooms of his heavily damaged offices in Ramallah surrounded by Israeli tanks, Powell demanded that Arafat take "actions, not just words" to stop the terrorism, though the Secretary of State did not clarify what actions he thought Arafat could take under such circumstances.[82] Says Palestinian analyst Mouin Rabbani, "The unconditional U.S. support for Israel's offensive led many in the region to wonder if Israel had merely secured a green light from Washington or was in fact doing its bidding."[83]

Graham Fuller, former vice-chairman of the National Intelligence Council at the CIA, observed how Israeli intelligence officers have regularly pointed out that massive repression will not work and that Sharon's escalating military repression "has in fact multiplied terrorist attacks." As a result of such Israeli military offensives, he observed, "The terror is now totally decentralized as the Palestinian government infrastructure is destroyed."[84] The BBC reported how during the offensive, "the campaign climaxed with the bombardment of the Preventive Security Headquarters near Ramallah, the institution responsible for security coordination with Israel, which was the backbone of the Oslo Agreement. Now there is no one to enforce a cease-fire, should one be declared."[85] Even Israeli Defense Minister Eliezar admitted, at the end of the offensive in late April, "It is impossible to eradicate the terrorist infrastructure"[86] and that "The operations themselves become the hothouse that produces more and more new suicide bombers. The military actions kindle the frustration, hatred and despair and are the incubator for the terror to come."[87]

While the Bush Administration was, at least on record, calling for an Israeli pullback, Senator Joseph Lieberman—the 2000 Democratic vice presidential candidate—and other leading members of Congress sought to undercut the Bush Administration's call for restraint by hosting Benyamin Netanyahu, the rightist former Israeli prime minister, to address legislators on Capitol Hill in support of Israel's military offensive. Democratic and Republican leaders criticized Bush for failing to express stronger support for Israel's actions. Meanwhile, both houses of Congress passed bipartisan resolutions by overwhelming margins in support of the Israeli offensive, blaming the Palestinians exclusively for the violence and insisting that the Israeli attacks were only in self-defense. The vast majority of both liberals and conservatives supported these resolutions, which also commended President Bush's "leadership" in addressing the conflict; there were only two "no" votes in the Senate and only twenty-one "no" votes in the House. At the peak of the offensive, Democratic Congressional leaders such as House Minority Leader Dick Gephardt, Assistant House Minority Leader Nancy Pelosi, Senate Majority Leader Tom Daschle and Assistant Senate Majority Leader Harry Reid—spoke at a series of rallies and forums supporting Sharon's policies and condemning the Palestinians.

In contrast to Congress—which blamed the violence exclusively on the Palestinians and vindicated the Israelis—public opinion polls during this period indicated that most Americans believed that both sides were to blame. For example, a May 2002 poll indicated that a majority of Americans opposed Sharon's invasion and his refusal to heed President Bush's request to withdraw from the re-occupied Palestinian towns. It also showed that two-thirds of those polled believed the United States should be strictly even-handed in its approach to the conflict.[88] According to Steven Kull, director of the Program on International Policy Initiatives at the University of Maryland, "What this poll makes clear is that recent actions by Congress are out of step with the American public and their views on the crisis in the Middle East. Americans clearly hold both sides equally responsible for the current situation and are willing to increase pressure on both sides to achieve a peace deal."[89]

Furthermore, a Time/CNN poll indicated that, in response to Israel's offensive, 60% of Americans believed some or all U.S. aid to Israel should be suspended, while only 1% believed it should be increased.[90] However, in an effort to reward Israel for its offensive, Representative Nita Lowey, the leading Democrat on the House Appropriations Subcommittee, pushed for an additional $200 million in military aid for Israel in addition to the more than $2 billion of military assistance already allocated to Sharon's government for the fiscal year. Initially opposed by President Bush due to budget limitations, the administration gave in under Democratic pressure and the supplemental funding passed by an overwhelming margin.

While there has always been a strong bias in Congress and in successive administrations in support for the Israeli government, the events since the breakdown of the peace process do show a qualitative shift. Only a few years earlier, Ariel Sharon had been considered to be on the extreme right wing of Israeli politics due to his strident opposition to the Oslo process and was also widely viewed as a war criminal. By 2002, however, the administration and an overwhelming majority of both parties in Congress had solidly thrown their support behind Sharon and his policies.

Putting the Impetus on the Palestinians

On June 24 of that year, in the face of a new wave of terrorist attacks by Palestinian extremists inside Israel and the re-conquest of Palestinian cities by Israeli forces, President Bush gave a major policy speech in the White House Rose Garden on Israel and Palestine. In it, the president described what steps the United States would insist were necessary to bring the peace process forward.

After more than thirty years of rejecting the international consensus that peace requires the establishment of a Palestinian state alongside a secure Israel, President Bush made the most explicit statement by an American president to date affirming that principle. However, his speech focused upon the idea that while Israel's right to exist is a given, Palestine's right to exist—even as a mini-state on the West Bank and Gaza Strip—is conditional. Perhaps the most striking element of the speech was his assertion that U.S. support for Palestinian statehood was predicated on major internal reforms by the Palestinian Authority to the point of insisting that "Peace requires a new and different Palestinian leadership, so that a Palestinian state can be born."[91]

The irony is that, whatever the many faults of Yasir Arafat and the Palestinian Authority, the Palestinian negotiating position on the outstanding issues in the peace process—regarding Jerusalem, the rights of refugees, Israeli withdrawal from occupied territory and the Jewish settlements—is far more consistent with international law and United Nations Security Council resolutions than that of the Israelis. Despite that, President Bush was insisting that it was the Palestinians, not the Israelis, who needed to have new leadership in order for the peace process to move forward. Similarly, President Bush focused his speech primarily on Palestinian violence against Israeli civilians, despite the fact that Israeli occupation forces were responsible for far more Palestinian civilian deaths than were Palestinian terrorists for Israeli civilian deaths.

The administration's priorities could not have been more apparent than in the fact that, in the course of his speech, the president mentioned terrorism eighteen times but did not mention human rights or international law even once. Nor did he mention the peace plan of Saudi Prince Abdullah—endorsed by the Palestinian Authority and every single Arab government—which offered Israel security guarantees and full normal relations in return for withdrawal from the occupied territories seized in the 1967 War. Not only did President Bush fail to demand a total withdrawal of Israeli occupation forces, he called only for a freeze on additional Israeli settlements, when international law—reiterated in UN Security Council resolutions 446 and 465—requires Israel to abandon the existing settlements as well.

Turning the understanding of most observers on its head, President Bush insisted that it was Palestinian terrorism that was preventing the Palestinians from achieving their freedom, not that the denial of Palestinian freedom was resulting in terrorism. There was no apparent awareness of the near absence of terrorism from the Palestinian side for more than a decade from the mid-1980s to the mid-1990s, while—during this period—Israel refused to withdraw from most of the occupied territories or curb the dramatic expansion of Jewish settlements on confiscated Palestinian land. Nor was there any promise of a specific timetable or a full Israeli withdrawal. While Palestinians were ordered to stop their violence immediately, his call for a freeze on Israeli settlement construction and even a pullback to lines prior to the outbreak of fighting in September 2000 was to occur "as we make progress toward security,"[92] a process that could be held up indefinitely by just one suicide bomber. There are also serious questions as to how the free and fair elections in the West Bank and Gaza Strip could proceed as Palestinian population centers were under siege or under full military occupation.

While many if not most Palestinians would love to see Arafat go, President Bush's insistence that the United States has the right to say who the Palestinians choose as their leader resulted in widespread resentment from across the Palestinian political spectrum. Even Israeli Foreign Minister Shimon Peres was quoted saying "Making the creation of a Palestinian state dependent upon a change in the Palestinian leadership is a fatal mistake. Arafat has led the Palestinians for 35 years, kept their head above the water in the international arena. No, no, you can't just brush him aside with one speech."[93] The more right-wing Israeli Environmental Minister Tzahi Hanegbi suggested giving the American president honorary membership in the Likud Party.[94] President Bush's criticisms of Arafat's regime, however valid, have never been the reason the United States has opposed the Palestinians' right to self-determination. They are simply the excuse.

Undermining Israel's Real Security Interests

According to former CIA official Graham Fuller,

> Only when the Palestinians have a genuine stake in the new state and its sovereign freedom—something to lose—will the atmosphere of society change. Only then will radicals be perceived as damaging to their state, society and future. Only then can a

Palestinian government start its own crackdown internally on the remaining radicals, as the value of violence fades under new conditions.[95]

Indeed, Jewish terrorist groups active in early Zionist struggle, like the Irgun and Stern Gang, disappeared soon after Israel became independent. Similarly, Hamas and Islamic Jihad—either on their own or through what would then be a widely supported crackdown by the Palestinian government—would also likely cease to be a threat if the Palestinians had a viable state of their own.

In addition, Israel would be far more secure with a clearly delineated internationally recognized border than with the current patchwork of settlements and military outposts on confiscated land amidst a hostile population. Despite claims of being concerned about Israel's security, Clinton's peace proposal presented in December 2000 would have left Israel with narrow indefensible peninsulas of territory within the West Bank. With a full Israeli withdrawal, the terrorist attacks inside Israel would be substantially reduced if not eliminated, since it is the occupation and the Palestinian Authority's inability to achieve a viable independent state through negotiations which is what primarily motivates the radical Islamists who commit their acts of terrorism.

Temporarily seizing territory of hostile neighbors to create a buffer zone pending the establishment of security guarantees may have made some strategic sense for Israel back in 1967. At that time, troops from Arab states were massing on Israel's borders threatening to attack and Palestinian guerrilla groups were engaged in cross-border raids against civilian targets. Today, however, there are no armies massing on Israel's border. Israel is at peace with Egypt and Jordan and peace with Lebanon and Syria would be forthcoming once Israel withdraws from the occupied Syrian territory in the Golan Heights. The Palestinians have offered guarantees that their future mini-state on the West Bank and Gaza Strip would be largely demilitarized and no foreign forces hostile to Israel would be allowed. Like Egypt and Syria, they have offered to accept international monitors, and have even gone a step further by agreeing to allow Israel to station some of its own monitors in Palestinian territory.

Nor does the occupation enhance Israel's security from unconventional threats such as terrorism. Palestinian terrorists who engage in suicide bombings do not require a territory from which to operate. All they need is enough frustration and anger to motivate themselves to strap explosives to their bodies, something which decades of foreign military occupation helps make possible.

In short, there is no longer any strategic rationale for Israel holding on to any land beyond its internationally recognized borders. From the Arab perspective, Americans who try to portray Israel's territorial land grab as necessary for the country's security interests are simply rationalizing for the colonization of one country by another through military force and repression.

U.S. support for Israel's ongoing occupation simply does not help Israel address its legitimate security needs. The vast majority of Israelis killed since the uprising began in September 2000 have been in the occupied territories, an indication of how holding onto the West Bank and Gaza Strip does not enhance the security of Israelis, but rather threatens it. And, despite U.S. claims to the contrary, the unfortunate reality is that Israeli occupation and repression does more to encourage terrorism than it does to prevent it.

The archipelago of illegal settlements amidst occupied Palestinian territory essentially constitutes a 2000-mile border, five times longer than Israel's internationally recognized pre-1967 boundaries. Israeli armed forces have deployed more divisions protecting these 400,000 settlers outside of Israel than it has protecting its five million citizens within Israel. A majority of Israelis have told pollsters that they would support removing settlers and would even support the use of force against their own fellow citizens if necessary to accomplish this.[96] The Mitchell Commission Report encouraged Israel to withdraw from the most remote settlements. President Bush's refusal to simply insist that Israel withdraw from these isolated settlements, however, raises questions as to whether the United States is really concerned about the safety of Israelis.

Given that the U.S. government appears to oppose creating such conditions where Israel would be safe from terrorism and other threats to its security, should U.S. policy, then, really be considered "pro-Israel?" A strong case can be made that U.S. support of Sharon's policies actually endangers Israel's legitimate security needs because it gives the Israeli government little outside incentive to make peace. As Israeli writer Gideon Samet complained, "Instead of calming things down and balancing the pressure on Arafat with demands on Sharon to start talking with the Palestinians seriously, Uncle Sam is writing a script for a horrifying Western of the good guys against the bad guys, to death."[97] As General Peled once put it, "The United States is making Israel less and less secure by encouraging the reckless agenda of the Israeli right."[98] More recently, long time Israeli peace and human rights activist Gila Svirsky observed,

> For decades, we in the Israeli peace movement have been struggling to get Israelis to compromise on the issue that feeds the conflict with the Palestinians. And then our work for peace gets doused twice: once by a prime minister who believes brutality will convince the Palestinians to give up, and then by a U.S. president who supports him on this. Bush has become a big part of the problem. He has to make up his mind: either he's for peace, or he's for Sharon. He can't be both.[99]

Some, like Avnery, already believe that they know the answer and have given up: "Those of us who desire an Israeli-Palestinian peace cannot rely on America. Now everything depends on us alone, the Israelis and the Palestinians."[100]

There has been a pattern over the years of the U.S. government encouraging some of the more chauvinistic and militaristic elements in Israeli politics. The rise of the rightist Likud Bloc in Israel and the rightward drift in the Labor Party since 1967 is in large part due to this large-scale American support. Rightist Israeli political leaders such as Menachem Begin, Yitzhak Shamir, Benyamin Netanyahu and Ariel Sharon would certainly have existed without U.S. backing, but they would have likely been part of a small right-wing minority in the Knesset and would have never become prime ministers. Were it not for the United States protecting successive Israeli governments from international sanctions resulting from their violations of international law as well as the negative fiscal consequences of their costly militarization and occupation, the Israeli people would have long ago concluded the occupation simply was not worth the costs. Any small country that tried to pursue the policies that Israel has followed—extraordinarily high levels of militarization, territorial conquest, suppression of minorities, flaunting of international law, and gross and systematic human rights violations—would have to pay the consequences. The inevitable repercussions are self-defeating: such policies would eventually result in economic collapse, military defeat, debilitating international sanctions, or internal rebellion. However, the Israeli leadership has been able to maintain its otherwise self-destructive direction because it has been backed diplomatically, financially, and militarily by the world's dominant superpower. The need to compromise by allowing the Palestinians to exercise their national rights in a viable state has not yet become apparent to the majority of Israelis, knowing they have an American umbrella under which to hide from the consequences of their actions.

Zionism, like other nationalist movements, has historically been quite diverse politically, including both chauvinistic and pluralistic elements. In

addition to its powerful right wing, the Zionist movement also included progressive elements interested in sharing Palestine on an equitable basis with the
Palestinians. However, the carte blanche from the world's one remaining
superpower has allowed these more hard line militaristic factions to dominate.

This is significant. Some Israelis, for religious or nationalist reasons,
oppose the necessary compromises for peace. Other Israelis, for moral or
pragmatic reasons, support the necessary compromises for peace. The
majority of Israelis, however, are in the middle. Historically, Israeli voters
have tended to lean towards the peace camp if they feared Israel's close
relationship with the United States and the resulting largesse of aid was
threatened by a particular policy and lean towards the right if they felt
Israel could get away with it. A blank check from the United States for the
government to do whatever it pleases, therefore, significantly hurts the
peace forces within Israel. By contrast, pressure from the United States has
traditionally enhanced the position of Israeli moderates, since it enables
them to convince the Israeli public that failure to compromise would jeop-
ardize their country's close relationship with the United States.
Unfortunately, by publicly claiming during the summer of 2000 that the
Israelis had made greater sacrifices than the Palestinians had in the peace
talks, the Israeli right was able to portray the government of Prime Minister
Ehud Barak as having offered too much. Similarly, when top administration
officials and congressional leaders claimed that Arafat had turned down a
generous peace offer, Israelis got the message that the Palestinians were not
really interested in peace, therefore a tough military strongman was needed to lead the country. As a result, many Israelis fault the Clinton
Administration's reaction to the failure of the Camp David talks as directly contributing to the election of Ariel Sharon.

The fact is that the Israeli public takes a far more moderate viewpoint
than do the Israeli or American governments. In a public opinion poll
taken in May 2002, a sizeable majority of Israelis supported peace talks,
believing the problem of terrorism could not be solved without it, and 60%
believed that a withdrawal that was not acceptable to both sides would not
lead to a peace accord. Most significantly, 59% said they would support—
if accompanied by American security guarantees—an Israeli withdrawal to
the 1967 lines with minor mutual and agreed-upon adjustments, evacuation of most of the settlements and compromise on Jerusalem.[101]

With the United States arming and financing Israel's occupation and
colonization drive and blaming the Palestinians exclusively for the violence, however, Sharon and future Israeli leaders can essentially do as they

please. This buying time will likely end up being disastrous for Israel since it further isolates the Jewish state from other Middle Eastern countries and much of the rest of the world, provides an opening for anti-Semitic ideologies, and creates a greater dependency on the United States. And, as noted above, the ongoing occupation and the dimming hopes that the Palestinians will have a viable state of their own are just what breed extremists prone to commit acts of terrorism.

How Did we Get Here? The Roots of U.S. Policy

What, then, motivates this strong American bias against the Palestinians? One is the sentimental attachment many Americans—particularly liberals of the post-World War II generation—have for Israel. There is a great appreciation for Israel's internal democracy, progressive social institutions (such as the *kibbutzim*), the relatively high level of social equality, and Israel's important role as a sanctuary for an oppressed minority group that spent centuries in the Diaspora. Through a mixture of guilt regarding Western anti-Semitism, personal friendships with Jewish Americans who identify strongly with Israel, and fear of inadvertently encouraging anti-Semitism by criticizing Israel, there is enormous reluctance to acknowledge the seriousness of Israeli violations of human rights and international law. Many American liberals of this generation have an idealist view of Israel that is both as sincere and inaccurate as the idealized view of Stalin's Russia embraced by an earlier generation of American leftists.[102] To many Americans who are middle aged and older, Israel is seen as it was portrayed in the idealized and romanticized 1960 movie *Exodus*, starring a young Paul Newman. Contributing to this view is the widespread racism in American society against Arabs and Muslims, often encouraged in the media. This is compounded by the identification many Americans have with Zionism in the Middle East as a reflection of their own historical experience in North America as immigrants and pioneers. In both cases, European migrants—many of whom were escaping religious persecution—built a new nation based upon noble, idealistic values while simultaneously suppressing and expelling the indigenous population seen as violent and "primitive."

An increasingly important factor shaping U.S. policy is the Christian Right, with tens of millions of followers and a major base of support for the Republican Party, which has thrown its immense media assets and political clout in support for Ariel Sharon and other right-wing Israeli leaders. Based in part on a messianic theology that sees the ingathering of Jews to the

Holy Land as a precursor for the second coming of Christ, the battle between Israelis and Palestinians is, in their eyes, simply a continuation of the Biblical battles between the Israelites and the Philistines. God is seen as a kind of cosmic real estate agent who has deemed that the land belongs to Israel alone—secular notions regarding international law and the right of self-determination notwithstanding.

Furthermore, as illustrated in Chapter Two, the arms industry—which contributes more than twice as much money to congressional campaigns and lobbying efforts as does the American Israel Public Affairs Committee (AIPAC) and other pro-Israel groups—has considerable stake in supporting massive arms shipments to Israel and other Middle Eastern allies of the United States. It is far easier, for example, for a member of Congress to challenge a $60 million arms deal to Indonesia than the more than $2 billion of arms sent annually to Israel, particularly when so many congressional districts include factories that produce such military hardware.

Still another factor is the failure of progressive movements in the United States to challenge U.S. policy toward Israel and Palestine in an effective manner. For many years, most mainstream peace and human rights groups avoided the issue, not wanting to alienate many of their Jewish and other liberal constituents supportive of the Israeli government. There was also concern that their criticism of Israeli policies might be seen as anti-Semitic or that it might even inadvertently encourage anti-Semitism. As a result, without any countervailing pressure, liberal members of Congress have had little incentive not to cave in to pressure from supporters of the Israeli government. Meanwhile, some groups on the far left and others have taken a stridently anti-Israel position that did not just challenge Israeli policies but also questioned Israel's very right to exist, severely damaging their credibility. In some cases, particularly among some of the more conservative individuals and organizations critical of Israel, a latent anti-Semitism has come to the fore in wildly exaggerated claims of Jewish economic and political power, further alienating potential critics of U.S. policy.

As significant as these factors may be, however, none of these should be considered the driving force behind U.S. policy.

The most common explanation for U.S. policy towards the conflict is the political influence of the American Jewish community. However, while this is another important component in the shaping of the U.S. position, it would be a mistake to exaggerate this factor, either.

Jews make up less than 4 percent of the U.S. population and are hardly monolithic on the question of U.S. policy in the Middle East. In the late 1990s, while the Clinton Administration was putting pressure almost exclusively on the Palestinian Authority to compromise, polls showed that over 80% of American Jews believed the United States should be willing to apply pressure on both the Palestinians and the Israelis to help bring about a peace settlement.[103] Despite the turn to the right since then, nearly three-quarters of American Jews still believe it to be in Israel's interest for the United States to serve as a "credible and effective facilitator," even if it means disagreeing with the Israeli government.[104] Perhaps most telling, as the percentage of Jews in the overall U.S. population and their level of support for the Israeli government has declined, U.S. support for the Israeli government has increased. Many of the most outspoken members of Congress supportive of Israel's occupation policies are from states or districts with very small Jewish populations.

Though the "Jewish vote" may not be that significant, how about the "pro-Israel lobby?" Groups like AIPAC and its related political action committees have certainly influenced members of Congress. Mainstream and conservative Jewish organizations have mobilized considerable lobbying resources, financial contributions from the Jewish community, and citizen pressure on the news media and other forums of public discourse in support of the Israeli government. At times, they have even created a climate of intimidation against many who speak out for peace and human rights and support the Palestinians' right of self-determination.

However, the strength of the lobby is often greatly exaggerated. For example, some of the most outspoken congressional supporters of the Israeli government are from some of the safest districts in the country and need no support from pro-Israel PACs to be re-elected. Furthermore, Congress only rarely plays a crucial role in the development in foreign policy; recent decades have seen foreign policy become increasingly the prerogative of the executive branch. Congress during this period has played a limited, and largely reactive, role in foreign policy. Indeed, it is a naive assumption to believe that foreign policy decision making in the United States is pluralistic enough so that any one lobbying group, particularly one associated with a small ethnic minority, can have so much influence.[105]

Blaming the pro-Israel lobby also assumes that U.S. policy towards the Middle East would somehow be more enlightened than it is towards other Third World regions where the United States has strategic interests. A look at recent U.S. foreign relations reveals that there has never been a need for a strong domestic ethnic lobby to support an ally that invades and occupies neighboring countries. For example, no ethnic lobbies played a role in convincing the United States to support Indonesia during its brutal twenty-four year occupation of East Timor or to support Morocco as it continues its occupation of Western Sahara.

It also would be wrong to assume that the U.S. commitment to Israel has primarily a moral basis as claimed by its supporters.[106] U.S. support for Israel is certainly not a case of defending a democracy battling for its very survival. Were this actually the primary motivation for supporting Israel, American aid would have been highest in the early years of the existence of the Jewish state—when its democratic institutions were strongest and its strategic situation most vulnerable—and would have declined as its military power grew dramatically and its repression against Palestinians in the occupied territories increased. Instead, the trend has been in just the opposite direction: major U.S. military and economic aid did not begin until after the 1967 War. Indeed, 99 percent of all U.S. military assistance to Israel since its establishment came only after Israel proved itself to be far stronger than any combination of Arab armies and after Israeli occupation forces became the rulers of a large Palestinian population.

In the hypothetical event that all U.S. aid to Israel was immediately cut off, it would be many years before Israel would be under significantly greater military threat than it is today. Israel has both a major domestic arms industry and an existing military force far more capable and powerful than any conceivable combination of opposing forces. A cutoff of U.S. military and economic support might force Israel to negotiate a settlement with the Palestinians, since it would make the expensive patchwork of Israeli military control and subsidized settlements in the occupied territories prohibitively expensive for such a small country. However, even with such a suspension of U.S. aid, there would be no question of Israel's survival being at risk militarily in the foreseeable future.

One of the most fundamental principles in the theory of international relations is that the most stable military relationship between adversaries (besides disarmament) is strategic parity. Such a relationship provides an effective deterrent for both sides against the other launching a pre-emptive attack. If the United States was concerned simply with Israel's security, the goal would be to maintain Israeli defenses to the point where they would be approximately equal to any realistic combination of Arab armed forces. Instead, leaders of both American political parties have insisted that rather than help maintain a military balance between Israel and its neighbors, the United States must insure a qualitative Israeli military superiority.[107]

When Israel was less dominant militarily, there was no such consensus for U.S. backing of Israel. The continued high levels of U.S. aid to Israel does not come out of concern for Israel's survival, but more likely from a desire for Israel to continue its political dominion over the Palestinians and its military dominance of the region.

Why, then, this extraordinary support for Israel?

The primary reason is the role Israel plays for the United States. In a region where radical nationalism could threaten U.S. control of oil and other strategic interests, Israel successfully has prevented victories by radical nationalist movements, not just in Palestine, but in Lebanon and Jordan as well. They have kept Syria, with a radical nationalist regime once allied with the Soviet Union, in check. Their air force is predominant throughout the region.

Another function Israel provides is that its frequent wars have allowed for battlefield testing of American arms. In addition, Israel's own arms industry has provided weapons and munitions for governments and opposition movements supported by the United States. Moreover, Israel has been a conduit for U.S. arms to regimes and movements too unpopular in the United States for openly granting direct military assistance, including South Africa under the apartheid regime, Iran's Islamic republic, Guatemala's rightist military juntas, and the Nicaraguan Contras. Israeli military advisors have assisted the Contras, the Salvadoran junta, and other movements and governments backed by the United States. The Israeli intelligence agency Mossad has cooperated with the CIA and other U.S. agencies in intelligence gathering and covert operations. Israel has missiles capable of reaching the former Soviet Union and has cooperated with the U.S. military-industrial complex with research and development for new jet fighters and anti-missile defense systems, a relationship that is growing every year.[108] As one Israeli analyst described during the Iran-Contra scandal, where Israel played a crucial intermediary rule, "It's like Israel has become just another federal agency, one that's convenient to use when you want something done quietly."[109]

The pattern of U.S. aid to Israel reveals striking attention to the utility of Israel for U.S. interests. Immediately following Israel's spectacular victory in the 1967 War, when it demonstrated its military superiority in the region, U.S. aid shot up by 450 percent. Part of this increase, according to the *New York Times*, apparently was related to Israel's willingness to provide the United States with examples of new Soviet weapons captured during the war.[110] Following the 1970-71 civil war in Jordan, when Israel demonstrated its ability to help curb revolutionary movements outside its borders, aid increased another sevenfold. During the 1973 Arab-Israeli war, advancing Arab armies successfully were countered by the largest U.S. military airlift in history, enabling Israel to demonstrate its power to defeat surprisingly strong Soviet-supplied forces; as a result, military aid increased by another 800 percent. These increases paralleled the British decision to withdraw its forces from areas east of the Suez. Along with the Shah of Iran, who also received massive arms and logistical cooperation as a key component of the Nixon Doctrine, Israel too became an important force in the wake of the British absence.

This pattern continued when aid jumped again in 1977, following the election of the first right-wing Likud government in Israel, and rose yet again soon after the fall of the Shah and the ratification of the Camp David Treaty. Aid increased still further soon after the 1982 Israeli invasion of Lebanon. In 1983 and 1984, when the United States and Israel signed memoranda of understanding on strategic cooperation and military planning and conducted their first joint naval and air military exercises, Israel was rewarded by an additional $1.5 billion in economic aid, as well as another half billion dollars for the development of a new jet fighter.[111] During and immediately after the Gulf War, U.S. aid increased an additional $650 million.[112] In the subsequent decade—as concern has risen about the threat of terrorist groups, Islamic extremists and so-called "rogue states"—aid has increased still further. The more conservative estimates of U.S. aid for FY2003 stand at well over $2 billion in military assistance and approximately $1.4 billion in economic support.

In short, the stronger, more aggressive, and more willing to cooperate with U.S. interests that Israel has become, the higher the level of aid and strategic cooperation. A militant Israel is seen to advance American interests. Indeed, an Israel in a constant state of war—technologically sophisticated and militarily advanced, yet lacking an independent economy and dependent on the United States—is far more willing to perform tasks that might be unacceptable to other allies than would be an Israel at peace with its neighbors. As Kissinger once put it, in reference to Israel's reluctance to make peace, "Israel's obstinacy...serves the purposes of both our countries best."[113]

"The Godfather's Messenger":
Anti-Semitism with a Twist

Throughout Europe in past centuries, the ruling class of a given country would, in return for granting limited religious and cultural autonomy, set up certain individuals in the Jewish community to become the visible agents of the oppressive social order, such as tax collectors and money lenders. When the population would threaten to rise up against the ruling elites, the rulers could then blame the Jews, sending the wrath of an exploited people against convenient scapegoats, resulting in the pogroms and other notorious waves of repression that have taken place throughout the Jewish Diaspora over the centuries. Unfortunately, one of the more unsettling aspects of U.S. policy today is how closely it corresponds with this historic anti-Semitism.

The idea behind Zionism was to break this cycle of the centuries through the creation of a Jewish nation-state where Jews would no longer be dependent on the ruling class of a given country. But in a tragic irony, as a result of Israel's inability or unwillingness to make peace with its Arab neighbors, Israel's role over the decades has been to perpetuate this cycle on a global scale. Israel has been used by Western powers—initially Great Britain and France[114] and more recently the United States—to maintain their interests in the Middle East. In a horrible echo of the past, autocratic Arab governments, Islamic extremists, and others are blaming Israel, Zionism, or the Jews for their problems, leaving largely untouched the broader exploitative global economic system and their own elites who benefit from and help perpetuate such a system.

The ramifications of U.S. policy are quite apparent when it comes to the suffering of Palestinians. But it also has a negative impact on Israel. The late respected Israeli intellectual Yishayahu Leibowitz observed,

> The existence of the Jewish people of 60 to 80 generations...was a heroic situation. We never got from the goyish world a cent. We supported ourselves. We maintained our own institutions. Now we have taken three million Jews, gathered them here and turned them over to be parasites—parasites of America. And in some sense we are even the mercenaries of America to fight the wars of what the ruling persons in America consider to be American interests.[115]

This view is not uncommon. In the Israeli press, one can find comments like those in *Yediot Ahronot* that describes their country as "the Godfather's messenger," since Israel undertakes the "dirty work" of the

Godfather, who "always tries to appear to be the owner of some large respectable business."[116] Israeli satirist D. Michael describes U.S. aid to Israel as a situation where "My master gives me food to eat and I bite those whom he tells me to bite. It's called strategic cooperation."[117] Progressive Zionists have argued that the growing Israeli dependency on the United States violates the principle of non-alignment, once a cornerstone of the Labor Zionist movement, and has undermined the last vestiges of Labor Zionism's commitment to socialism and solidarity with the Third World. They fear that Israel's close ties with what they perceive as an imperialist power like the United States alienates Israel's potential allies in the Third World and leaves Israel vulnerable to the whims of U.S. foreign policy. Like the Jews of medieval Europe, they fear Israel could be suddenly abandoned by the West after being set up to become the visible agent of an oppressive world order.[118]

Increasingly, critics of U.S. support of Israel—such as conservative political leader Patrick Buchanan, former Congressman Paul Findley and retired State Department officials like Richard Curtiss—are claiming that the U.S.-Israeli relationship is a case of the "tail wagging the dog." This analysis argues that tiny Israel—through its agents in the American Jewish community—is manipulating U.S. foreign policy. However, in reality, the situation is just the opposite: In a classic case of exactly this type of anti-Semitic scapegoating, members of Congress and their aides will claim—always off the record—that they or their boss has to take pro-militarist and anti-human rights positions towards the Israeli-Palestinian conflict because of the need for Jewish campaign contributions.[119] Similarly, as a means of diverting Arab criticism from U.S. policy makers, American diplomats routinely tell representatives of Arab governments that wealthy Jews essentially dictate U.S. Middle East policy.[120] The senior President Bush made it clear that such scapegoating is acceptable when—during the debate on the proposed $10 billion loan guarantees to Israel in 1992—he claimed that he was just "one lonely little guy" standing up to "a thousand lobbyists" swarming on Capitol Hill.[121]

Such scapegoating of Jews serves a purpose. As University of Michigan political scientist A.F.K. Organski observed,

> The belief that the Jewish lobby...is very powerful has permitted top U.S. policy makers to use "Jewish influence" or "domestic politics" to explain the policies...that U.S. leaders see as working to U.S. advantage, policies they would pursue regardless of Jewish opinion on the matter. When Arab leaders or officials of allies protest, U.S. officials need give only a helpless shrug, a regretful sigh, and

explain how it is not the administration's fault, but that policy makers must operate within the constraints imposed by powerful domestic pressures molding congressional decisions. Presidents, and those who speak in their names, have followed this strategy time and time again. Congressmen employ this same device....[122]

The reality is very different. As Organski puts it,

> ...the United States has used its relationship with Israel as a means to control its client. When American leaders crack the whip, Israel responds and the Israeli show of resistance is just that—a show. The real constraint on American leaders has been their fear of weakening an important ally...[T]here has been no question in either the patron or the client's mind that is in control. When it comes to important questions, Israel does as she is told.[123]

The results of U.S. policy could be tragic, not just for the Palestinians and other Arabs who are the immediate victims of the diplomatic support and the largess of American aid to Israel, but ultimately for Israel as well. The fates of American client states have often not been positive. Though differing in many respects, Israel could end up like El Salvador and South Vietnam, whose leadership made common cause with U.S. global designs in ways that ultimately led to the countries' self-destruction. Israeli leaders and their counterparts in many American Zionist organizations have been repeating the historic error of trading short-term benefits for their people at the risk of long-term security.

However, it has long been in the interests of the U.S. government to maintain a militarily powerful belligerent Israel dependent on the United States. Real peace could undermine such a relationship. The United States therefore has pursued a policy that could bring greater stability to the region while falling short of real peace. The United States is working towards a Middle East where Israel can be a key component in projecting American military and economic interests, which requires suppressing challenges to American-Israeli hegemony.

Unfortunately, this policy has seemed to only provoke a kind of reaction that threatens any kind of stable order, much less justice. U.S. policy has resulted in dividing Israelis and Arabs—both Semitic peoples who share the same God and the same love for the land as well as a history of subjugation and oppression—from one another. The so-called peace process, then, is not about peace, but about imposing a Pax Americana.

The Fundamental Issue: Self-Determination

Israeli commentator, author and peace activist Uri Avnery observed, "We are in their territory, not they in ours. We settle on their land, not they on ours. We are the occupiers, they are the victims. This is the objective situation, and no minister of propaganda can change that."[124] As accurate as that may be, it has not stopped U.S. administrations and members of Congress of both parties from doing their best to convince the American people otherwise. Ordinary Americans are confused, as they watch the Palestinians' legitimate quest for freedom mixed with acts of murder against innocent Israeli civilians and Israel's legitimate quest for security mixed with the destruction of Palestinian institutions and society.

By the spring of 2002, it was apparent that both the administration and Congress, in facilitating the destruction of the Oslo process and failing to support Saudi Prince Abdullah's initiative, had abandoned decades of U.S. policy based on the premise of land for peace. Instead, the United States has thrown its support behind the far right wing in Israel that rejects meaningful territorial compromise. Such a position runs counter not just to a broad international consensus, which includes most of the United States' allies in Europe and elsewhere, but also the position of most independent scholars of the region in the United States and even most State Department and CIA analysts. And, despite Israeli public opinion swinging to the right as a result of the upsurge in terrorism, 52% of Israelis polled supported the Saudi peace plan calling for the full withdrawal from all occupied territories in exchange for peace with the Arab world.[125] Unfortunately, Israeli commentator Gideon Samet, writing in *Haaretz*, noted how the United States has become "more Israeli than the Israelis.... Continuing to rage, raining abuse on 'the other,' and demonizing the Palestinians" comparable to the former terrorist leader and Israeli Prime Minister Menachem Begin.[126]

American support for a permanent takeover by Israel of Palestinian territory seized in the 1967 War is not new, however. In 1989, Congress passed a resolution that effectively endorsed Israel's annexation of greater East Jerusalem, the Palestinian part of the city and surrounding areas seized by the Israeli army in 1967. This vote was in direct defiance of a 1968 UN Security Council resolution invalidating the Israeli annexation of East Jerusalem and its environs,[127] using similar language to the 1990 resolution invalidating Iraq's annexation of Kuwait. A number of subtle policy shifts by the Clinton Administration beginning in 1993 demonstrated that the

United States effectively had recognized Israel's unilateral annexation of greater Arab East Jerusalem. For example, in the government's annual report on Israeli settlement activity in the occupied territories, the Clinton Administration stopped including Israeli settlements in greater Jerusalem, thereby implying that they were located within Israel. In April 1994, the United States abstained from a section of a UN Security Council resolution condemning a massacre committed by an Israeli soldier in the occupied West Bank city of Hebron. The United States objected to a paragraph that referred to the Arab part of Jerusalem as occupied territory; Vice-President Al Gore declared that had the mention of Jerusalem been an operative paragraph rather than simply as part of the preamble, the United States would have vetoed the entire resolution.[128] In an indication of how isolated the United States is in its Middle East policy, no other government besides Israel has taken any issue with conferring the status of occupied territory on East Jerusalem. On three occasions since then, the United States has vetoed otherwise-unanimous UN Security Council resolutions opposing Israeli settlement activities in Israeli-occupied Arab East Jerusalem.

The United States rationalized for this position by arguing that the Declaration of Principles signed between Israel and the Palestine Liberation Organization in September 1993 relegated the issue of Jerusalem—along with settlements and military locations—to "permanent status negotiations." Then-Secretary of State Warren Christopher insisted that since Jerusalem is "a final status matter...any effort to prejudge that issue in a UN resolution would find the opposition of the United States."[129] But this argument that Jerusalem's status should not be prejudged runs in only one direction. President Clinton, as well as the vast majority of members of Congress who attacked the UN resolutions as "pre-judging" the status of Jerusalem by criticizing Israeli colonization of illegally confiscated Palestinian land were also on record unilaterally declaring Jerusalem the unified capital of Israel, a clear pre-judgment of the city's status.[130]

More importantly, whatever the final outcome of negotiations, the residents of Arab East Jerusalem never voluntarily ceded to Israeli sovereignty through a referendum or other democratic methods; their part of the city was seized by military force. Israeli occupation forces patrol the streets and human rights abuses against residents who oppose Israeli rule continue. By any definition, this constitutes a military occupation.[131] The status of Jerusalem is a particularly emotional topic for the world's Muslims who—like Jews and Christians—see it as a holy city. The U.S. insistence that it be under the effective control of only one of the three monotheistic faiths for whom it is religiously significant has dramatically contributed to the rise of anti-Americanism in the Islamic world.

Yet the Clinton Administration's acquiescence to the Israeli occupation went beyond the boundaries of greater Jerusalem. Upon coming to office, President Clinton promised to block any UN resolution that referred to the West Bank and Gaza Strip as "Palestinian" and similarly to oppose any UN resolution critical of Israel that did not criticize Arabs as well.

Furthermore, the Clinton State Department began referring to the Israeli-occupied territories as "disputed territories" and actively encouraged the media to do the same, an effort that was largely successful. Unlike an "occupied territory," a "disputed territory" implies that both sides have a legitimate claim to the land in question. (There have been disputed territories in the history of the conflict. These include the Taba Strip between Israel and Egypt—which was resolved by international mediators in Egypt's favor in 1989—and the Shebaa Farms area between Lebanon and Israeli-occupied Syria, which is the scene of ongoing clashes between Israeli occupation forces and the Lebanese Islamic militia Hizbullah. Such tiny parcels of territory, however, have nothing to do with the effort by the Clinton Administration to reclassify the Israeli-occupied West Bank, Gaza Strip and Golan Heights.)

Viewed as a conflict over disputed territories—as the U.S. government wants to see it—there are other implications. Persons living under a foreign military occupation are protected by the Fourth Geneva Convention, whereby the occupying power is obliged to uphold certain standards of human rights; this would not be the case with a disputed territory. Another implication is that if they are simply disputed territories, with competing legitimate claims, it would appear that Israel has indeed made the most concessions and the Palestinians need to learn the art of compromise. However, virtually the entire rest of the world sees the West Bank and Gaza Strip as the occupied territory that it is. Israel's control over these territories, therefore, is no more legitimate than Iraq's 1990-91 takeover of Kuwait or Indonesia's 24-year occupation of East Timor.

Leading American officials see things otherwise, however. Secretary of Defense Rumsfeld has defended Israel's control of the West Bank and Gaza Strip, which he has referred to as the "so-called occupied area" emphasizing that Israel was just a "sliver" of a country prior to its 1967 conquests and that the West Bank and Gaza Strip were "won" as "the result of war."[132] Tom DeLay, assistant majority leader in the House of Representatives, declared that in his visits to the West Bank, East

Jerusalem and the Golan Heights, "I didn't see any occupied territory. I saw Israel."[133] House Majority Leader Dick Armey also claims that the occupied Palestinian territories are actually part of Israel and has even advocated the removal of Palestinians from this expanded Jewish state. In defending his call for ethnic cleansing, Armey noted "there are many Arab nations that have many hundreds of thousands of acres of land, soil, and property and opportunity to create a Palestinian state." In order to facilitate such a forced population transfer, says Armey, "we're perfectly content to work with the Palestinians in doing that."[134] One reason for Congressional Republicans' lack of concern about international law is the widespread belief within their ranks that the solution was spelled out by a higher authority thousands of years ago. For example, Senator James Inhofe, in a floor speech in the U.S. Senate in December 2001, insisted that the West Bank belongs to Israel because God promised it to Abraham. Israel, according to the Oklahoma Republican, "has a right to the land...because God said so.... This is not a political battle at all. It is a contest over whether or not the word of God is true."[135]

Putting aside the rhetoric of fundamentalists of all faiths, at the core of the Israeli-Palestinian conflict—from Israeli settlements to U.S. aid and from Israeli security concerns to the question of which side's violence constitutes terrorism—is a simple but profound issue: the right of self-determination. The bipartisan consensus in the United States has been rock-solid for years: that the fate of the Palestinians is up to their Israeli occupiers. While the United States has grudgingly accepted the possibility of some sort of Palestinian state, statements by both the Clinton and Bush Administrations and Congressional resolutions passed by huge bipartisan majorities have long made clear the U.S. position: Whether and under what form Palestinian independence will take place is to be defined not by the international community or international law, but by Israel. Given that the Israeli government is under the leadership of Ariel Sharon's far right Likud Party, that has long opposed Palestinian self-determination, the United States is essentially endorsing continued Israeli military occupation and the violent reaction and repression which inevitably results. More than eighty years after President Woodrow Wilson helped establish the right of national self-determination as a cornerstone of international law and U.S. foreign policy and more than ten years after the senior President Bush declared that a New World Order had come into effect based upon such principles, both the Democratic and Republican parties are now adhering to a very different principle: the right of conquest.

Many Arab leaders, ranging from heads of government to terrorists, have used the Palestinians as political pawns to promote their agenda. They do this because they know the Palestinian cause has a lot of sympathy throughout the Arab and Islamic world. U.S. support for Israel and its occupation forces continues to be one the foremost reasons for Arab anger at the United States and has become a favorite cause for Islamic extremists, particularly with the advent of satellite television enabling millions of Arabs to view graphic scenes of Israeli human rights abuses in the occupied territories and American officials defending the Israeli actions.

Historically, the United States has defined Israeli security primarily in terms of American arms transfers, which may be lucrative for U.S. arms exporters and enhance the U.S. domination of the region, but does not address Israel's core security concern, namely the violent reaction of a population resentful over three and half decades of military occupation.

It should be apparent that such militarization does not promote American security interests either. Zbigniew Brzezinski, the hawkish former National Security Advisor, has noted that Israel, "a symbol of recovery of a people who were greatly persecuted now looks like a country that is persecuting people. Meanwhile, the United States and Israel are becoming isolated internationally. This could hurt America's ability to conduct its war on terrorism."[136] Tragically, it appears that the increased solidarity Americans feel with Israelis—long the victims of terrorist attacks—since September 2001 has included the propensity to pursue some of the same misguided and tragically ineffective policies in response to terrorism that the Israelis have pursued over the decades, policies which have only made matters worse: producing more martyrs and victims among the oppressed populations and thereby creating more recruits for ever more fanatical and dangerous terrorist organizations.

Chapter Five

The Rise of
Extremist Islamic Movements

The terrorist attacks of September 11, 2001 tragically reinforced many of the racist stereotypes in the United States regarding Islam. How can we realistically assess the phenomenon of terrorism that seems to be rising out of the Islamic world? It's a vital question: the security of the United States and other nations depends in no small part on getting the answer right.

There is a widespread assumption that Muslim terrorists are religious fanatics beyond the reach of reasoning, where no offer of negotiation or deterrence will bring them out of their insanity. The details of recent history and current events, however, reveal a more complex picture: the growth of extremist movements is oftentimes proportional to the suffering inflicted on the populations from which they arise. In many instances, that suffering is inflicted or supported by the United States.

As with Christianity, Judaism and most major religious faiths, the killing of innocent civilians is considered a major sin in Islam. Similarly, there is nothing in traditional Islamic teachings that justifies suicide in any situation, much less suicide bombings. Nor do Muslims or Arabs engage in terrorism more frequently than any other peoples: Sub-Saharan Africans have engaged in the most widespread acts of terrorism in recent years, and Hindu Tamils from Sri Lanka have traditionally held the record for suicide bombings. The worst single terrorist atrocities in the Middle East in recent decades were committed by Christians: the Phalangists, a Lebanese Maronite militia, were responsible for the massacres of thousands of Palestinians at the Tal al-Zataar refugee camp in June 1976 and the Sabra and Shatila refugee camps in September 1982.

Yet it is the spread of radical Islamic movements throughout the Middle East and beyond that has placed political Islam at the forefront of concerns of Western nations, including the United States. This is particularly true when such movements have engaged in acts of terrorism against the interests of the United States and its allies. One unfortunate aspect of this newfound attention has been in the way it has strengthened ugly stereotypes of Muslims already prevalent in the West, which thereby has allowed the U.S. government to engage in questionable military campaigns against such movements with little public opposition. Even though the vast majority of the world's Muslims oppose terrorism, religious intolerance and the oppression of women, these remain the most prevalent images of the Muslim faith throughout the Western world. In the United States, there are now twice as many Muslims as there are Episcopalians, yet much of the media attention regarding American Muslims is related to their alleged connections to international terrorism. Similarly, few Americans realize that the vast majority of the world's Muslims are not Arabs and that there are significant non-Muslim minorities in the Arab world. While the Bush Administration has made public calls for Americans to refrain from racist attacks against Muslims and others of Middle Eastern and South Asian background, U.S. law enforcement agencies engage in the widespread use of racial profiling.

While most U.S. officials acknowledge that violence is not inherent to Islam, the idea that Muslims are a people continually involved in conflict and violence continues as the prevailing stereotype in the United States. The comparative record is revealing. Over the centuries, Western countries have experienced far more warfare, instability and intolerance than has the Muslim world. There has traditionally been a marked preference by Muslims for order and nonviolent solutions to conflicts. The dramatic spread of Islam in the seventh century occurred not as much through Arab militarism as the absence of formidable opposition. More often than not, the way was open to them. Indeed, the Arabs of that period had little military professionalism, techniques or organization. Their generals tended to be merchants, poets or tribal chieftains. Their culture did not have the militaristic caste tradition of the Spartans, Prussians, Janissaries or Karalis, nor did they build up a military organization comparable to other empires such as the Greeks, Romans, Byzantines or Persians. Until the creation of Israel, Jews found the Islamic world to be far safer than Western Christendom and while they—like Christians and other religious minorities—were rarely granted full equality to Muslims, they seldom experienced outright persecution.

Part of this misperception in the West regarding Islamic militarism is confusion over the concept of *jihad*. Rather than a holy war in the sense often conceptualized in the West, *jihad* for Muslims is seen as the ongoing struggle of both the individual and the Muslim people as a whole to do

God's work. Indeed, the highest form of *jihad* is considered the internal struggle for righteousness against the temptation of sin. *Jihad*—which relates to an overall struggle—is distinct from *qital*, the fight. Whether a particular *jihad* must take the form of a *qital* is debatable, but belief in *jihad* does not presuppose the use of violence in the quest. This has not stopped the U.S. government from misrepresenting the meaning of the term to advance its political agenda, however. For example, in September 1997, the U.S. Senate unanimously passed a resolution affirming that "the United States should provide no monetary or other assistance to the Palestinian Authority" until it ceases making "statements encouraging a...'jihad' against Israel."[1] To this day, anti-Palestinian Congressional leaders often cite Arafat's call for his people to struggle (to make *jihad*) to free their country from foreign military occupation as a means to justify their assertion that the Palestinians simply want to destroy Israel.

The term *jihad* can be used, for example, in regard to the fight against drugs, crime, litter or AIDS, just as Americans regularly use the word "crusade" in such contexts (which, coincidentally, is a similarly loaded term for Muslims.) President Bush initially used the word "crusade" to describe the American-led effort against Middle Eastern terrorism, a choice that ended up feeding the propaganda efforts of Osama bin Laden and other Islamic extremists who seek to portray their struggle as being between Islam and the West. Even many moderate Muslims saw it more as a mindset than as a slip of the tongue.

Despite this common misunderstanding of the term, it is important for those in the West to understand why a small but increasingly dangerous minority of Muslims have embraced extremist ideologies and violent tactics—and really do see *jihad* as, at least in part, a violent struggle or even war. Part of the reason is historic: From the time of the Crusades, through the European colonial era, to the wholesale bombing of Iraq in 1991, to the ongoing "war on terrorism," Western Christians have killed far more Muslims than Muslims have killed Western Christians. Muslims generally carry a stronger sense of history than do their Western Christian counterparts, and this fact is not lost on them. Despite the important contributions by Muslims in bringing Europe out of the Dark Ages as a result of the Islamic world's advances in science and technology while Europe stagnated, many Muslims see a Western world that, rather than being grateful, seems to carry an inherent hostility towards Islam.

More recently, when predominantly Muslim countries have sought to create democratic secular governments, hard line Christian militias have attacked them with either the acquiescence or outright support of Western nations. For example, in the 1970s, when the predominantly Muslim but secular Lebanese National Movement tried to overturn the country's undemocratic sectarian-based political system originally imposed by French colonialists, they were defeated by the right-wing Christian Phalangists, clandestinely backed by the French, Israelis, and Americans. In 1992, when the predominantly Muslim government of Bosnia-Herzegovina tried to establish a pluralistic non-sectarian nation-state as an alternative to the autocratic and militaristic ethno-chauvinism of the neighboring ex-Yugoslavian states of Serbia and Croatia, Serbian Christians attacked. The West stood by for more than three years while tens of thousands of Bosnian civilians were slaughtered, even preventing the Bosnians from procuring arms to defend themselves.[2] Military intervention by NATO and Croatian forces lifted the Serbian siege on Bosnian cities in the fall of 1995, though Western governments eventually pressured the Bosnians to abolish their secular unitary system for an effective partition of their country along religious lines. Most Muslims believe that had the situation instead been one of Muslims slaughtering Christians, Western countries would have come to the defense of democracy and international law far earlier.

Regardless of these facts, however, there is undeniably a strain of Islamic extremism that is indeed violent and chauvinistic, sees the Western world—and the United States in particular—as the enemy, and has embraced terrorism as a method of struggle. This requires an examination of what is nurturing Islamic terrorism and what can be done to stop it.

U.S. Support for Islamic Extremism

Though the U.S. government has used the threat of "Islamic fundamentalism" as a justification for keeping a high military profile in the Middle East for over twenty years, the United States at times has actually supported Muslim extremists when they were perceived to support U.S. interests. For example, during the 1980s, the United States sent large amounts of military aid to the oppressive Islamist military government in Pakistan and even supplied weapons clandestinely to the Ayatollah Khomeini's revolutionary Islamic regime in Iran.

The Taliban's five-year reign in Afghanistan represented the most extremist Muslim state in modern history, in terms of its strict interpretation of Islamic codes, repression of women, suppression of religious minorities and reactionary political orientation. The nature of the regime was emphasized repeatedly during the fall of 2001 to help justify the heavy bombing of that country by U.S. forces. However, the next most repressive Muslim state in modern times, Saudi Arabia, has always been accorded very different treatment for the simple reason that the kingdom is an important U.S. ally. As discussed earlier, the United States is a major trading partner with Saudi Arabia and sells the Saudi monarchy billions of dollars worth of highly sophisticated U.S. military equipment every year.

The kind of Islam traditionally practiced in Afghanistan bears little resemblance to what was imposed under the Taliban. The Taliban emerged out of the *madrassas*—religious schools supported by the Saudis and others that were set up in the refugee camps in Pakistan to teach the ultra-conservative interpretation of Islam from the *wahabi* tradition, which grew out of Saudi Arabia. The Saudis have funded such religious education throughout the Islamic world, often in places where it has not only been the sole religious education available, but sometimes also the only formal education of any kind provided. The U.S.-backed Saudi regime, then, is more responsible than any other government for the spread of this dangerous turn to the right in Islamic theology in recent decades. The global reach of this reactionary interpretation of Islam is made possible in large part by the movement's generous funding, which is a result of the billions of petrodollars flowing to Saudi Arabia from the West—in particular, the United States.

The U.S. role in bringing the Taliban to power, however, goes beyond simply buying oil from a regime that uses this income to support reactionary interpretations of Islam: The United States began arming the anti-Communist Islamic resistance movement in Afghanistan, known as the *mujahadin*, in July 1979, six months prior to the Soviet invasion. In a 1998 interview with the French magazine *Le Nouvel Observateur*, Zbigniew Brzezinski, who had been the National Security Advisor for President Jimmy Carter, said that he and Carter went ahead with the decision to arm the *mujahadin* despite that they "knowingly increased the probability" that the Soviets would invade. However, according to Brzezinski, he actually considered this a positive development, since "It had the effect of drawing the Russians into the Afghan trap" thereby draining their rival superpower's resources.[3] Over the next nine years, the United States poured over three billion dollars in support for the Islamic insurrection, perhaps the most intensive aid program to an insurgent force in world history. This anti-Communist insurgency was led by a fractious coalition of tribal militias, virtually all of which advocated an ultra-conservative interpretation of Islam.

U.S. support extended beyond money. An important component of the U.S.-backed rebellion was to support the recruitment of as many as 35,000 Muslims from around the world, particularly Arab countries, to fight in what was depicted as a holy war against the Communist government of Afghanistan and its Soviet sponsors. The United States, working closely with Pakistani intelligence, armed and trained Afghan exiles and their foreign Muslim allies in refugee camps in Pakistan and elsewhere. One of those recruits was a young Saudi businessman named Osama bin Laden. It was during this period, as part of the U.S.-backed war effort in Afghanistan, that bin Laden received the training and made the contacts that eventually led to the forming of the Al-Qaeda network in the early 1990s. Some of the bases later bombed by the United States in August 1998 and in October 2001 were actually funded by the United States during the 1980s to support the *mujahadin*. Most of the contact on the ground in Afghanistan with the *mujahadin*, including the training, was through Pakistani intelligence, not directly through the CIA. Strictly speaking, then, the United States may not have actually "trained Osama bin Laden" as some have charged, but U.S. intelligence operatives did at least train his trainers, supply his arms and provide much of the funding.

The terrorist attacks of September 11, 2001 were not the first time that U.S. support of these radical elements came back to haunt Americans. Sheik Omar Abdul-Rahman, the blind Egyptian cleric convicted of planning the 1994 truck bombing in the parking garage at the base of one of the World Trade Center towers, as well as a series of additional terrorist attacks in the New York City area that were foiled, is an interesting illustration. The CIA and other American agencies also supported Sheik Omar during the 1980s for his work on Afghanistan, including the recruitment of Muslims to join the struggle. In fact, the CIA provided him a visa allowing him into the United States even as the Immigration and Naturalization Service had him on a terrorist watch list that would otherwise have barred him from entering the country.[4]

Of the seven Afghan *mujahadin* groups resisting the Soviets and their proxy regime during the 1980s, the United States gave most of its aid to the extremist Hekmatyar faction. One reason was that much of the aid to the Afghan resistance was funneled through Pakistani intelligence at a time when Pakistan, then under a right-wing Islamic military dictatorship, favored the Hekmatyar. Perhaps more importantly, however, the United States believed that the Hekmatyar would be the least likely to reach a negotiated settlement with the Soviets, which would thereby prolong the war and the damage inflicted upon America's superpower rival. The United States did not consider the suffering of the Afghan people as a result of this policy to be a relevant factor. Some Afghans, in looking back on their recent history, recall the old African proverb, "When elephants fight, the grass gets trampled."

In 1989, Soviet troops withdrew after losing 15,000 of their soldiers.[5] The Afghan Communist regime fell in 1992. At this point, the United States found it had little further interest in the war-devastated country, in which over one million Afghans were killed, six million were made refugees and half of the country's villages were destroyed.[6] Despite several efforts by the victorious *mujahadin* to form a viable coalition, the Hekmatyar group, with its sizable arsenal of American weapons, launched a series of bloody attacks against the capital city of Kabul in an attempt to overthrow the more moderate post-Communist Islamic government. The assaults not only caused many thousands of civilian casualties, but they also forced those in power to include the Hekmatyar in government leadership and to impose some reactionary interpretations of Islamic law in an unsuccessful attempt to appease their rightist challengers, who continued their assaults. Due to the inability to form a stable government, ethnic militias and warlords ruled Afghanistan for four years, resulting in a chaotic period of banditry, a dramatic increase in the opium trade and ongoing internecine violence. Out of this anarchy rose the Taliban, composed mostly of young religious students educated in the *madrassas* set up in the refugee camps in neighboring Pakistan. According to Pakistan's prime minister of that time, Benazir Bhutto, these Taliban training centers were "paid for by the United States and Britain."[7] (This backing of religious movements with extreme anti-Communist ideologies was also manifested in the clandestine U.S. support during the 1980s of right-wing Protestant fundamentalist missionaries in conflict-ridden Central American countries as a counter to the growing influence of the progressive liberation theology within the Roman Catholic Church.) The Taliban militia launched their military operations in 1994 along the Afghan-Pakistani border. They grew rapidly and added some former Hekmatyar fighters to their ranks. Desperate for stability and order, the Afghans initially welcomed the Taliban, which swiftly took over the country and put an end to the reign of the warlords. Following the Taliban victory in September 1996, the deposed warlords and ethnic militias, joined by some tribal factions that had once backed the communists, were able to hold on to only a small territory in northeastern Afghanistan. Later known as the Northern Alliance, they retook most of the country, including the capital of Kabul, during the fall of 2001 as a result of heavy U.S. air strikes against the Taliban. In December, they agreed to share power in a broader-based coalition that was reorganized and institutionalized in June the following year.

During the Taliban's rise to power and soon after its 1996 takeover of most of the country, the United States quietly supported the extremist militia. So strong was the U.S. desire for stability that, until their connections with bin Laden and Al-Qaeda became apparent, there was little American opposition to the Taliban. The theocratic fascism they imposed upon the Afghans themselves was of no obvious consternation to the U.S. government. Clinton Administration officials saw the Taliban as a hard-line fundamentalist dictatorship, but one that would generally be favorable to U.S. interests. As one U.S. diplomat put it, "The Taliban will probably develop like the Saudis did. There will be...pipelines, an emir, no parliament and lots of Sharia law. We can live with that."[8] Assistant Secretary of State for South Asia Robin Raphael visited the Afghan city of Kandahar in early 1996 to meet with Taliban officials just prior to their takeover of Kabul. There they discussed a proposal by the U.S. oil company Unocal to construct an oil pipeline through Afghanistan that would connect the oil fields of the former Soviet Central Asia to a Pakistani port for shipping. Soon afterwards, feminists, Greens and other human rights activists in the United States launched a campaign against U.S. ties to the Taliban. By 1997, the Taliban's ties to Al-Qaeda became apparent to the Clinton Administration and the United States successfully encouraged the United Nations Security Council to impose sanctions on the Taliban government in November 1998 for its refusal to extradite bin Laden. Despite this, and the imposition of even stricter unilateral sanctions in 1999, contacts continued. As late as May 2001, the Bush Administration sent $43 million to the Taliban as a thank you for their support of drug eradication efforts. Bush State Department official James Callahan praised what he called the Taliban's "consensus-building" approach and the fact that their ban on drugs was "in very religious terms."[9]

Some evidence suggests that U.S. interest in the possible pipeline deal may have been one of the factors that led to the early U.S. appeasement of the Taliban regime. French intelligence officer Jean-Charles Brisard and journalist Guillaume Dasquie, in their 2001 book *Bin Laden, La Verite Interdite* document a cozy relationship between President Bush and the Taliban. They quote John O'Neill, former director of anti-terrorist operations for the FBI, who believes the State Department, acting on behalf of

American oil interests, interfered with FBI efforts to capture bin Laden.[10] Some leftist critics of U.S. policy have gone further, alleging that the oil interests were the primary motivation for the 2001 U.S. bombing of Afghanistan, noting that both the president and vice-president, as well as other prominent government officials, are former oil company executives. However, Central Asian oil, located primarily around the Caspian Sea, is far more easily routed to ports through Iran and Russia. Given the precarious nature of U.S. relations with those two countries, Unocal and other oil companies saw diverting the oil through a stable Afghanistan as an option worth considering. Yet, since the Afghan route was always more of a backup option for one oil field rather than a cornerstone of U.S. energy policy, it is rather doubtful whether this was the major factor in the U.S. decision to go to war in Afghanistan.

In any case, this review of U.S. policy makes clear that it would be a mistake to assume that the United States is morally opposed to fundamentalist governments or extremist Islamic movements. The degree of U.S. opposition or support for reactionary Islamists is related not to their level of violence and repression, but their perceived willingness or unwillingness to cooperate with American political and economic interests.

Encouraging the Islamic Backlash and the Future Risk

Even where the United States has not supported Islamic extremist movements directly, the U.S. has often engaged in policies that have led directly to the rise of such movements. The classic case of this phenomenon is Iran.

The move by the nationalist Iranian Prime Minister Mohammed Mossadegh to nationalize the British-owned oil monopoly in the early 1950s sparked direct U.S. involvement in the country's internal affairs. Fearing the possibility of this precedent spreading to Saudi Arabia—where U.S. oil companies were in effective control of that country's oil reserves—the United States joined Great Britain and other Western countries in boycotting Iranian oil, resulting in a major economic and political crisis. Concerned that the political unrest was increasing the influence of the communist Tudeh Party and desiring control of the country's vast oil wealth, the United States sent in the CIA to facilitate the overthrow of Iran's constitutional government in 1953. In its place, the United States installed Shah Mohammad Reza Pahlavi—who had fled into exile barely a week earlier after losing a power struggle with Mossadegh—as an absolute monarch. Over the next twenty-five years, the United States armed and trained the military and the SAVAK, the dreaded secret police of the Shah, which emerged as one of the most repressive internal security organizations of the era. It comes as no surprise, in light of this, that the revolution that finally ousted the monarchy in February 1979 was stridently anti-American. Furthermore, since the Shah's repressive apparatus had largely succeeded in wiping out the secular opposition to the regime, it was religious opponents—who survived as a result of the greater cohesion made possible through the mosques—who spearheaded the revolutionary movement. Thus, the radical Islamic orientation of the revolution was greatly influenced by the Shah's American-backed efforts to maintain control through repression.

Just eight months after the triumph of the revolution, the exiled shah entered the United States for medical treatment. Fearing he might be plotting with American officials to try to return to power, radical Iranian students, backed by elements in the Islamic government, seized more than fifty American hostages at the U.S. embassy, promising to release them only if the shah was extradited to Iran for trial. They held the American hostages for 444 days. During that time, the United States successfully petitioned the International Court of Justice to demand their release, made threats of war, staged an unsuccessful military raid to free them, seized Iranian assets overseas, and helped secure international sanctions against Iran. The hostage crisis dominated the attention of the Carter Administration during its last fourteen months in office and brought the attention of the United States for the first time to the threat from anti-American Islamic movements. The Shah died of cancer in July 1980. A series of difficult negotiations, brokered by the government of Algeria, eventually led to the hostages' release on January 20, 1981, the day Ronald Reagan was inaugurated president.[11]

That spring, the Islamic leadership in Iran began a violent series of purges that eliminated most of the revolution's progressive and moderate elements and thereby assumed a brutal and reactionary character. Hundreds of royalists, leftists, nationalists and moderate Islamists were executed. The Iranian people found themselves under the rule of a regime at least as repressive as that of the ousted Shah, and the United States found itself faced with the largest country in the Middle East, until recently a key regional ally, under the control of a hostile anti-American regime. To this day, the United States sees Iran as one of the most dangerous countries in the world.

The U.S. support for the Shah often is cited as a classic example of "blowback," the phenomenon where the United States engages in policies supporting political repression for short-term political expediency only to find that, in the long term, an extreme anti-American reaction results.

What is the risk of more "blowbacks" like Iran in the future, as the United States continues supporting autocratic regimes and pushes economic reforms that lead to widespread social dislocation and gross inequalities? Egypt and—to a lesser extent—Tunisia are two countries where these grievances have been embraced by extremist Islamic movements. With some notable exceptions, attacks by radical Islamic groups in Egypt have been launched not toward religious opponents *per se*, but primarily toward those who are linked to a political and economic system seen as unjust and corrupt. The leaders of Egypt's Islamic movements are often Egyptians from poor families who have gone on to obtain advanced academic degrees, only to find most career options have been closed off to those of more humble backgrounds as a result of the corruption and nepotism. In such countries undergoing growing economic stratification, Islamic movements have essentially been waging a kind of class warfare; twenty years ago, many of their leaders would have been Marxists. (And at least a few of them once were!) These Islamic movements are stronger than the leftist movements of previous decades, however, since the message of social justice in the Koran has far greater appeal among the masses than does comparatively arcane Marxian dialectics. The failure of the bureaucratic-authoritarian brand of socialism advocated by Nasser and other Arab nationalists of his era, as well as serious problems with the more recent experiments in neo-liberal economics, have given rise to those seeking to impose an Islamic alternative.

Sudan provides another example of how imperial powers have fomented the backlash of fundamentalists. During the late nineteenth and early twentieth centuries, British colonialists destroyed Sudan's self-sufficient economy by imposing an agricultural system of cash crop production centered on cotton exports from which the country has yet to recover. The resulting widespread social dislocation made the embrace of a reactionary brand of Islam by the country's military palatable to many Sudanese. United States policy in recent decades extended this dynamic. U.S. support for the regime of Jafaar Nimeiry during most of his repressive sixteen-year rule of Sudan between 1969 and 1985 led to the destruction of much of that country's civil society. This made his successors' efforts to build a viable democratic system, following the dictator's overthrow in the largely nonviolent uprising of 1985, virtually impossible. The result was a coup by right-wing Islamist military officers three years later that have ruled with extreme brutality ever since.

As discussed in Chapter Two, the ongoing purchase of U.S. arms by Middle Eastern states—strongly encouraged by both private companies and the U.S. government—has diverted billions of dollars from potential development projects to the American arms industry. This has increased both human suffering and popular resentment of the United States and its allied regimes. Such a misallocation of resources was, for example, a major factor in the downfall of the Shah of Iran.

Similarly, American encouragement of neo-liberal economic policies in Islamic countries has brought increased prosperity for some but has worsened the plight of much of the poor and increased economic inequality and injustice. Central Asia nations, in their rush to liberalize their economies after decades of Soviet Communism, have embraced disruptive and corrupt privatization schemes that have resulted in small elites enriching themselves as the majority experiences increased economic deprivation. Meanwhile, throughout the Islamic world, popular understanding of capitalism is manifested by the most crass and vulgar examples of American-style consumerism and materialism enjoyed by a handful of elites while most people live in poverty. In this context, it is small wonder that globalization under the model pushed by the United States and its allied international financial institutions has been a major factor in encouraging the anti-American backlash led by Islamic extremists.

In Pakistan and other Islamic countries, the costs from purchasing American arms combined with structural adjustment programs pushed by the United States have resulted in dramatic cuts in government spending for domestic programs, in which state-funded education is a major casualty. As a result, due to the poor quality or absence of public schools in many areas, lower middle and middle class families have sent their boys to Saudi-funded *madrassas* in increasing numbers, where they are exposed to ultra-conservative Islamic teachings that have made many susceptible to extremist anti-American ideologies.

When a people have lost their identity—whether it be through foreign military occupation, relocation through war, the collapse of traditional economies, or other reasons—there is a great pull to embrace something that can provide the structure, world view, and purpose through which to rebuild their lives. In Islamic countries undergoing great social disruption, the mosque is one of the few constants. While some strains of Islamic thought are relatively apolitical, many interpretations of Islam put forward a clear sense of social justice, a feeling of empowerment and a belief in one's obligation to challenge those who cause the injustice.

How people live out their faith can range widely in terms of ideology, strategy and tactics. Much depends on what obstacles are faced by such movements. For example, in countries like Turkey, Jordan and Yemen, where Islamic parties have at times been allowed to compete in a relatively open political process, they have generally played a responsible—if somewhat conservative—role in the political system. By contrast, in Egypt, Palestine and Algeria, the Islamic movements have taken on a violent and extremist orientation, clearly a reflection of the denial of their right to participate in political discourse. Were Islamic groups allowed to function in an open democratic system instead of under siege, they would likely divide into competing political parties ranging across the ideological spectrum.

Despite occasional emancipatory rhetoric, many Islamic-identified movements subscribe to a reactionary and misogynist worldview. Justifiably repulsed by this, many erstwhile skeptics of U.S. foreign policy, such as writer Christopher Hitchens and most liberal Democrats in Congress, have been outspoken in their support of military interventionism to fight such movements, particularly after the September 11 attacks. They compare these movements—not unfairly, in many respects—to the European fascist movements of the 1930s and therefore argue that they must be violently suppressed. However, if the U.S. response is primarily through political repression and military force, a solution that does nothing to address the underlying injustices that feed these movements, American efforts to crush them will not only likely fail, but perhaps contribute to the growth of the very groups seeking to harm the United States and its citizens.

The implications of U.S. actions are clear: the rise of radical Islamic movements is a direct result of major social dislocation—through war, through traumatic economic transitions, and/or through political repression. U.S. policy—from supporting such movements for political expediency, to propping up repressive regimes, to supporting economic reforms that result in greater social stratification—is in no small part responsible for this dynamic. Two prominent examples of where the United States has contributed to a dangerous backlash by Muslim extremists, which reveal much when examined in detail, are Lebanon and Palestine.

The United States and Islamic Extremists in Lebanon

Islamic extremists were never much of a factor in Lebanese politics until the 1980s. The "Muslim" side of the Lebanese civil war in the mid-1970s was actually a largely secular grouping known as the Lebanese National Movement (LNM) which, while consisting primarily of Sunni

Muslims and Druzes, also included leftists and nationalists from virtually all of Lebanon's communities. Seeking to block the LNM's demands for constitutional reform to create a more representative political system that would likely enact policies less sympathetic with the West, the United States clandestinely supported the Phalangist militia, a neo-fascist grouping based in the country's Maronite Christian community. The PLO—which had a sizable armed presence based in the Palestinian refugee camps in that country—eventually joined the civil war on the side of the LNM, helping them to gain ground until the Syrians, with quiet U.S. support, invaded to block their incipient victory in 1976. The war continued on and off for nearly fifteen years.

Meanwhile, the Israelis were engaged in frequent air strikes against both military and civilian targets in Lebanon throughout the 1970s, ostensibly in retaliation for terrorist attacks against Israel by exiled Palestinian groups based in that country. Despite the high civilian death toll and damage to Lebanon's economy, particularly in the southern part of the country, the United States largely defended the Israeli actions. In 1978, Israel invaded southern Lebanon in a devastating military thrust launched in retaliation for a Palestinian terrorist attack that killed dozens of Israeli civilians north of Tel Aviv. The United States voted with the rest of the UN Security Council in calling on Israel to cease all military action and withdraw immediately.[12] President Carter threatened to suspend some U.S. aid if Israel did not pull back its forces, resulting in a partial withdrawal to what Israel later referred to as a "security zone," a twelve to twenty-mile strip of Lebanese territory along Israel's northern border. Nine subsequent resolutions reiterated the demand that Israel withdraw completely, but the United States blocked the Security Council from enforcing it.

Over the next three years, Israel—along with an allied right-wing Lebanese militia known as the South Lebanese Army—periodically bombed and shelled Palestinian forces and civilian areas in southern Lebanon while Palestinian forces lobbed shells into civilian areas in northern Israel. Israel, with its vastly superior firepower, tended to inflict a lot more damage. In June 1981, following a particularly heavy Israeli bombing raid on a crowded Beirut neighborhood that resulted in hundreds of civilian casualties, the United States brokered a cease-fire.

One year later, however, Israel launched a full-scale invasion of Lebanon, occupying nearly half the country and laying siege to the Lebanese capital. The United States vetoed a series of UN Security Council resolutions demanding an Israeli withdrawal. Subsequent resolutions simply calling for a cease-fire were also blocked by U.S. vetoes. In the three months of Israel's war on Lebanon, heavy Israeli bombardment resulted in the deaths of more than 17,000 Lebanese and Palestinian civilians. American Congressional leaders, particularly on the Democratic side, vigorously defended Israel's invasion and rewarded the right-wing government of Prime Minister Menachem Begin by increasing military aid.

In September, the United States brokered an agreement where the PLO would evacuate its fighters and political offices from Beirut in return for an Israeli pledge not to occupy the city. Part of the agreement included the deployment of a U.S.-led peacekeeping force to, among other things, protect the Palestinian refugee population from the Phalangist militia, which had engaged in a series of massacres against Palestinians in previous years. U.S. forces were pulled out after only a couple of weeks, however, following the election by the Lebanese parliament of Phalangist militia leader Bashir Gemayel as president. Days later, Gemayel was assassinated in a bombing by unknown assailants. Israel used the assassination as an excuse to break its pledge and occupy the Lebanese capital. At that point, the Israelis sent Phalangist militiamen into Sabra and Shatila, two Palestinian refugee camps on the southern outskirts of the city. There, the Phalangists massacred over a thousand civilians under the watch of Israeli occupation forces, who did nothing to stop the atrocity and even lit flares to allow the Phalangists to continue the assaults into the night.

Along with smaller contingents of French and Italian forces, U.S. troops then returned and Israeli forces withdrew to just south of Beirut. Bachir Gemayel's brother Amin, the political leader of the Phalangists, assumed power, soon to be faced with a popular uprising against his far right-wing government. U.S. forces intervened in his support, exchanging fire with Muslim rebels in suburban Beirut slums, engaging Syrian forces in the Bekaa Valley, and bombing and shelling Druze villages in the Shouf Mountains. The American air strikes and the utilization of the big guns from the battleship *New Jersey* resulted in large-scale civilian casualties.

It is hardly surprising that radical anti-American Islamic movements arose out of this chaos. During this period and for a few years afterwards, nearly a dozen Americans were kidnapped and held hostage by Islamic radicals, in some cases for years. There were also several assassinations, including Francis Meloy, the U.S. ambassador, and Malcolm Kerr, a well-respected Middle East scholar who served as president of the American University of Beirut.

On April 18, 1983 suicide bombers struck the U.S. Embassy in Beirut,

killing 63 people. On October 23, a suicide bomber attacked a Marine bar-
racks near the Beirut Airport, killing 241 servicemen. Not long afterwards,
the United States withdrew its forces from Lebanon.

The utilization of terrorism by elements of disempowered populations
is usually a reflection of the violence and injustice inflicted upon them by
more powerful forces. The rise of Hizbullah and other anti-American
Islamic terrorist groups in Lebanon during the 1980s came only after the
U.S.-backed 1982 Israeli invasion and the subsequent U.S. intervention in
support of the right-wing minority Phalangist government installed under
Israeli guns. Though it is easy to portray terrorists as fanatical and irrational, the personal histories of many display an understandable source to
their anger, however immoral their subsequent actions may be. One example is particularly noteworthy in this regard: In June 1985, radical Lebanese
Muslims hijacked a TWA airliner and held the passengers and crew hostage
for several days on the tarmac of the Beirut airport, murdering a U.S. Navy
officer on board. One of the two principal hijackers had lost members of his
family when the U.S. Navy shelled his village two years earlier.

In a 1989 interview, former President Jimmy Carter observed,

> We bombed and shelled and unmercifully killed totally inno-
> cent villagers, women and children and farmers and housewives, in
> those villages around Beirut. As a result, we have become a kind of
> Satan in the minds of those who are deeply resentful. That is what
> precipitated the taking of hostages and that is what has precipitated
> some terrorist attacks.[13]

In the wake of the forced departure of the PLO and the destruction of
the LNM by successive interventions from Syria, Israel, and the United
States, Hizbullah and older Islamic militias like Amal rose to fill the vacuum. By 1985, guerrilla warfare by various Lebanese groups forced the
Israelis to withdraw their occupation forces from central Lebanon to as far
back as the strip in the southern part of the country originally occupied in
1978. In the south of Lebanon, dominated by the PLO and its leftist
Lebanese allies until they were driven out in 1982 by the Israelis, the
Hizbullah came to exercise almost full control and began an armed struggle against Israeli occupation forces. Israel, with American backing, continued its occupation of southern Lebanon, now claiming it was necessary
to protect Israelis from the Hizbullah. Yet this threat from Hizbullah was
very much an outgrowth of U.S. and Israeli policy: the group did not even
exist until four years after Israel began its occupation of southern Lebanon
in 1978.

Israel tried to maintain its occupation through both frequent armed clashes with the Hizbullah as well as assaults against towns and villages from where they were believed to operate. The Israelis periodically would extend these attacks throughout Lebanon, targeting bridges, dams, power plants, and other segments of the country's civilian infrastructure, often many miles from areas of Hizbullah control. Throughout this period, much of the ordinance and many of the delivery systems used by the Israelis against Lebanese civilians were from the United States.

Successive U.S. administrations rejected demands by human rights groups that such military aid be made conditional on an end to Israeli attacks against civilian targets. The United States repeatedly defended the Israeli assaults, vetoing UN Security Council resolutions condemning the violence, and questioning the credibility of human rights groups and UN agencies that exposed the extent of the humanitarian tragedy. To cite one critical example, the Israelis attacked a UN compound in 1996 near the Lebanese village of Qana that was sheltering refugees, killing more than one hundred civilians. Reports by the United Nations, Amnesty International, and other investigators all indicate that the bombardment was deliberate. However, the United States insisted that the massacre at Qana was an accident, though the Clinton Administration was unwilling to provide any evidence challenging the other findings.

There is a horrible symmetry that often escapes notice in the United States. Through its massive attacks on Lebanon, Israel resorted to the same tactics that Hamas and other extremist groups have employed targeting Israel: terrorizing innocent civilians in order to influence government policy. Yet just as the attacks by Arab terrorists against Israeli civilians have only hardened Israeli attitudes towards the peace process, so Israel's attacks against Lebanese civilians, which resulted in far greater casualties, made it more difficult for Lebanon and Syria to further compromise with Israel.

During the early 1990s, following the end of the Lebanese civil war, a revived central Lebanese government and its Syrian backers disarmed most of the other militias that had once carved up much of the country. By contrast, as the Israeli attacks continued, Hizbullah not only remained intact, it grew. Years of heavy Israeli bombardment led hundreds of thousands of Lebanese Shiites to flee north, filling vast slums in the southern outskirts of Beirut. It is from these refugees and others who suffered as a result of these U.S.-supported Israeli assaults that Hizbullah received the core of its support. The Hizbullah militia became heroes to many Lebanese, particularly as the U.S.-led peace process stalled.

The Hizbullah also periodically fired shells into Israel proper, some of which killed and injured civilians. Virtually all these attacks, however, were in direct retaliation for large-scale Israeli attacks against Lebanese civilians, and the Hizbullah pledged to cease such shelling of Israeli territory should Israel end its occupation. In any case, the United States condemned Hizbullah not just for occasional attacks inside Israel but also for its armed resistance against Israeli soldiers within Lebanon, despite the fact that international law recognizes the right of armed resistance against foreign occupation forces. The United States was apparently hoping that enough Israeli pressure against Lebanon would force the Lebanese to sign a separate peace treaty with Israel and thereby isolate the Syrians. U.S. officials greatly exaggerated the role of Syria in its control and support for Hizbullah, seemingly ignoring the fact that Syria had historically backed Amal, a rival Shiite militia. By contrast, the radical Iranian Revolutionary Guards did play a significant role in the initial formation of Hizbullah in 1982, though most direct Iranian support diminished substantially. The emphasis by the United States in subsequent years on Hizbullah's ties to Iran was largely to discredit a movement that had widespread popular support for its resistance efforts against a foreign occupation condemned across Lebanon's diverse confessional and ideological communities.

By the mid-1990s, increasing casualties among Israeli Defense Forces in occupied southern Lebanon led to increased dissent within Israel over Israeli policy. In response to public opinion polls showing that the vast majority of Israelis wanted the IDF to withdraw unilaterally, Martin Indyk—President Clinton's ambassador to Israel who had also served as his Assistant Secretary of State for the Middle East—publicly encouraged Israel to keep its occupation forces in Lebanon. In other words, the United States, while defending its sanctions and bombing against Iraq on the grounds of upholding UN Security Council resolutions, was encouraging Israel—against the better judgement of the majority of its citizens—to defy longstanding UN Security Council resolutions that demanded Israel's unconditional withdrawal. When asked about his ambassador's comments at a press conference, President Clinton replied, "I believe it is imperative that Israel maintain the security of its northern border and therefore I have believed that the United States should be somewhat deferential under these circumstances."[14] In an interesting display of double standards, the wording of the 1978 resolution demanding Israel's withdrawal from Lebanon that the United States was being deferential about was virtually identical to the resolution passed twelve years later demanding Iraq's withdrawal from Kuwait, for which United States went to war.

The Hizbullah finally drove the Israelis and their proxy force out of Lebanon in a hasty retreat in May 2000. In the wake of the failure of those advocating a more moderate ideology and a diplomatic solution, the military victory by the Hizbullah has greatly enhanced its status. Since then, except for a few minor incidents, the Israeli-Lebanese border has been quiet. There has been periodic fighting, however, between Hizbullah and Israeli occupation forces in the disputed Shebaa Farms area along the Lebanese-Syrian border in the Israeli-occupied Golan Heights northeast of the Israeli-Lebanese border. Meanwhile, the number of Hizbullah fighters is down to around 1000 and the movement functions today primarily as a political party with elected representatives serving in the Lebanese parliament.

The U.S. support for Israel's 22-year occupation of southern Lebanon and its efforts to undermine the authority of the United Nations has led many Palestinians to believe that reliance on UN Security Council resolutions or a U.S.-brokered peace process will fail. By contrast, the military victory by Hizbullah led many Palestinians to believe that the only way to free themselves from Israeli control is, like the Lebanese, to wage a sustained armed resistance led by an extremist Islamic movement. For a number of reasons—particularly the great difference in Israeli perspectives regarding the significance of the occupied Palestinian territories as compared with southern Lebanon—it is a very inappropriate comparison. Despite this, however, it is now a widely held view among the Palestinian population; Palestinians engaged in the ongoing anti-Israeli violence often cite Lebanon as their model. The United States is largely to blame for this radicalizing shift in Palestinian attitudes as a result of its policy in Lebanon.

The United States and Islamic Extremists in Palestine

In many respects, the Palestinians would seem to be among the least likely Arab people to embrace radical strains of Islam. With the most highly-educated population in the Arab world, Palestinians have exhibited a relatively high degree of tolerance towards the many peoples and cultures with whom they have come in contact over the centuries in their homeland, a crossroads of civilizations. Unlike neighboring Lebanon, the Muslims in Palestine have lived with their country's Christian minority quite peacefully. Prior to the advent of Zionism a century ago, Palestine's small Jewish community also fared relatively well.

Yet, given that radical Islamic movements have grown to prominence where there has been great social dislocation, it is not surprising that Islamic extremism is on the rise among the Palestinians, a people forcibly uprooted from their land more than five decades ago and much of the population still living as refugees. Most others have been living since 1967 under a repressive Israeli military occupation—supported diplomatically, militarily and financially by the United States—which has also denied them the basic economic opportunities of their fellow Arabs in neighboring countries. Such conditions inevitably breed extremist movements. Though the ideology of Hamas and related Palestinian Islamic groups is undeniably reactionary, it has attracted the adherence of a surprisingly broad cross-section of Palestinian society as a result of the lack of a credible alternative.

Israel, with U.S. support, has helped move opposition to its occupation toward more extreme responses and away from alternative and less violent means of resistance. In the early 1980s, the Israelis actually encouraged Islamic groups in the occupied territories in an effort to split the Palestinian movement. While supporters of the secular PLO were denied their own media or any right to hold political gatherings, Israeli occupation authorities allowed radical Islamic groups to hold rallies, publish uncensored newspapers and even have their own radio station. For example, in the occupied Palestinian city of Gaza in 1981, Israeli soldiers—who had shown no hesitation in brutally suppressing peaceful pro-PLO demonstrations—stood by when a group of Islamic extremists attacked and burned a PLO-affiliated health clinic in Gaza. In 1988, Israel detained, tortured, and forcibly exiled Palestinian activist Mubarak Awad, a Christian pacifist who advocated peace with Israel and the use of Gandhian-style resistance to the Israeli occupation.[15] At the same time, however, Israeli occupation authorities were allowing Hamas founder Sheik Ahmed Yassin to circulate anti-Jewish hate literature and publicly call for the destruction of Israel by force of arms.

Since the PLO formally chose the diplomatic path in the 1993 Oslo Accords with Israel, the material conditions of the Palestinians have worsened considerably. Israeli occupation forces have placed most Palestinian areas under siege. Meanwhile, well over 1,500 Palestinians have been killed, including hundreds of unarmed civilians. Israel's military offensive in the spring of 2002 destroyed much of the West Bank's civilian infrastructure. As a result, many Palestinians are quite susceptible to the contention of radical Islamic movements like Hamas and the smaller Islamic Jihad that nonviolent methods get you nowhere.

While the Palestinian Authority struggled to supply their population with even the most basic of social services, Hamas and its allied groups received millions of dollars from sources in Saudi Arabia, Kuwait, Qatar, and the United Arab Emirates, countries that the United States considers to be its close Arab allies. Ironically, the oil-rich Muslim nations backing these extremist groups have long been labeled as "moderate" by the U.S. government, even as successive American administrations refused to include the increasingly conciliatory PLO in the peace process prior to 1993. Indeed, in a strange twist, for several years prior to the signing of the Oslo Accords, U.S. officials in the consular office in Israeli-occupied East Jerusalem were meeting with Hamas leaders while being barred from meeting with anyone from the PLO. This policy was implemented despite the fact that the PLO had renounced terrorism and unilaterally recognized Israel as far back as 1988. Meanwhile, Hamas' impressive health clinics, schools, cultural institutions and other social work became effective recruiting centers for thousands of young Palestinians.

One of the early major boosts for Hamas came when the Israeli government expelled more than 400 Palestinian Muslims from their homes in the occupied territories in late 1992. While most of the exiles were associated with Hamas-affiliated social service agencies, very few had been accused of any violent crimes. Since such expulsions are a direct contravention of international law, the UN Security Council unanimously condemned the action and called for their immediate return. The incoming Clinton Administration, however, blocked the United Nations from enforcing its resolution by falsely claiming that an Israeli offer to eventually allow some of the exiles back constituted a fulfillment of the UN mandate. The result of the Israeli and American actions was that the exiles became heroes and martyrs; the credibility of Hamas in the eyes of the Palestinians grew enormously—and so did their political strength.

Beginning in 1994, Hamas and Islamic Jihad began a series of terrorist campaigns launched against Israeli settlers in the occupied territories as well as against Israelis inside Israel itself, primarily through the use of suicide bombers. Scores of Israelis were murdered in these attacks over the next seven years. When Ariel Sharon came into office in early 2001, the attacks dramatically escalated, with the death toll soaring into the hundreds. As examined in Chapter Four, the governments of Israel and the United States blamed the Palestinian Authority, either through negligence or intent, of encouraging the terrorism through its failure to crack down on Islamic terrorists by arresting known militants and for releasing some suspects already under arrest.

Part of the dilemma for the Palestinian Authority is that in abiding by U.S. and Israeli demands to get tough on terrorism, Palestinian president Arafat has periodically attempted to crack down against a wide range of dissident groups, even those without any direct connection with terrorist violence. This has resulted in serious human rights violations, including having his police fire into crowds of Islamist demonstrators. Some Palestinians argue that the Israelis and Americans have made the Palestinian Authority jailers in their own prison. This attitude only enhances the status of the radical Islamic groups.

More problematic is that the lack of direct U.S. economic aid—combined with the Palestinian Authority's own corruption and ineptitude—has severely limited Palestinian access to basic social services outside of Islamic charities, many of which are controlled by Hamas and its sympathizers. If the Palestinian Authority casts too wide a net in its crackdown against extremist Islamic groups, they will face the wrath of their own population for denying them access to health care clinics, child care centers, food banks and pensions. Such social services are made all the more important due to the ongoing U.S.-backed Israeli sieges. If the Palestinian Authority is too conservative in its crackdown, terrorists will continue to operate out of its territory to engage in attacks against Israeli civilians, both inside Israel and among Israeli settlers. The result will likely be further Israeli retaliation against Palestinians as a whole.

Ultimately, those Palestinians who choose to commit acts of terrorism for the same reasons as did Kenyans, Algerians and Zimbabweans: they feel that they are prevented from attaining their national freedom through peaceful means. Indeed, the Zionist movement produced its share of terrorist groups during the Israeli independence struggle in the 1940s, with two prominent terrorist leaders—Menachem Begin and Yitzhak Shamir—later becoming prime ministers whose governments received tens of billions of dollars worth of United States military and economic aid. In suppressing demands for national freedom by the Palestinians, the United States is fueling the very kind of terrorism and radical Islamism it claims to oppose.

Since the shift towards a more stridently anti-Palestinian position by the Israeli and American governments in 2001-2002 and the escalation of attacks against Palestinian civilian areas, there has been a corresponding shift by the Palestinian public in support of terrorism. Despite the obvious ways the terrorists' actions are both morally reprehensible and politically counter-productive, there is an attitude that—after decades of suffering under the world's longest ongoing foreign military occupation—they no longer care. For a people who have given up hope in a peace process that most now feel was rigged against them, there is a perverse sense of empowerment that comes from suicide bombing—it is an attitude that if they are to suffer and die anyway, they might as well take some Israelis with them.

The majority of Palestinians in the West Bank and Gaza Strip have known nothing but Israeli occupation. It is hard to imagine that had these young Palestinians instead grown up in an independent viable Palestinian state, they would decide one day to sneak into the neighboring country of Israel and blow themselves up along with innocent Israeli civilians.

Even beyond Palestine, there are Muslim leaders who had denounced suicide bombings as anti-Islamic in the past who—in the face of the U.S.-backed Israeli assaults on Palestinian population centers—are now on record defending the practice. There is little question that U.S. policy has contributed to this dangerous shift in attitudes.

Chapter Six

Responding to the Threat of Terrorism

Beginning in the early 1980s, the U.S. government has claimed that international terrorism, primarily of Middle Eastern origin, is a major threat to the country's national security, and that the war against terrorism should be a major focus of U.S. foreign policy. This seemed to be hyperbole to many observers until the tragic events of September 11, 2001.

Still, the United States was not ready. Despite a great deal of attention from the highest levels of government in recent years, there appears to have been little coherency in actual policy. As recently as 1998, Richard Davis of the General Accounting Office reported, "There does not seem to be any overall strategy to guide how we're spending money on counter-terrorism" and, despite Congressional eagerness to fund such efforts, there seems to be "no oversight, no priorities, no strategy, and much duplication."[1] The decision by Congress to grant over $20 billion of unrestricted funds to the Bush Administration to combat terrorism in the wake of the September 11 catastrophe raises fresh questions about how wisely such resources will be spent. More important, however, than the efficiency with which the money is distributed is whether overall U.S. counter-terrorism strategy will reduce the problem, as is claimed, or exacerbate it.

Prior to the September 11 attacks, the Bush Administration pursued a number of policies that seriously harmed international efforts against terrorism. During his first seven months in office, President Bush reiterated his opposition to the establishment of an International Criminal Court, walked out of a conference designed to strengthen the 1972 Biological and Toxic Weapons Convention, and refused to support an effort by other advanced industrialized countries to strengthen regulations against tax havens and money laundering. In addition, the Bush Administration successfully weakened a United Nations effort to control the transfer of small arms to irregular groups. As the largest supplier of arms to the Third World, and to the Middle East in particular, the Bush Administration and its predecessors have allowed potential terrorists easy access to weapons.

Rather than change such policies, however, the Bush Administration—with bipartisan support in Congress—has instead imposed a series of controversial initiatives, including tougher immigration laws, higher military spending, restrictions on civil liberties, increased arms shipments, and expanded training programs for the police and military of repressive governments. None of these policies, however, addresses the underlying causes of anti-American terrorism.

The Politicization of the Campaign Against Terrorism

American credibility in the war against terrorism has been hampered by the way the U.S. government has politicized the struggle against terrorism, using this very real threat as an excuse to advance its foreign policy agenda.

Syria provides an example of how this dynamic unfolds. U.S. officials have repeatedly claimed that Syria's links to terrorist groups are a major obstacle in improving relations. Yet the United States has admitted that it has no proof of direct ties by the Syrian government to terrorism since 1986. U.S. officials acknowledge that Syria has pressed radical Palestinian groups to refrain from terrorism, that Syria was instrumental in securing the release of American hostages held by Muslim extremists in Lebanon and that Syria has offered support in the fight against the Al-Qaeda network. The major remaining stumbling block, according to American officials, is that individuals with ties to terrorist groups are still being granted sanctuary in Syria and that this alone is grounds for keeping Syria on its list of terrorist nations. However, this is a stricter criterion for keeping the country on the State Department's list of state supporters of terrorism than it is for almost any other government. Repeated U.S. offers to drop Syria from the list of terrorist states—which would offer a variety of benefits, including access to certain technology exports—in return for certain political concessions reveal that the United States is primarily concerned with forcing Syria to cooperate with U.S. strategic and economic interests in the region. In short, the terrorism label placed on Syria has remained not on its own merit, but as a wedge through which to apply U.S. diplomatic pressure.[2]

Meanwhile, in a further extension of this dynamic where countries are treated as pariahs or as allies based on their allegiance to U.S. strategic interests, at least one staunch U.S. ally suffers no sanctions despite clear evidence that at least some leading officials in government advance the agenda of terrorists: Saudi Arabia has contributed more funds to extremist

Islamic groups connected with terrorism than has Iran or any of the other so-called "rogue states."[3] As has been noted, fifteen of the nineteen hijackers of September 11 were Saudis, as was Osama bin Laden. Yet there is no talk of routing out terrorists in Saudi Arabia through military force.

During the summer of 2002, news leaks from administration officials, commentary by conservative talk show hosts, a report from the influential RAND Corporation, statements by members of Congress, and a lawsuit from survivors of the attacks on September 11 finally began raising disturbing questions regarding Saudi connections to Al-Qaeda and other Islamic extremists. It also became increasingly common to hear reports about human rights abuses, the poor treatment of women and other formerly rare criticisms of the Saudi regime, long protected by its close relationships with the U.S. government and American corporations. While the Bush Administration remained supportive of the Saudi regime on the record, these criticisms did mark a notable shift in attitudes by certain sectors of elite opinion. What appears to have prompted much of the newfound concern, however, was not an increase in Saudi repression or support for terrorism, but Saudi Arabia's leadership in opposing U.S. plans to invade Iraq and its diplomatic efforts in relation to the Israeli-Palestinian conflict based on the principle of land for peace. In other words, it appears that instead of being an overdue response to Saudi extremism, it was a reaction to Saudi moderation.

There is little debate that the attacks against the United States on September 11, 2001 were acts of terrorism and that the Al-Qaeda network is indeed a terrorist organization. The problem is that the open-ended mandate granted the Bush Administration by Congress to fight terrorism allows President Bush and his successors enormous latitude in interpreting what constitutes a terrorist group. Given that President Bush has declared that any government harboring terrorists will be treated as the terrorists themselves, this broad definition raises the prospect of U.S. military intervention against any number of countries simply because they resist American political demands. Such a possibility was underscored in June 2002 when President Bush announced his willingness to launch pre-emptive strikes against any government that the United States deems even a potential threat.

A telling example of the problems with a military-based response to terrorism involves Libya, the oil-rich North African state ruled for more than three decades by the enigmatic dictator Muammar Qaddafi. Prior to the rise of Al-Qaeda, Libya was considered the primary Middle Eastern target of the United States regarding international terrorism, leading to the U.S. bombing of two Libyan cities in 1986. Earlier that year, citing concerns about terrorism, the United States imposed comprehensive sanctions on Libya, including the freezing of Libyan assets and the banning of all trade and financial dealings with the country. It also forbade Americans, including journalists and academics, from traveling to Libya without permission from the U.S. government. Throughout the 1980s and 1990s, the U.S. government issued a series of reports, widely circulated in the media, designed to discredit and demonize the Libyan government. These included charges of a Libyan hit squad targeting American officials, coup attempts against Qaddafi and the presence of a large underground chemical weapons factory. Subsequent investigations found all of these reports to have been false.

In 1992, two Libyan officials were indicted in the 1988 bombing of an American airliner over Scotland. The British and American governments demanded their extradition. The Libyans, noting the absence of extradition treaties with either government and claiming they would not get a fair trial in these traditionally hostile countries, offered instead either to try them in Libya (as allowed by the 1970 anti-hijacking Montreal Convention); send them to trial in Switzerland or some other neutral country; or have them tried before Scottish judges at the World Court.

The United States and Great Britain initially refused to consider such a compromise and the question went before the International Court of Justice.[4] Rather than waiting for the verdict, however, the United States took the case to the UN Security Council and successfully pushed through two resolutions imposing strict sanctions on Libya. (The World Court ended up acknowledging Libya's right to refuse extradition was indeed safeguarded by international law, but declared that they would not challenge the already-implemented decision of the Security Council on the matter.)

What made the Libyans particularly reluctant to give into these demands initially was the realization that, even if they complied, the United States would oppose the lifting of sanctions, believing that the U.S. government's target was never really the indicted men but the regime itself. While sanctions against Libya have never had the serious humanitarian consequences of the sanctions against Iraq, they did retard the country's economic development and isolated the regime internationally, thereby discouraging liberalizing influences. As with Iraq, the regime's opponents have largely opposed the sanctions on the grounds that they have played into the hands of the Libyan dictator.[5]

A particularly problematic manifestation of U.S. sanctions has been the 1996 D'Amato Act, designed to prevent companies from doing business with governments the United States defines as supporting terrorism. As noted, the motivation for such a designation may be more an effort to exert U.S. pressure on weaker countries than to curb terrorism. The act gives the president the power to "determine" that a person, company or government is in violation of the law. In what many feel is an alarming departure from the concept of checks and balances, the aggrieved party has no recourse to challenge the president's determination in court or through any other means. With such wide latitude of interpretation, a president can impose sanctions or other punitive measures based more on political considerations than any objective criteria. This strengthens the tools by which the United States can force foreign countries to cooperate with its strategic and economic agenda. The law provides for an array of sanctions, including banning the sale of products of culpable foreign firms to the United States.

Even with these pressures on foreign companies, however, other countries are likely to pick up on lost American business. Thus, it has not been these regimes that have been hurt by U.S. policy, but American business— and American credibility. As with similar extraterritorial efforts regarding Cuba and Iran, even the United States' strongest allies have raised vehement objections to the law, noting how it violates the rules of the World Trade Organization regarding non-economic barriers to trade. Ironically, when Middle Eastern states have applied similar secondary boycotts on U.S. firms because they did business in Israel, the United States has been vehement in its opposition.

In 1999, Libya, Great Britain and the United States agreed to have the Libyan suspects tried in the Netherlands before three Scottish judges. When the two Libyan suspects were extradited for trial, United Nations sanctions against Libya were indefinitely suspended. The judges made their ruling in January 2001, convicting one suspect and acquitting the other. It is still unclear whether the destruction of the Pan Am jet was a rogue operation or was ordered by higher-ups, possibly including Qaddafi himself.

Despite efforts by the Libyan government to assist in counter-terrorism efforts in the aftermath of the September 11 attacks, the United States still opposes permanently lifting the UN sanctions and has maintained its own strict unilateral sanctions on Libya. The U.S. also continues to pressure other nations to limit their commercial contacts with the North African country, even though there is little evidence to suggest whether such economic pressure and other moves to isolate Libya actually reduces the threat from terrorism.

U.S. Support for Terrorism

Just what constitutes "terrorism"? The noted linguist and social critic Noam Chomsky likes to quote the famous story told by St. Augustine regarding a notorious pirate who was placed before the emperor following his capture. When the emperor asked him why he engaged in such theft and pillage, the pirate replied that, except for the fact that his actions were on a smaller scale, they were no different than the crimes committed by the empire; they only went by another name. The clear analogy, Chomsky observes, is in regard to U.S. policy towards terrorism in the Middle East and elsewhere. Indeed, the attacks of September 11, 2001 are not unprecedented in terms of scale, but they are in terms of the target—the United States. In effect, as of that September morning, the guns are now turned the other way as well. This is new for Americans. The United States has been responsible for the large-scale killings of civilians in the past, but no Vietnamese or Nicaraguan or any other victim of U.S. policy ever flew planes into American buildings. The United States has bombed twenty-six different countries since the end of World War II, but Americans are not used to being bombed themselves.

The U.S. State Department defines terrorism as "premeditated, politically motivated violence perpetrated against non-combatant targets by subnational groups or clandestine agents, usually intended to influence an audience." [6] When the definition is expanded to include the usually more widespread killings by sanctioned organs of the state against equally innocent people, there is little question that the United States has supported terrorism. In the past, the United States backed military governments in Guatemala, El Salvador, Indonesia, Turkey, Zaire, the Philippines, Brazil, Argentina, South Korea and literally dozens of other countries that practiced state terrorism. Even today, the U.S. continues to support governments that engage in widespread acts of terror against their own populations by their military, intelligence units, or paramilitary forces, such as Colombia, the largest recipient of U.S. military aid after Israel and Egypt. A strong argument could be made that Israel practices a kind of state terrorism in the occupied territories. In addition, the United States has often failed to cooperate with international efforts to prosecute state terrorists when attempts are made to bring them to justice, such as with Chilean General Augusto Pinochet.

More striking is that even by the more restricted use of the term "terrorism," relegating it to exclusively non-state actors, the United States has demonstrated a propensity to ignore its own role in encouraging such political violence.

In recent decades, the U.S. has sponsored terrorist attacks and assassi nations, either directly or through intermediaries, against several countries. In the 1960s, right-wing Cuban exiles were organized by the CIA to con-duct a series of attacks inside Cuba that resulted in widespread civilian casu-alties. During the 1980s, the U.S. government created, financed, armed and trained the Nicaraguan Contras. Based in Honduras and led primarily by officers from the dreaded National Guard of the Somoza dictatorship that had been ousted in a popular revolution in 1979, their cross-border attacks against Nicaraguan villages and cooperatives resulted in more civilian deaths than those killed by Al-Qaeda. With close cooperation with the CIA and American armed forces, the Contra attacks were largely targeted at noncombatants, especially teachers, health care workers, union organizers and suspected supporters of the leftist Sandinista government.

In a statement that horrified many, Libya's Qaddafi referred to radical Palestinians supported by his government who gunned down passengers in the Rome and Vienna airports in December 1985 as "freedom fighters." That same month, and not long after a group of Contras massacred mem-bers of a wedding party in Nicaragua, President Reagan used exactly that same term to describe these U.S.-backed terrorists. By this standard, if Libya's support of Abu Nidal—the Palestinian terrorist group responsible for the airport massacres—really could justify the 1986 U.S. air strikes against Tripoli and Benghazi as the U.S. government claimed, U.S. support of the Contras could have justified Nicaraguan air strikes against Washington and Miami.

It is noteworthy that the most serious single terrorist bombing against a civilian target in Middle East history was the March 1985 blast in a sub-urban Beirut neighborhood that killed 80 people and wounded 200 others. As described in detail by investigative reporter Bob Woodward in his book, Veil, this attack was ordered by CIA director William Casey and approved by President Reagan as part of an unsuccessful effort to assassinate an anti-American Lebanese cleric. The U.S. role in the attack was widely reported throughout the Middle East and elsewhere. The initial report of U.S. involvement made the leading front page headline of the New York Times and other newspapers. Yet this incident is rarely mentioned in discussions on Middle Eastern terrorism in the United States, seemingly erased from public memory.

U.S. double standards extend to the issue of extradition and sanc-tions. For example, the successful U.S. effort to impose UN sanctions against Libya for its initial refusal to extradite two of its agents in the 1988 Lockerbie bombing contrasts with another case of terrorists blowing up a passenger plane: In 1976, right-wing terrorists blew up a Cuban airliner on a regularly scheduled international flight, killing all 73 passengers and crew. Four men, all Cuban exiles who had been trained by the U.S. Central Intelligence Agency and had ongoing associations with CIA covert activities, were indicted in Venezuela for the crime. The mastermind of the bombing, Luis Posada Carriles, had worked for the CIA in the 1960s as a saboteur against a variety of Cuban targets. After his escape from custody in Venezuela, the CIA hired him again to help direct arms shipments for the Nicaraguan Contras from a Salvadoran air base. Like the Libyans, the United States showed its willingness to keep terrorists on the government payroll. And, like the Libyans, the U.S. blocked extradition of its terrorists. This is not the only case of its kind: The United States has refused to extradite John Hull, an American CIA operative indicted in Costa Rica for the 1984 bombing of a press conference in a Nicaraguan border town in which five journalists were killed.[7] Similarly, the United States refuses to extradite Emmanuel Constant, head of the dreaded FRAPH under the Haitian dictatorship in the early 1990s, who had worked closely with U.S. intelligence agencies and who is believed to be responsible for the murder of upwards of 5000 people.[8]

On September 19, 2001, President Bush spoke to the nation and the world, declaring, "From this day forward, any nation that continues to harbor or support terrorism will be regarded by the United States as a hostile regime."[9] But the U.S. position regarding extradition of these alleged terrorists has not changed, which helps explain why so many people outside the United States believe a double standard is at work and that the U.S. government is also complicit in the harboring of terrorists.

Just three days after the September 11 terrorist attacks, the U.S. Senate approved on a voice vote the nomination of John Negroponte as U.S. ambassador to the United Nations. Negroponte was President Reagan's ambassador to Honduras during the 1980s when that Central American country was the primary base for the Contras. He actively supported the Contra terror campaigns across the border in Nicaragua as well as the repression against Honduran dissidents by the U.S.-trained Honduran internal security forces, even to the point of covering up evidence of atrocities from the U.S. Congress.[10] The *Los Angeles Times* called his pro forma hearing before the Senate Foreign Affairs Committee, which allowed no opposition witnesses, as "little more than a sham."[11] At the very time the United States was loudly condemning terrorism to the world, its actions—in choosing this prominent supporter of terrorism to be the U.S. representative to the world body—spoke louder. Similarly, Otto Reich, who has had close ties with both Cuban and Nicaraguan exiles involved in terrorist activities for decades, was named in December 2001 as the new U.S. Assistant Secretary of State for Latin America.

The United States has opposed efforts by the United Nations General Assembly to define terrorism in an apparent fear that such U.S. support for terrorism would become more difficult to deny. The adage "One man's terrorist is another man's freedom fighter" is as true for U.S. foreign policy makers as it is for ideologues of the far left or far right.

The links between the U.S. government and terrorist groups in recent years are better known outside the United States than they are within. Such apparent hypocrisy raises the question as to whether the U.S. is really opposed to terrorism in general or just to terrorism when it targets the United States and its allies. This does not mean that the threat from Al-Qaeda and other terrorists should be dismissed, as some on the left have implied, on the grounds that "we do it too." However, it must be recognized that these kinds of double standards have greatly harmed the ability of the United States to gain as much international support and cooperation in the struggle against terrorism as might otherwise have been possible.

Military Force: The Right Tool to Combat Terrorism?

The United States has long preferred unilateral initiatives for combating terrorism and has often opposed efforts by the United Nations and other international agencies to address the problem. For example, in December 1987, the United Nations General Assembly passed a strongly-worded resolution that "unequivocally condemns, as criminal, all acts, methods and practices of terrorism wherever and by whomever committed" and spelled out specific ways states had to assist each other in preventing terrorism. Concerned at the way some governments have labeled legitimate national liberation struggles as "terrorist" even when their actions were directed solely at armed forces, the General Assembly also said that "nothing in the present resolution could in any way prejudice the right to self-determination, freedom and independence, as derived from the Charter of the United Nations, of peoples forcibly deprived of that right referred to in the Declaration on Principles of International Law concerning Friendly Relations and Co-operation among States in accordance with the Charter of the United Nations, particularly peoples under colonial and racist regimes and foreign occupation or other forms of colonial domination."[12] Angered at the clause regarding the right to self-determination, Israel and the United States voted against the resolution. With the exception of Honduras, which abstained, all the remaining 153 nations voting in favor.

In recent decades, the U.S. response to international terrorism has placed a strong emphasis on military solutions, based primarily on bombing raids by cruise missiles and fighter aircraft against targets in foreign nations. Though such air strikes have played well with the American public because they give the impression that the United States is taking decisive action to strike back at terrorists, there have been times when the U.S. war against terrorism is just another example of foreign policy by catharsis.

One problem with targeting alleged terrorist bases, which are often in close proximity to populated areas, with air strikes is that it risks casualties among innocent civilians. In 1986, for instance, the U.S. bombed two Libyan cities in retaliation for suspected Libyan involvement in a terrorist attack against a Berlin discotheque that killed two American servicemen. More than 60 civilians were killed in the bombing, including Qaddafi's baby daughter. Though the air strikes were very popular in the United States, they were widely condemned in the international community. The high civilian casualties from the attacks and the serious damage caused to the French embassy and other diplomatic facilities provoked outrage throughout the world, bolstering Qaddafi's standing both at home and abroad.

More problematically, rather than stop Libyan-backed terrorism, the Libyans retaliated. In December 1988, Libyan agents blew up Pan Am Flight 103 over the Scottish town of Lockerbie, killing 270 people, 189 of them Americans.

Another problem is that such air strikes can be based on faulty intelligence and thereby result in tragic consequences. For example, in August 1998, the United States bombed the al-Shifa pharmaceutical plant in Sudan, claiming it was a chemical weapons facility controlled by bin Laden. The Clinton Administration subsequently refused to release the "evidence" it claimed to have that prompted these strikes and blocked the United Nations from proceeding with an investigation as requested by the Sudanese government. The plant produced more than half the antibiotics and vaccines in this impoverished African country and left the country with no supplies of choloroquine (the standard treatment for malaria)[13] or of drugs treating tuberculosis.[14] Though there were few casualties from the attack itself—which took place at night in a suburb of the capital Khartoum—the sudden absence of these needed medications created a humanitarian disaster. Germany's ambassador to Sudan, when asked his estimate of the death toll resulting from the U.S. destruction of the Al-Shifa plant, replied "several tens of thousands seems a reasonable guess."[15] In addition, the brutal military dictatorship, closely linked with a hard-line Islamic movement, had been on the verge of collapse and was in negotiations with opposition forces to open up the political process and end its brutal civil war against black Christians and animists in the southern part of the country. According to the British newspaper *The Guardian*, "Then al-Shifa was bombed, and overnight Khartoum was plunged into the nightmare of impotent extremism it had been trying to escape."[16] The anti-American fervor that resulted from the U.S. attack allowed the regime to reconsolidate its hold on power.

Also, angry over the missile attack on the pharmaceutical plant, the Sudanese government released two top Al-Qaeda operatives they had recently arrested and had offered to turn over to the United States along with substantial files of information about the group's operations.[17] According to a CIA analyst, in reference to the September 11 terrorist attacks against the United States three years later, "It is reasonable to say that had we had this data we may have had a better chance of preventing the attacks."[18]

The Clinton Administration quietly paid damages to the Al-Shifa owner, but never publicly apologized for or even acknowledged its mistake. In an interesting irony, the U.S. military commander of the attack against the Al-Shifa pharmaceutical plant was Anthony Zinni, whom President Bush named as his special Middle East envoy in 2001.

Rather than curbing terrorism, such strikes often escalate the cycle of violence as terrorists seek further retaliation. Meanwhile, as a result of the U.S. strategy of military retaliation, Libyans, Iraqis, Sudanese, Palestinians, Afghans, and other peoples victimized by U.S. bombing raids are likely to become more hostile toward the United States—and more sympathetic to the terrorists.

There are serious legal questions regarding such reliance on military responses to terrorism as well. International law prohibits the use of armed force except under narrow circumstances. The United States has claimed that Article 51 of the UN Charter allows such military actions, but Article 51 deals only with self-defense; neither retaliatory strikes nor preemptive strikes are included. Furthermore, the unilateral use of armed force is allowed only in "self-defense if an armed attack occurs...until the Security Council has taken measures necessary to maintain international peace and security."[19] In other words, a military response is legitimate only until the UN Security Council has time to convene to take action in the name of collective security, which is generally only a matter of hours.

The War Against Afghanistan: Dubious Victory

Despite such moral and legal questions and recent examples pointing to the dubious efficacy of responding to terrorism by large-scale military operations, it was immediately clear that the United States would launch a major military operation as the centerpiece of its response to the terrorist attacks of September 11, 2001.

The Bush Administration insisted that it launched its war against Afghanistan only after the Taliban regime had refused to accept non-military means of resolving the conflict, such as through acceding to the U.S. demand that the Taliban hand over bin Laden. Unfortunately, the absence of an International Criminal Court, delayed in large part due to U.S. objections, made it impossible for the Taliban to find a face-saving means of bringing bin Laden to justice without handing him over to a hostile foreign government. Furthermore, the United States refused requests by the Taliban to show them evidence that bin Laden was connected with the terrorist attacks, even though presenting such evidence is normally expected before complying with an extradition request.

In addition, Pakistani and British newspapers reported that in late September and early October, leaders of Pakistan's two Islamic-identified parties negotiated a deal that could have avoided war. According to these reports, the Taliban would extradite bin Laden to Pakistan to face an international tribunal that would then decide whether to try him or hand him over to the United States. However, the U.S. ambassador to Pakistan Wendy Chamberlain pressured that country's military ruler, General Pervez Musharraf, to kill the deal. An American official was later quoted saying that "casting our objective too narrowly" risked "a premature collapse of the international effort if by some luck chance Mr. bin Laden was captured."[20] In short, the United States actually preferred going to war than bringing bin Laden to justice.

Other U.S. demands were even more difficult for the Taliban to accept: the U.S. required the expulsion of all Al-Qaeda fighters, even though most of them had nothing to do with foreign terrorist operations but instead were brought in by bin Laden as a mercenary force that served as the backbone of the Taliban's defense against the Northern Alliance. The additional demand of unfettered U.S. inspections throughout the country was seen as an unreasonable encroachment of Afghan sovereignty.

Furthermore, the Bush Administration failed to take advantage of deep divisions within the Taliban and restive political leaders in the south-eastern part of the country in ways that could have provided a non-military solution to the impasse.

In any case, when the Taliban refused to give into U.S. demands, the United States—with support from Great Britain—began a major bombing campaign against Afghanistan on October 7, four weeks after the attacks against the United States. The physical devastation from twenty years of conflict on what was already one the poorest countries in the world led the United States to make war on what was, in the words of some strategic analysts, "not a target-rich environment."[21] General Richard Myers, chairman of the Joint Chiefs of Staff, acknowledged that by the third day of the air strikes, U.S. planes were returning with the ordinance since they could not find obvious targets. Secretary of Defense Rumsfeld added, to the laughter of assembled journalists, "We're not running out of targets. Afghanistan is."[22]

The U.S. military operation resulted in widespread civilian casualties. During the heaviest phases of the air strikes that fall, American bombs struck a Red Cross food convoy, a military hospital, a boys school, an old age home, several small villages and residential neighborhoods, and twice attacked a Red Cross food distribution center. Amnesty International demanded "an immediate and full investigation into what may have been violations of international and humanitarian law such as direct attacks on civilian objects or indiscriminate attacks" by the U.S. military. [23] A study by Carl Conetta of the Project on Defense Alternatives estimates that, by the end of the year, civilian deaths from the bombing ranged between 1000 and 1300.[24] Another study, by Professor Marc Herold of the University of New Hampshire, estimated that the civilian death toll had risen to above 3700.[25] In addition, conservative estimates are that the U.S. air campaign created more than a half million additional refugees as well as an additional 3200 civilian deaths from starvation, exposure and related illness and injury sustained while trying to flee from the bombing.[26] These civilian deaths are particularly tragic given that the Afghan people were the first and primary victims of the Taliban, perhaps the world's most totalitarian regime during its five years of rule. There is little question that the number of civilian casualties—from both the bombing as well as from the resulting refugee crisis—surpassed the numbers killed in the Pentagon, the World Trade Center and on the four hijacked airliners.

U.S. officials repeatedly denied and covered up credible reports by the international media regarding civilian casualties. In December, reporters from the *New York Times, The Independent,* and other media eyewitnesses on the ground in Afghanistan found evidence of widespread civilian casualties from American bombings in the Tora Bora region. In a Pentagon briefing, Rear Admiral John Stufflebeem responded that such reports were "orchestrated by the Taliban" and that the three villages hit were "legitimate military targets."[27] In other cases, concerns were dismissed on the grounds that civilian casualties were inevitable in a war of this magnitude, ignoring the question as to why the United States did not pursue a more limited military response focussed on those responsible for the September 11 attacks and their cohorts. General Tommy Franks, when confronted by the media regarding a U.S. military operation on January 23, 2002 that killed sixteen Afghan civilians in Hazar Qadam, declared, "I will not characterize it as a failure on any type."[28] A few weeks later, a U.S. commanding officer threatened to kill a *Washington Post* reporter for trying to enter a U.S.-occupied village where three civilians had been killed.[29]

A case can certainly be made that there is a significant difference in moral culpability between terrorists who kill civilians on purpose and military personnel who kill civilians accidentally. However, many Muslims and other observers note that most of the bombing raids took place when there was no serious enemy fire and the Americans had plenty of time and technology to avoid such mistakes.[30] Manslaughter may not be as bad as murder, but it is still a crime. The use of anti-personnel cluster bombs in urban areas and the targeting of the civilian infrastructure—such as the Kajakai dam power station, Kabul's telephone exchange and media centers—is indicative of the low value the United States placed on avoiding civilian casualties. The emphasis on high altitude bombing was less a strategic necessity as it was an effort to avoid casualties among U.S. pilots, an understandable trade-off when facing enemy soldiers but widely seen to be as unethical when the result is increasing the death toll on the civilian population. The high rate of civilian casualties among Afghan civilians seemed particularly unfair to many Muslims and other observers since none of terrorists involved in the hijackings and none of their leaders were Afghans; they were outsiders who had taken advantage of the country's political tragedy that had been rooted in foreign intervention. Similarly, they did not elect the Taliban and had no part in the decision to provide sanctuary for bin Laden and his followers. Whether some Afghans will in turn seek vengeance over the deaths of their civilians at the hands of U.S. forces remains to be seen.

Most estimates of Taliban casualties range from 3,000 to 4,000 fighters killed. The Taliban collapsed only after the U.S. military campaign began to provide direct support for the Northern Alliance and other anti-Taliban Afghan militias. The last urban Taliban holdout of Kandahar surrendered on December 6, and most of the remaining mountain outposts were overrun a few weeks later. However, U.S. bombing raids continued, including an attack on a convoy of tribal elders en route to the newly installed Afghan president's inauguration on December 20. Scores of civilians were killed, including inhabitants of a nearby village.[31] By April 2002, U.S. forces had moved into tribal areas of neighboring Pakistan, attacking the village of Darpa Khel along with Pakistani forces.[32] Periodic bombing raids and small-unit ground operations in eastern Afghanistan continued throughout the spring and summer. In mid-May, American jets killed dozens of villagers at a wedding party in Bul Khil in the Sabri district of Khost Province and a similar attack in early July killed scores more in the Uruzgan province's Dehrawad district; in both cases, the celebratory shooting of guns into the air may have been mistaken for hostile fire.[33]

A war against a terrorist group is not as straightforward as a war against a foreign government, with clear fixed targets such as command and control centers, intelligence headquarters, heavy equipment, major weapons stockpiles, large concentrations of troops or major military complexes. Due to the nature of attacks organized by small groups using clandestine methods, so-called "terrorist bases" generally contain none of these. As a result, such air raids make little sense strategically. A loose network of terrorist cells just does not have the kind of tangible assets that can be seriously crippled by military strikes. As a result, such air campaigns have a mixed success rate at best, particularly in poor rural countries that have few obvious targets to destroy or damage. This is particularly true for Afghanistan, which saw much of its infrastructure already incapacitated by the Soviet invasion and the civil war between the *mujahadin* factions that followed.

Furthermore, while the Taliban regime in Afghanistan gave bin Laden and his supporters sanctuary, this was not a typical case of state-backed terrorism. As a result of bin Laden's personal fortune and Al-Qaeda's elaborate international network, Al-Qaeda did not need and apparently did not receive direct financial or logistical support from the Afghan government. If anything, Al-Qaeda had more influence over the Taliban than the Taliban had over Al-Qaeda. Whether losing most of their sanctuary in Afghanistan will substantially reduce Al-Qaeda's ability to inflict damage remains to be seen. Some analysts speculate that the further decentralization of Al-Qaeda operations resulting from the loss of their base in Afghanistan will make it even harder to track down and eliminate their operatives.

Approximately 600-800 Al-Qaeda fighters were also killed, though only about one-quarter of Al-Qaeda fighters in Afghanistan were believed to be committed members of the organization; most were foreign volunteers—in many cases, mercenaries—brought into Afghanistan by bin Laden to support the Taliban in their civil war. Most Al-Qaeda leaders escaped; indeed, Herold estimates that for every Al-Qaeda leader killed, approximately 130 Afghan civilians were killed. Though Al-Qaeda's ability to engage in global acts of terrorism has undoubtedly suffered, this setback may be temporary since, according to Conetta's report, "Most of the organization's capabilities to conduct far reaching terrorist acts resided and resides outside of Afghanistan, and thus fell beyond the scope of Operation Enduring Freedom." Furthermore,

> The essential importance of Afghanistan to the extra-regional goals and activities of Al-Qaeda was *not* that it provided a sanctuary and training site for terrorists. Instead, Afghanistan served the organization's global activities principally as a *recruiting ground for future cadre*. The capacity of Al-Qaeda to repair its lost capabilities for global terrorism rests on the fact that terrorist attacks like the 11 September crashes do not depend on the possession of massive, open-air training facilities. Warehouses and small *ad hoc* sites will do. Moreover, large terrorist organizations have proved themselves able to operate for very long periods without state sanctuaries—as long as sympathetic communities exist....Thus, Al-Qaeda may be able to recoup its lost capability by adopting a more thoroughly clandestine and "stateless" approach to its operations, including recruitment and training.[34]

Indeed, the key figures in the September 2001 attacks lived in residential neighborhoods in Hamburg, Germany, not in the bombed-out "terrorist bases" in Afghanistan. Similarly, they received more training from flight schools in Florida than from military camps in Afghanistan.

There are no other countries outside the Taliban's Afghanistan that formally grant the Al-Qaeda network sanctuary. But that has not prevented these terrorists from operating. High-altitude bombing—even putting the legal and moral arguments aside—is a very blunt and not particularly effective instrument in the fight against terrorism. Terrorism—even such large-scale atrocities as the September 11, 2001 attacks—should not be seen as acts of war, but as international crimes. The war analogy has serious problems: For one, it elevates the mass murderers who commandeered the airplanes from thugs to warriors. Secondly, it gives license for a crack-down on civil liberties and other individual rights domestically. The biggest problem, however, may be in that the decentralized, clandestine and elu-sive nature of the enemy bears less resemblance to a conventional inter-state war or even a traditional counter-insurgency campaign than it does to the failed "War on Drugs." Like the Colombian drug lords, the chain of command is not formal or hierarchical.

More serious is that the Bush Administration has made clear that the "war on terrorism" goes well beyond the violent cult of Al-Qaeda. This, in turn, leads to the question as to when the United States can ever declare victory, raising the specter of an indefinite militarization of U.S. foreign policy and the resulting negative impact upon civil liberties, immigrant rights, federal budget priorities and other important political concerns. For example, Secretary of State Powell, when asked in a Congressional hearing to define "victory" in the war on terrorism, replied, "it can be identified by reaching a state where people are no longer afraid of terrorist activities, where they can go about their lives not concerned about the kinds of things that happened on the 11th of September or the kinds of car bombings that take place in Jerusalem or the kinds of terrorism that [are] meted out by [left-wing guerrillas] in Colombia." As Powell acknowledged, "It will take us a long time to reach that state."[35]

A more immediate problem is this: Fighting international terrorism requires international cooperation. To track down and break up bin Laden's terrorist cells, which exist well beyond the borders of Afghanistan, the United States needs the active support of Muslim countries. The bombing campaign against Afghanistan damaged the unity needed to deal with the very real threat posed by Al-Qaeda operatives and distracted world atten-tion away from the crimes of September 11 toward questions regarding the appropriateness or inappropriateness of the American attacks. If there was any logic to the terrorists' madness, it was to have the United States over-react and turn large segments of the Islamic world against the West. Launching a major military operation against Afghanistan and threatening to pursue such actions into other countries has enhanced Osama bin Laden's standing among many, which may have been exactly what he had hoped. In the struggle against terrorism, then, the bombing of Afghanistan only marginally improved the military equation but may have significantly set back the far more important political equation.

The image of one of the richest nations in the world bombing one of the world's poorest nations has contributed to the growing anti-American resentment, particularly in the Islamic world, regardless of the nature of the Taliban government or their support for Al-Qaeda. The *New York Times* noted four weeks into the bombing campaign how "Portraits of the United States as a lonely, self-absorbed bully taking out its rage on defenseless Afghanistan are on the rise."[36] After the September 11 attacks, the United States had unprecedented sympathy—and opportunity. It was an opportunity to forge an international coalition of disparate nations in the common determination to fight against such crimes against humanity. As a result of the bombing campaign, however, much of this good will has been lost. Both fairly and unfairly, the United States is being seen as responsible for killing thousands directly through bombing and indirectly risking the lives of millions by exacerbating Afghanistan's humanitarian crisis.

Much of this could have been avoided had the United States found a means of avoiding military action in Afghanistan or if the military response had been limited to special operations and selective air strikes. Indeed, the most urgent actions related to the post-September 11 defense needs were related to Al-Qaeda cells outside of Afghanistan, which would be primarily the responsibility of intelligence and law enforcement agencies. Even if an international consensus had developed to oust the Taliban regime, it would have been far better to have taken the time to lay the groundwork politically for a post-Taliban government and to have had the post-war peacekeeping troops and development aid readied prior to the launch of military action. This was the strategy supported by most American allies, but was opposed by the Bush Administration. As Conetta observed, "The lack of proper political preparation makes it harder to achieve military success and raises its cost."[37] It is probably no accident that there was very little attention to the political side of the equation regarding the future of Afghanistan relative to that of the military side. For example, Afghan scholar Barnet Rubin noted, in reference to the Bush Administration, "They've got one part-time upper-middle-level figure working on the political side, and they've got all of the Joint Chiefs of Staff working on the military side."[38]

The U.S. victory over the Taliban regime was more difficult than some hoped but quicker than others feared. Unlike the Soviets, who faced as many as 100,000 Afghan resistance fighters armed with sophisticated American equipment, the Taliban were a small ragtag group of a few thousand tribesmen. The United States helped install Hamid Karzai, a U.S.-educated former consultant for Unocal, as its new president little more than two months after the start of the bombing campaign and his leadership was ratified by a *loya jirga* (a traditional mass assembly of disparate Afghans) in June 2002. Ridding the world of perhaps the most oppressive and misogynist regime on the planet could be considered a worthwhile result whether or not it enhances the struggle against terrorism. However, questions remain as to whether the regime would have collapsed from within in the ensuing months as some had been predicting, whether the suddenness with which opposition forces came to power will result in a weak government and long-term instability, or whether the devastation from the U.S. assault will create a reaction that will lead to the rise of new extremists in the future.

While many Americans celebrated the country's triumph over a few thousand Pushtun tribesmen in Afghanistan, there are still questions as to whether involvement in such a tribal war has really made the United States more secure. The United States has little to show but the overthrow of the weak and impoverished Taliban regime in Afghanistan and was unable to even capture bin Laden. As one veteran British journalist noted, "There is no victory in Afghanistan's tribal war, only the exchange of one group of killers for another."[39] There have been a number of reports of massacres of Taliban prisoners by Northern Alliance forces, some of which may have taken place with the knowledge of U.S. officials.[40] The U.S. ambivalence towards such atrocities was illustrated by Secretary of Defense Rumsfeld's declared hope, in reference to non-Afghan fighters in Afghanistan, that "they will either be killed or taken prisoner," indicating no preference either way.[41]

Meanwhile, there has been a breakdown of law and order in large parts of the country and war lords have re-emerged to claim their fiefdoms beyond the reach of the central government. There has also been a dramatic growth in opium production in Afghanistan. This is not surprising, since Hazrit Ali and Haji Mohammed Zaman—who led the Afghan ground attack along with U.S. forces against the Al-Qaeda holdout in Tora Bora—are the biggest heroin and opium magnates in the Pushtun areas of Afghanistan. Just ten years ago, Afghanistan had supplied 90% of the heroin entering Europe. When the Taliban came to power, they imposed the greatest curtailment of opium production in a half century. Not surprisingly, as much as 90% of the crop that remained were in areas under control of the Northern Alliance. Even putting aside the impact of increased opium production on addicts worldwide, this resumption of large-scale Afghan opium production is a major threat to Afghanistan's stability since it is one of the major sources of the warlordism that has wreaked such havoc on the region.[42] Interestingly, as the new Afghan government has tried to curb the power of the warlords, the United States has deliberately strengthened their power due to their help in fighting the scattered remnants of the Taliban and Al-Qaeda.

There are international implications of U.S. policy as well. The impulse to go to war following the atrocities of September 2001 obscured the broader repercussions of military actions on regional stability and other important factors. For example, the conflict over Kashmir and in Israel/Palestine increased in part as a result of the war. The Pakistani military regime, under intense American pressure, acquiesced to supporting the U.S. war efforts despite widespread internal opposition, raising questions about the stability of a government that possesses nuclear weapons against challenges by its own radical Islamic groups.

This lack of concern over the broader political question is illustrated in the near-absence of U.S. support for post-Taliban Afghanistan. The United States has refused to provide forces for the European-led United Nations peacekeeping operation, and the U.S. economic assistance in rebuilding the country is only a fraction of what was spent to bomb it. This follows a trend seen in recent years of the United States taking leadership in bombing a country but leaving it to the United Nations to provide the subsequent humanitarian relief and the Europeans to provide post-war security. The hesitancy in getting involved in peacekeeping operations does not indicate an unwillingness to engage in other military operations beyond chasing down Al-Qaeda fighters, however. The U.S. air force has engaged in air strikes against rival forces of the Afghan government that had no affiliation with Al-Qaeda or the Taliban, despite Congress not having authorized the use of military force beyond those responsible for the September 11 attacks or those harboring them.[43]

Military victories can be illusory. The Gulf War was a spectacular victory in narrow military terms, yet that war and the resulting U.S. military role in Saudi Arabia led directly to Osama bin Laden developing his fanatical anti-American ideology. The first U.S. "victory" in Afghanistan in 1992, with the triumph of the U.S.-backed anti-Communist *mujahadin*, was directly responsible for the rise of Al-Qaeda. What this second "victory" in Afghanistan will mean in the long term remains to be seen.

Broader Implications

Despite these important questions regarding the appropriateness of the American military response to the threat from Al-Qaeda, the United States position has remained, in President Bush's words, that "You are either with us or with the terrorists."[44] This has made even the most thoughtful and nuanced critiques of American policy appear to some supporters of U.S. policy as tantamount to defending mass murderers. As a result, at the very time thoughtful questioning of U.S. counter-terrorism policy is most important, it has effectively been banished from mainstream political discourse. This, however, will only make the prospect of further terrorism against the United States more likely.

Another implication of this black and white view of the world is that a country's willingness to support the U.S. war on terrorism will, in the eyes of U.S. policy makers, take priority over concerns about human rights, fighting corruption, protecting the environment, international law or even nuclear non-proliferation. One of President Bush's first acts after September 11 was to waive sanctions imposed on the governments of Pakistan and India in 1998 in response to their nuclear weapons tests. What this means, says Thomas Donilon, former Secretary of State Christopher's chief of staff, is that "the central organizing principle" of U.S. foreign policy "will be the effort against terrorism."[45] Human Rights Watch, in a open letter to Secretary of State Powell, warned how governments could "cynically take advantage of this cause to justify their own internal crackdowns on perceived political opponents, 'separatists' or religious activists, in the expectation that the United State will now be silent." Human Rights Watch also noted how "There already is a sense that the United States may condone action committed in the name of fighting terrorism that would have been condemned just a short time ago."[46] Since September 2001, the United States has silenced its previous opposition to Russian repression in Chechnya and Chinese repression against what the Communist government calls "separatists and terrorists" in Tibet and Xinjiang. The United States has also renewed military support—previously suspended on human rights grounds—to Indonesian forces engaged in serious human rights violations in Aceh and Irian Jaya. As mentioned in earlier chapters, the widespread human rights abuses by Israeli occupation forces have been defended as part of the war against terrorism, not just by the Bush Administration, but by leading Congressional Democrats, including those who had formerly been outspoken defenders of human rights. A subsequent Human Rights Watch report emphasized that the U.S. anti-terrorist campaign "risks reinforcing the logic of terrorism unless human rights are given a far more central role." The report also noted the increased use of double standards by the U.S. government, where "rebel or insurgent attacks on civilians are condemned, but government attacks on civilians...are ignored." Of particular concern was how U.S. support for repressive allies like Egypt and Saudi Arabia leaves their people "with the desperate choice of tolerating the status quo, exile or violence." The result, says Human Rights Watch, is that the failure of the United States to use its leverage against its allies has contributed to the radicalization of the region.[47]

Related to this are U.S. efforts to re-politicize the lending practices of the World Bank, International Monetary Fund and other international financial institutions that—since the end of the Cold War—had been increasingly basing their decisions on exclusively economic criteria.

This comes on the heels of the American abrogation of the Kyoto Protocols on global warming and the 1972 treaty on strategic arms limitation as well as the rejection of the International Criminal Court and other international treaties, such as those banning land mines or the use of child soldiers. With the United States now formally rejecting the requirement under the Geneva Convention that all member states must abide by international treaties they have signed and ratified, the United States is appearing to increasing numbers of people as a kind of rogue superpower. The goal of U.S. policy in the Middle East, acknowledges top Bush Administration officials, is to "shape" the world "to preclude the rise of another global rival for the indefinite future." The only way to proceed in making this possible is through war, since—according to one top Bush advisor—"in that part of the world, nothing matters more than resolute force and will."[48] It is an attitude that more closely resembles Cecil Rhodes and Rudyard Kipling than Woodrow Wilson or John F. Kennedy, a fact not lost to many Muslims whose most paranoid fears of an America determined to effectively run the world appear to be coming true. It is perhaps not surprising, therefore, that the United States is witnessing such an unprecedented backlash.

Chapter Seven

Towards a New Middle East Policy

The United States faces a stark choice between continuing with its strategy of Pax Americana and building real peace and security. The first option requires the continued oppression of large populations, from stateless peoples like the Palestinians, Sahrawis and Kurds; to those victimized by repressive allied regimes, like the Saudis and the Egyptians; to those suffering as a result of American antipathy towards their governments, like the Iraqis and the Iranians. This will continue to breed an inevitable hatred by these peoples against those who they believe are responsible for their suffering. When outlets for redress are systematically sealed off, whether by occupation armies or dictatorial regimes, some portion of the oppressed population will almost certainly respond with terrorism. Acts of terrorism by oppressed Middle Eastern peoples have been going on for years, long before the United States became the target in the attacks of September 2001, striking such countries as Turkey, Lebanon, Israel, Egypt and Algeria, among others. The propensity for targeted populations to engage in acts of terror is particularly high when the oppression they face is itself a form of terrorism, in terms of the large-scale killings of civilians. Americans cannot expect that those on the receiving end of state violence will refrain from treating Americans in a manner similar to how they see themselves as being treated, particularly as the United States, directly or through allied governments, brings destruction to their countries and death to their people.

On the day of the attacks against the World Trade Center and the Pentagon, CNN decided to repeatedly show video clips of a small number of Palestinians celebrating. Though their sentiments represented only a small minority of Palestinians and other Arabs,[1] these West Bank residents were probably not alone in the Third World in feeling a perverse sense of satisfaction: Finally, the United States knows what it is like to lose thousands of civilians in an act of political violence, getting a taste of what it has been like for those who have been the victims of U.S. foreign policy.

For such massive loss of civilian lives is not new to the Palestinians, nor is it to the people of Vietnam, El Salvador, Nicaragua, Angola, East Timor, Iraq or Lebanon, who know the feeling all too well, not in small part due to the policies of the United States. The heart-rending scenes in the days following the tragedy of anguished New Yorkers holding up pictures of their missing loved ones bore a striking resemblance to similar scenes in Latin America during the 1970s and 1980s of the relatives of *los desaparecidos*, the thousands of "disappeared," victims kidnapped and murdered by military regimes backed by the U.S. government.

While the United States has been responsible, both directly and indirectly, for inflicting enormous violence throughout the globe, that can never justify violence against American civilians. The unfortunate reality, however, is that such violence is likely to continue unless there is a change in U.S. policy. In addition to the strong moral imperatives that have led peace and human rights activists to challenge U.S. policy over the decades, there is now the additional incentive of self-interest: bringing about a more enlightened foreign policy is necessary for national security.

The Challenges for Critical Voices in the New Political Environment

For years, there have been calls by peace and human rights activists in the United States for the withdrawal of American troops from the Persian Gulf, a more even-handed policy toward the Israelis and Palestinians, a cessation of support for repressive governments, an end to the punitive sanctions against the people of Iraq and a halt to the massive arms shipments to that already overly-militarized region. If those in power had heeded these demands, it would have likely prevented the rise of anti-American terrorism in the Middle East; thousands of Americans and others killed on September 11, 2001 would still be alive today. It is ironic, then, that the very militarists whose policies led to the current crisis have successfully manipulated the threat that they helped create to their own political advantage while marginalizing the prophetic progressive voices who warned that such consequences might be forthcoming if such misguided policies continued.

Indeed, many Americans concerned about peace and human rights barely had time to grieve the tragedies of September 11 without having to start worrying about the frightening political implications of the government's response. In addition to the threat of war, few doubted that there would soon be assaults on such areas as civil liberties, immigration, funding for social programs, human rights, international law and arms control. This has put many activists on the defensive and has made it difficult to focus on the urgent need to challenge U.S. Middle East policy.

From fiscal policy to civil liberties to trade issues to environmental concerns, the agenda of the political right is being advanced in the name of fighting terrorism. "Anti-terrorism" has become what "anti-Communism" was during the Cold War: the manipulation of an outside threat to pursue a right-wing political agenda, including the suppression of legitimate dissent. Also, as they did during the Cold War, most prominent liberals in Congress and the media have timidly accepted many of the assumptions and policies put forward by right-wing Republicans. This has made thoughtful debate on the policies that contributed to this terrorist threat extremely difficult.

Part of the difficulty in building an anti-war movement has been the nature of the Bush Administration's initial military response. On the one hand, had the U.S. military response been a limited and targeted paramilitary action under international auspices, or even if the bombing raids had been targeted exclusively at Al-Qaeda facilities and nearby anti-aircraft batteries, there would not have been much reason for concern. On the other hand, massive attacks against a series of Middle Eastern and Central Asian countries with the concomitant large-scale civilian casualties would have resulted in such a backlash that the self-defeating nature of the U.S. military response would have been obvious enough to have created a credible anti-war opposition. Instead, the U.S. response has been somewhere between the two: excessive enough to raise serious moral, legal and political objections, but limited enough so that the immediate negative consequences are not readily apparent to most Americans. Indeed, despite the failure to capture Osama bin Laden and destroy the Al-Qaeda network, U.S. military operations have at least partially, if perhaps only temporarily, crippled the operations of the terrorist group and succeeded in overthrowing a brutal totalitarian regime. While the U.S. military operations were not as quick or successful as many in the Bush Administration had hoped, dire predictions from the left that the United States would be dragged into a quagmire comparable to the Soviet experience of the 1980s also proved to be incorrect.

A good case can be made for some form of targeted military action in the face of the threat of terrorism on the magnitude represented by Al-Qaeda. Similarly, at least some aspects of the utilization of such force in the fall of 2001 had some initial positive results. Unfortunately, however, this view only feeds the militarization of U.S. foreign policy that has played such a major role in creating the anti-American backlash so frighteningly manifested in the Al-Qaeda movement and other extremist activities.

So, there are some unprecedented challenges facing critics of U.S. foreign policy. For more than half a century, opponents of U.S. military intervention abroad could challenge the fabricated and exaggerated threats to national security put forward by the U.S. government, academia and the media to justify war and repression. Now, however, for the first time in the lives of most Americans, the United States has found itself under attack and even traditional critics of U.S. foreign policy must acknowledge that a very real threat exists.

Despite this, there is a significant minority of Americans who seriously question the wisdom of the U.S. military response. Some of these dissidents come from the pacifist tradition, who take a principled position in support of nonviolent alternatives, believing that violence necessarily begets only more violence. Other opponents come from the far left, arguing that the nature of the United States' role in the world, and the powerful special interests that possess such an inordinate amount of influence on policy making, result in any such military intervention being inherently imperialistic. Some opponents are from the libertarian tradition, believing that military action should be restricted to the most narrow requirements of national self-defense and fear that there may be a self-defeating overreach in American military power. Still others emphasize utilitarian arguments against the use of large-scale bombing and other blunt instruments of military force where more targeted police or commando operations might be more appropriate. The problem is that, however valid such principled or pragmatic objections to excessive military force may be, the current political climate makes such critics appear to many to be naively acquiescing to dangerous forces that have demonstrated both the willingness and ability to do enormous harm to many thousands of innocent Americans.

Perhaps the strongest case that critics have is that current policy undermines national security. Fundamentally, a U.S. Middle East policy based more on the promotion of human rights, international law and sustainable development and less on arms transfers, air strikes, punitive sanctions, and support for occupation armies and dictatorial governments, would make Americans a lot safer. For the United States does not become a target for terrorists because of its values, as President Bush and others claim, but when it strays from its values.[2]

Challenging U.S. Counter-terrorism Strategies

Perhaps the greatest contribution responsible voices of dissent can make to the current situation in the short to medium-term is exposing how there are powerful elements in the Bush Administration that are using the crisis to advance their right-wing ideological agenda. For example, a series of threats have been issued by the Bush Administration to extend the war to Iraq, Somalia, Yemen, and elsewhere, in an apparent desire to use counter-terrorism as an excuse to punish regimes they don't like and to extend American military power. These threats come despite the fact that no other country besides Taliban-ruled Afghanistan has been shown to have harbored or given any other kind of direct support to Al-Qaeda. Such attacks on other countries would create a massive anti-American backlash in the region, jeopardizing important counter-terrorism efforts that require the support of other nations. Those opposing further large-scale American military interventions must emphasize that the struggle against terrorism is too important to be sabotaged by ideologues wishing to settle old scores.

Another example of how the crisis is being misused that is vital to address is the dubious justifications by the Bush Administration, with support from leading Congressional Democrats, for enormous increases in military spending. The claim is that the nearly $50 billion annual increase in military spending, already set at over $400 billion, is necessary to fund the war on terrorism. However, the vast majority of the proposed spending is for weapons systems and other expenditures that have nothing to do with counter-terrorism; indeed, many were originally designed to counter Soviet weapons that no longer exist or are being dismantled. Similarly, if the terrorist attacks of September 2001 proved anything, it is the folly of the assertion that a nuclear missile defense system can protect the American people from outside attack.

At a time of national crisis where a singularity of purpose is required, the two major parties are taking advantage of the American people and their tax dollars to subsidize the arms industry. The use of missiles, bombers and other heavy high-tech equipment may have been partially successful in Afghanistan, where there were some tangible, if limited, targets in the form of training camps for Al-Qaeda and military installations belonging to the allied Taliban regime. However, such weapons will be of little use against the majority of Al-Qaeda that remains intact as a network of decentralized underground cells. Meanwhile, this dramatic increase in military spending will take money away from valuable domestic programs supporting health care, education, housing, public transportation, environmental cleanup and other needs, as well as balloon the national debt and the costs of borrowing money for deficit spending. As a result of this first round of increases, the military budget now accounts for over half of all discretionary spending (money that Congress allocates each year.) Though two oceans and two weak friendly neighbors flank the United States, U.S. military budget consists of more than half of the estimated military spending for the entire world put together.

The threat of terrorism is real and requires a strong and effective response from the U.S. government. Yet, at the same time, there is a growing sense that the Bush Administration is cynically manipulating the country's genuine need for security for the sake of its rigid ideological constructs and its wealthy financial supporters. If this is indeed the case, it needs to be exposed and challenged.

Although there is no foolproof set of policies that will protect the United States and its interests from terrorists, there are a number of policy shifts that would likely reduce the frequency and severity of terrorist strikes.

Given that terrorism is an international problem, it needs international solutions. This means vigorously and collaboratively pursuing diplomatic, investigative and international police channels to identify, track down, arrest, and bring to justice members of terrorist cells responsible for these crimes. Precipitous and inappropriate military action could make many nations—particularly in the Middle East—whose support is needed to track down terrorists hiding within their borders, reluctant to cooperate in anti-terrorism efforts. Limiting military actions against suspected terrorists to small commando units, Special Forces and SWAT team-style operations could bring those responsible to justice and break up the terrorist cells that could commit attacks in the future, yet not result in the kind of backlash a more blunt use of force would create. This would be even more effective if done in cooperation with the United Nations and other international organizations, such as Interpol. The use of a multinational force, governed by international law, would come across as a just international effort in the global fight against terrorism. By contrast, further air strikes and other unilateral military actions by the United States that sacrifice civilian lives is certain to be portrayed by the extremists as a manifestation of American imperialism.

The United States should support international conventions and institutions that can track down and punish terrorists and prevent future terrorism, including the International Criminal Court, tighter controls to track money laundering, and curbing the small arms trade. In addition, the

United States must work with other nations to support treaties to curb chemical, biological and nuclear weapons and materials, including preventing their falling into the hands of terrorist networks or states that harbor these networks.

All terrorism is wrong, but since terrorism takes place in many forms, a more flexible response is needed. The United States must distinguish fringe groups whose primary function is inflicting violence against innocent people—such as bin Laden's Al-Qaeda network—and popular, multifaceted organizations that may also contain a terrorist component, such as Hamas. In the latter case, in addition to necessary security measures to prevent further attacks, a broader and more nuanced strategy is necessary. In the former case, more aggressive measures may be appropriate. Similarly, a careful distinction must be made between state-sponsored terrorist groups, groups that receive sanctuary without direct state support and those which operate independently underground. Each requires a different strategy.

Another policy shift must be for the United States to stop supporting irregular groups that may be prone to terrorism. Many of the most notorious terrorists in the world today originally received their training from the CIA as part of U.S. efforts to undermine leftist governments in Cuba, Nicaragua, Angola and Afghanistan. There must also be an end to any involvement by any branch of the military, intelligence agencies, or any other part of the U.S. government in acts of terrorism.

The United States is good at dropping bombs, firing missiles, and other displays of military force. However, even Bush Administration officials acknowledge that the most important aspects of the campaign against terrorism are non-military, including good intelligence, interdiction and the disruption of the financial networks that support terrorists. All of these require cooperation with other nations.

If there is evidence that terrorists are receiving support from any foreign government, the United States should take the case to the United Nations Security Council for appropriate action. The UN has been largely supportive of such requests in the past, passing U.S.-sponsored resolutions during the 1990s targeting Libya, Sudan and Afghanistan in response to these countries' role in harboring terrorists.

As has been noted by many analysts—particularly with the series of revelations in May and June 2002 about blunders by the FBI—the attacks of September 11, 2001 represent a massive U.S. intelligence failure. There needs to be thorough and independent investigations into why the CIA and FBI failed to better detect these terrorist networks, including their operations inside the United States, certainly before pouring massive amounts of money into these very agencies that failed so markedly.

Yet while tightening up cooperation between agencies and implementing some new security measures are necessary, the American public should not be lulled into thinking that improvements in intelligence alone can prevent terrorism. Any competent terrorist knows you have to keep plans secret. Terrorist groups have demonstrated their ability to do so throughout history, regardless of improvements in intelligence gathering techniques aided by new technologies so often touted by politicians as the solution.

There is a dangerous level of denial at the highest levels of government in assuming that terrorism is simply a military or law enforcement problem. A 2001 United Nations report on terrorism emphasized the need to focus on the underlying causes of terrorism, declaring that "were all states to do this in an unbiased way...the incidence of terrorist acts would dramatically decline."[3] The only real method of minimizing the possible recurrence of tragedies on the magnitude of those of September 11, 2001— or a series of smaller attacks that could be just as devastating in the long term—is to address these underlying causes.

Addressing the Root Causes of Terrorism

Arab nationalism, Marxism, and other ideologies that have come to the fore in recent decades have failed to free Islamic countries from unjust political, social and economic systems or from domination by Western powers. In many respects, political Islam has filled the resulting vacuum. The embrace of reprehensible tactics and ideologies by some radical Islamic movements does not negate the validity of some of the popular concerns that have given rise to such movements. One need not justify the reasons to understand them, yet these are concerns that the United States ignores at its own peril.

"The Arabs," observed Marine General Anthony Zinni, former head of the U.S. Central Command, "are a people obsessed with injustice."[4] Only by addressing the legitimate grievances will there be any hope of stopping the often-illegitimate methods and extremist ideologies of anti-American Islamic groups. Otherwise, the United States may find itself dealing with a series of conflicts that could eclipse the bloody surrogate Cold War battles that ravaged the Third World in previous decades.

From Afghanistan to Algeria and beyond, out of great social dislocation caused by war and misguided economic policies, radical Islamic move-

ments have grown to prominence. Policies designed to minimize such traumatic dislocation will be far more successful than military threats if the goal
is to encourage political moderation in Islamic countries. To effectively
challenge the threat from radical Islamic movements, the United States
must shift its focus from simply trying to crush such movements to pursuing policies that discourage their emergence.

Simply addressing the security aspects of terrorism, then, as U.S. policy currently does, confronts the symptoms rather than the cause. The struggle against terrorism cannot be won until the United States also ceases its
pursuit of policies that have alienated such large segments of the international community, particularly in the Middle East and elsewhere in the
Third World. The United States is a target of terrorists in large part due to
its perceived arrogance, hypocrisy, and greed. Becoming a more responsible
member of the international community will go a long way toward making
the United States safer and ultimately stronger. George Semaan, editor of
the London-based Arabic publication *Al Hayatt*, observed that the United
States cannot root out terrorism "unless it changes its attitude as to how to
develop and defend its interests by building a network of relations based on
respect of the interests of others, particularly the weak and those whose
rights have been denied."[5] The tactics of terrorists can never be justified,
whatever their grievances. Yet it is crucial to recognize that the most effective weapon in the war against terrorism would be to take measures that
would lessen the likelihood for the United States and its citizens to become
targets. This means changing policies that victimize vulnerable populations
in ways that currently result in them holding the United States responsible
for their suffering and thus becoming easy recruits for anti-American terrorists. For example, bin Laden's key grievances—U.S. support for the Israeli
occupation, the ongoing U.S. military presence on the Arabian peninsula,
the humanitarian consequences of the sanctions against Iraq, and support
for corrupt Arab dictatorships—have resonance among the majority of the
world's Muslims. Very few Muslims support terrorism of any kind, yet as long
as there is such widespread hostility to U.S. Middle East policy, it will not
be difficult for terrorists to find willing recruits.

Changing U.S. policy will not satisfy bin Laden and other extremists,
nor should it. The United States should never change any policy for the sake
of appeasing terrorists. However, changing policies that are already questionable on moral or legal grounds becomes all the more crucial when doing so
could also reduce the threat from terrorism, since it will substantially reduce
their potential following and—by extension—their ability to do damage.

The popularity of the United States in the Middle East is directly related to the perceived fairness of its policies towards the region. Support for the United States was highest in late 1956 when the Eisenhower Administration forced Israel, Great Britain, and France to halt their invasion of Egypt. Though ultimately motivated by fear of a pro-Soviet backlash in the Arab world if the United States did otherwise, this seemingly principled stand in support of international law and the right of self-determination against the wishes of America's closest allies won the United States enormous respect throughout the region. However, in more recent years, as the United States has tried to enforce its will on the region through militarization and support for what is widely perceived as repression and injustice, support for the United States has declined dramatically. This trust can be restored, but only if the United States shifts its policies to become more consistent with support for human rights, international law, sustainable economic development and demilitarization.

During World War II, President Franklin Roosevelt told the American public that any attempt by the United States to impose a peace "would bring no security for us or for our neighbors. Those who would give up essential liberty to purchase a little temporary safety deserve neither liberty nor safety."[6] The current idea that the United States must show its enemies who is more powerful will simply not work, since they know that already and they have planned their attacks accordingly. As Michael Klare observed, terrorists rationalize their actions because they see themselves as "strong and resolute in spirit but weak in military power against those who are weak or corrupt in spirit but strong in military power."[7] Instead of demonstrating that the United States is militarily stronger—which they already know—a more effective policy would be to show that America's values are better.

No extremist Islamic movement of major political consequence has ever evolved in a democratic society. By giving Islamic parties a stake in the political process, they would not be forced underground and thereby be tempted to support violent strategies to force political change. Supporting democracy would therefore be a major step in the direction of moderating political Islam. Anti-American sentiment is not inherent within Arab or Islamic culture. Indeed, there is much about the United States that is greatly respected in that part of the world. Rather than disdaining American democracy, most Arabs and Muslims envy it and wish the United States would stop supporting governments that deny them such freedoms. While the United States should not try to impose American-style democracy in the Middle East, the U.S. can at least stop supporting repressive regimes so the people of the region can have a chance to bring about more open and pluralistic societies based upon their own traditions and preferences. The United States must resist the temptation to consider all Islamic movements to be the enemy and put more emphasis on encouraging progressive Islamic movements by working for democracy, justice and economic equality.

The United States should support efforts to make the entire region free of weapons of mass destruction as called for by the United Nations, not just single out Iraq and Iran. This would require that the United States no longer bring nuclear weapons into the region on U.S. planes and ships and formally renounce the first use of any part of the U.S. nuclear arsenal. It may also require that the United States apply the necessary economic and diplomatic pressure to insure that all countries in the region—including U.S. allies like Israel—have dismantled their nuclear, chemical, and biological weapons and that credible international monitoring systems be established throughout the Middle East to insure that no country develops such weapons in the future. A more holistic program of non-proliferation might also include, for example, a five-year program where not just Iraqi missiles, but Syrian, Israeli and other missiles would also be phased out. UN Security Council resolution 687, which the U.S. claims to be enforcing through its sanctions and bombing of Iraq, calls not just for the dismantling of Iraq's WMD capability, but for "establishing in the Middle East a zone free from weapons of mass destruction and all missiles for their delivery...." Currently, as with its highly selective enforcement of other UN Security Council resolutions, the double standards in U.S. policy make even the most legitimate concerns, such as those regarding Iraqi WMD development, virtually impossible to pursue with any credibility.

All future arms transfers must be made conditional on a government's respect for internationally recognized human rights, political pluralism, compliance with United Nations Security Council resolutions and withdrawal from occupied territories outside their internationally-recognized borders. The United States should assist in the creation of a broader security regime for the entire region comparable to the Organization for Security and Cooperation in Europe. Jordan and some other Middle Eastern states have already proposed such a regime.[8] Foreign aid should be directed toward poorer countries and in support of grassroots development initiatives and away from support for the wealthier countries and/or corrupt and autocratic governments. The current emphasis on military aid must be replaced by appropriate and targeted development aid.

The current neo-liberal economic orthodoxy pushed by the United States through such international financial institutions as the International Monetary Fund and World Trade Organization exacerbates social divisions, resulting in great resentment among the poor at its perceived injustice. Instead, the United States must support sustainable economic development, so that the benefits of foreign investment, the market and globalization can be more fairly distributed with minimal social disruption. Stability requires economic policies that are more broad-based and sustainable, both in terms of the environment as well as in creating greater social equality from which the largest number can benefit from economic growth.

The United States should lessen its dependence on Middle Eastern sources of oil through conservation and conversion to safe, renewable forms of energy. This could be done at just a fraction of the costs it takes to maintain the large U.S. military presence in the Gulf designed to protect oil supplies. For example, had the Reagan Administration not eliminated automobile fuel efficiency standards scheduled to have gone into effect in 1989, it would have made up for all the U.S. oil imported at the time of the Gulf War from Iraq, Kuwait and Saudi Arabia combined.

There are other areas where the United States could also improve its popular standing in the Middle East as well as its moral standing overall. These would include better regulation of the exploitative practices by American oil companies and other multinational corporations, ceasing its highly prejudicial use of the UN Security Council, abiding by basic principles of international law, and finding non-military solutions to disputes with Middle Eastern countries.

In addition to these general principles, the United States can address some of the specific crisis areas in more beneficial ways as well.

U.S. Policy Towards the Gulf

On an international level, the United States must reverse its unilateralism and coordinate policy with the Europeans and others who share U.S. concerns. Enforcing already-existing safeguards against nuclear proliferation would be one particularly important area for such efforts. The United States must also seriously consider the perspectives of the democratic opposition in Iran and Iraq. Though the opposition in these countries is somewhat divided, most—while supporting the arms embargo and opposing direct support for their governments—strenuously object to the U.S.-led economic embargoes.

Regarding Iran, which is currently far more pluralistic than Iraq, supporting efforts at liberalizing the regime rather than overthrowing it entirely would be a more realistic, legal, and moral option, as well as one more likely to restore American credibility. Iran—due to its geography, the role of Shia Islam, and its close cultural and religious links to neighboring states—will continue to play an important and unique role in the politics of the region based on its own perceived self-interests. Despite persistent efforts to isolate the country, the United States cannot change that reality. It is important that the United States find a way to encourage Iran to become a more responsible member of the community of nations and to persuade it to end its internal repression of legitimate dissent. This will require, however, that the United States reevaluate its policies toward Iran and toward the region as a whole. Given the lack of credibility the United States has in the eyes of Iranians from across the political spectrum, the best the United States can reasonably do at this point is to avoid policies that might encourage more hard-line elements and retard current trends towards liberalization.

Regarding Iraq, the Bush Administration must halt its threat to invade the country. Furthermore, the ongoing U.S. air strikes against Iraq are illegal and counter-productive and must end. The United States should continue supporting the arms embargo but should respect calls from a growing number of countries in the Middle East and around the world, from France to Saudi Arabia, for a lifting of the economic sanctions that have brought so much suffering to Iraqi civilians.

The first step should be an American promise to lift the economic sanctions once the UN Secretary General recognizes that the Iraqi government is in effective compliance with Security Council resolutions. For sanctions to work, there must not just be pain inflicted but an offer to relieve the pain if policies change, that is, a carrot as well as a stick. In consultation with other members of the Security Council, the United States needs to be specific about what positive responses could be expected for what specific improvements in behavior. In addition, the United States must pledge to enforce other outstanding UN Security Council resolutions, and not simply single out Iraq. As long as the United States allows allied regimes like Turkey, Morocco and Israel to flaunt UN Security Council resolutions, any sanctimonious calls for strict compliance by the Iraqi government will be dismissed as hypocritical and ideologically-driven, whatever the merit of the actual complaints.

There is nothing inherently wrong with the United States or other countries supporting democratic opposition movements against autocratic regimes. Unfortunately, the United States has so thoroughly damaged its credibility that there is little good that could be done in actively supporting an Iraqi opposition without discrediting it in the eyes of most Iraqis, even those who oppose Saddam Hussein. In particular, support for any kind of military resistance would not only be futile, but would give the regime an excuse to crack down even harder against the country's already-suffering people. The lifting of economic sanctions and an end to the bombing would probably create the space for some kind of organized opposition to emerge. However, to be successful, it must be seen as a genuinely indigenous struggle, not the creation of yet another ill-fated intervention by a Western power. Furthermore, the United States must support democratization and human rights throughout the Gulf and beyond, not just in countries the United States regards as hostile. As long as the United States does not encourage greater freedom in countries it considers its allies, such as Saudi Arabia, the U.S. cannot effectively encourage greater freedom in states it regards as its enemies.

The United States should support the creation of a regional security regime in the Gulf that would lead to arms control and confidence-building measures that would bring real security to this strategically important region. As a first step, the United States needs to withdraw from its bases in Saudi Arabia and elsewhere in the Gulf. There is no military justification at this point for such a permanent military presence on the ground, particularly when it has proven to be so unnecessarily provocative.

U.S. Policy Towards Israel and Palestine

Peace between Israelis and Palestinians is possible because Israeli security and Palestinian rights are not mutually exclusive, but mutually dependent on the other. Israel will not be secure until the Palestinians are granted their legitimate rights and the Palestinians will not be granted their rights until Israel's legitimate security needs are recognized. An unsustainable peace agreement, like the United States was pushing in 2000, would be worse than no peace agreement at all. The U.S. government should support the Palestinians' right to a viable independent state alongside Israel while maintaining its moral and strategic commitment to the Jewish state to ensure its survival and legitimate strategic interests, including the defense of its internationally recognized borders. At the same time, however, the United States must also be willing to apply pressure—such as withholding military and economic aid—should the Israeli government refuse to make the necessary compromises for peace. This includes withdrawal from the occupied territories, the removal of its colonists from the illegal settlements in the occupied territories and recognizing—at least symbolically—the right of return for Palestinian refugees.

This includes an Israeli withdrawal from East Jerusalem, a major point of contention in the Islamic world. Both Congress and the executive branch should rescind resolutions and past statements that imply support for Israel's unilateral annexation of the occupied eastern part of the city and surrounding Palestinian lands. The United States must instead recognize the city's importance to all three monotheistic faiths—Judaism, Christianity and Islam—and support a shared Jerusalem that would serve as the capital of both Israel and Palestine, guaranteeing free access to holy places for all faiths. Such a policy shift would also have significantly positive security implications: it would remove a highly emotional and volatile issue from the arsenal of Islamic extremists, who exploit the widespread anger about U.S. support for the illegal Israeli occupation of a city that Muslims also see as holy.

Unlike some periods in Israel's past, the country's survival is no longer at stake. The Israeli military is far more powerful than any combination of Arab armies. Despite the threat and reality of suicide bombings, most Israelis are relatively secure within their country's internationally recognized borders. Where Israeli soldiers and civilians are most vulnerable is in the occupied Palestinian territories seized by Israel in the 1967 War. It is here, not within Israel itself, that Palestinian rioters and guerrillas allied with the Palestinian Authority have primarily targeted Israelis. Settlements and roads in these areas—reserved for Jews only—not only create an apartheid-like situation, but also make it extremely difficult for Israeli forces to defend against a hostile population angry that foreign occupiers have confiscated what is often their best land. Israel would be far more secure defending a clearly defined and internationally recognized border than a network of illegal outposts within Palestinian territory. If the United States is really concerned about the security of Israeli soldiers and settlers, the administration must insist that they return to Israel, behind their country's internationally recognized-borders, where they would be a lot safer. Only when the occupation ends will the threat from Palestinian terrorism finally have a realistic chance of being controlled.

The way to peace, then, is rather straightforward: Israel would repatriate its settlers and withdraw its occupation troops from lands seized in the 1967 War in return for security guarantees from the Palestinian

Authority and the right of access to Jewish holy places. Palestinian leader Yasir Arafat has already offered just such a deal in peace talks in early 2001. Furthermore, Israel has no choice if it is to obey international law and UN Security Council resolutions. The United States must support just such a peace settlement. It is unreasonable to demand that the Palestinians give up any more of the remaining 22% of Palestine outside of Israel's internationally recognized borders.

Regarding refugees, the United States should support the compromise similar to that proposed at the January 2001 talks in Taba, whereby Israel would formally recognize the Palestinian "right" to return, but provide financial incentives—and, if necessary, quotas—to insure that the vast majority move into territory of the new Palestinian state.

The United States should suspend arms shipments to Israel until it ends its ongoing violations of UN Security Council resolutions and internationally recognized human rights. This should be part of a comprehensive arms control process in the Middle East that would also require the suspension of military aid to any other country in the region that engages in similar violations.

No lasting peace settlement can be achieved until the fighting stops. The United States must cease its opposition to the deployment of an international peacekeeping force to separate the sides and of an impartial international commission to investigate the causes of the violence. The Palestinian Authority has already called for just such actions, even to the extent of supporting a state-building exercise comparable to the United Nations role in East Timor.[9] The U.S. government has traditionally opposed such a deployment and has blocked it with the power of its veto in the UN Security Council on the grounds that it is unacceptable to Israel. However, since the land in question is occupied territory, not legally part of Israel itself, Israel's permission is not required. With United Nations forces in charge, the Israeli-imposed curfews, closures, internal checkpoints and other hated aspects of the occupation would disappear, substantially reducing the possibility of Palestinian violence. These peacekeepers could also force the evacuation of some of the more hardcore Israeli colonists out of the illegal settlements, a likely necessary step that might be politically difficult if attempted by Israeli soldiers.

By contrast, troops sent in just to oversee a cease-fire between Israelis and Palestinians in the occupied territories with the Israeli occupation essentially intact and with little clear prospect of ending, would likely end up finding themselves as targets, as were the UN observers during Israel's

22-year occupation of southern Lebanon.

Ultimately, only when Israel sees its future with the Third World—made necessary by its geography, its Semitic language and culture, its large Sephardic population, and the Jews' history of exploitation by the Europeans—will Israel end its isolation and find the real security that it has been missing. Many of the so-called "supporters of Israel" in American politics are actually making Israel vulnerable by tying its future to the increasingly unpopular U.S. military role in the Middle East and preventing Israel from recognizing its natural alliance with the world's Afro-Asian majority. The combination of Israeli technology, Palestinian entrepreneurship and industriousness, and Arabian oil wealth could result in an economic, political, and social transformation of the Middle East. This would be highly beneficial to the region's inhabitants, but not necessarily to those in the U.S. government and its allied corporate interests that profit enormously from the continued divisions between these Semitic peoples. Israel's economic and military security ultimately will come not from the amount of territory it controls and colonizes nor from the amount of economic and military aid it receives from the United States, but from its willingness to make peace with its neighbors, particularly the Palestinians.

If the United States really wants to be a friend of Israel, the U.S. government must apply some "tough love." This would entail unconditional support for Israel's right to exist in peace and security, but with an insistence that Israel uphold its international obligations and withdraw its settlers and troops from the occupied territories. Only then will the violence end and peace become a reality. Some Israeli peace activists use the analogy of watching a drunkard stumble from the bar towards his automobile with the keys in his hand. They argue that a true friend does not stand by, but forcefully intervenes to stop the irresponsible behavior and make sure that the driver neither hurts himself nor anyone else. (This analogy would perhaps be more accurate if it depicted the current U.S. role as the bartender, irresponsibly pouring the alcohol with the full knowledge of the drunkard's intention to drive.)

The fate of the peace process may hinge upon whether a popular movement can emerge that will force the U.S. government to end its policy of providing Israel with the means to continue its destructive and ultimately self-destructive policies. Only if such a movement is successful will the United States be able to take on the mantle of a responsible mediator.

Changing U.S. Foreign Policy

It will be hard to change the policies of the current administration as long as the majority of even such liberal Capitol Hill bastions as the Progressive Caucus and the Human Rights Caucus support the status quo, as is currently the case. A widespread assumption is that the key to changing U.S. government policies is to replace these and other politicians by electing those interested in change. Supporting candidates with more enlightened views towards the U.S. role in the world certainly has its merits. The Green Party—that has a strong platform in support of peace and human rights in the Middle East—has been attracting large numbers of disaffected Democrats upset at their party's right-wing stance. Yet not only is the record of third parties mixed in terms of changing policies, but history has shown that it is ultimately less important whom the American electorate chooses as its political leaders as it is the choices that a well-mobilized citizenry give them once in office.

For example, the history of U.S. foreign policy in recent decades has been shaped markedly as a result of popular demands by large numbers of people putting pressure on elected officials through Congressional lobbying, legal protests, civil disobedience, and public education campaigns. For example, the Democratic Party in 1968 had a platform supporting the Vietnam War with the incumbent Vice-President Hubert Humphrey, a strong proponent of the war, as its nominee. By the next presidential election in 1972, the Democratic Party had a strong anti-war platform and an outspoken anti-war nominee in Senator George McGovern, which helped force the Nixon Administration to sign a peace treaty by January of the following year. There was much more than organizing people to vote responsible for this change. The four years in between saw massive anti-war mobilizations with hundreds of thousands of people protesting in Washington, DC and elsewhere, as well as large-scale civil disobedience campaigns, widespread draft resistance, and other forms of opposition.

There are many other examples: In 1980, Vice-President Walter Mondale and others in the Carter Administration strongly opposed the call for a freeze in the research, testing, and development of new nuclear weapons and delivery systems. By the time he ran for president in 1984, however, Mondale was an outspoken supporter of the proposed nuclear freeze. In the intervening four years, the Nuclear Freeze Campaign and disarmament activists had mobilized grassroots initiatives across the country, including the massive 1982 protest in New York City. Major arms control treaties were signed in the ensuing years.

In 1977, Andrew Young—the African-American clergyman and former aide to Martin Luther King who then served as President Carter's ambassador to the United Nations—vetoed a UN Security Council resolution calling for sanctions against South Africa. By 1986, the Republican-dominated Senate joined the Democratic-led House of Representatives in overriding a presidential veto to impose sanctions against the apartheid regime. This dramatic shift came as a result of the divestment campaigns and other actions of the anti-apartheid movement that sprung up on college campuses and elsewhere throughout the country. The imposition of sanctions proved to be instrumental in the downfall of white minority rule.

In the 1980s, massive protests against the U.S. military role in Central America forced the United States to accept the Arias peace plan, which brought an end to the bloody civil wars and resulted in the establishment of democratic governance in a region then dominated by repressive military-led regimes.

In the 1990s, a popular movement supporting self-determination for East Timor forced a reluctant Clinton Administration to cut off military aid to Indonesia, which in turn led to the withdrawal of Indonesian occupation forces and eventual independence.

The key to changing U.S. Middle East policy, then, is in building a popular movement comparable to these successful precedents. So far, the movement has been relatively small compared to these others. Given what is at stake, this is particularly tragic.

As with other movements, there are elements of the far left and others that sometimes fall into rigid ideological models based upon little empirical information about the conflict in question, often greatly simplifying complex historical dynamics and sometimes even buying into bizarre conspiracy theories. In addition, certain elements from the far right can infect movements critical of U.S. policy regarding Israel with anti-Semitic ideas. However, the biggest problem has been the timidity of the peace and human rights community to become more involved. For example, it is very unlikely that the scores of liberal members of Congress who support the bombing of Iraq or military aid to Israeli occupation forces would continue to do so if faced with the kind of mobilization that took place opposing U.S. policy in Central America.

Public opinion polls indicating popular support for President Bush's Middle East policy does not mean that most Americans actually support the policy. It merely means that they support what the policy is presented as being. Most Americans actually believe their government's rhetoric that the United States supports democracy, international law, demilitarization, economic development, and Israeli-Palestinian peace and that U.S. military involvement is focussed solely upon defending the United States. One of the first challenges for those wishing to change U.S. policy, then, is to expose the real nature of that policy. Once that is revealed, support for a new foreign policy can be mobilized into the kind of popular movement that has forced changes in foreign policy in the past.

There are many opportunities for a movement for peace and justice in the Middle East to build upon already existing popular movements. Those challenging the neo-liberal model of globalization can observe how the growing economic stratification in the Middle East and the declining access by the region's poor majority to basic needs resulting from such policies has contributed to the rise of extremist groups. Human rights campaigners can note the tendency of Islamic terrorists to emerge in countries where open and nonviolent political expression is suppressed. Peace activists can emphasize how the arms trade has contributed to the militarization of the region and the resulting propensity for violence.

The United States is at a crossroads symbolized by the Chinese character for "crisis," which is written as a compound word consisting of "danger" and "opportunity." The dangers of the current situation are obvious. And the threat from terrorism has in certain ways made change more difficult, as Americans become angry and defensive in the face of such violence and rage. Yet in other ways, the very seriousness of the threat has opened people up to learn more about the Middle East, about why so many people might hate America, and about what is in the real security interests of the nation. This represents a critical opportunity for those who want to change the direction of United States policy in the Middle East, both for the future of the long-suffering people of that region, as well as for ourselves.

Notes

Introduction

1 *Foreign Relations of the United States, 1945*, Vol. VIII, cited in Joyce and Gabriel Kolko, *The Limits of Power* (New York: Harper & Row, 1972), p. 45

2 Steven Spiegel, *The Other Arab-Israeli Conflict*, (Chicago: University of Chicago Press 1985), p. 51

3 See, for example, National Security Council Memorandum 5801/1, "Statement By The National Security Council Of Long-Range U.S. Policy Toward The Near East," January 24, 1958, *Foreign Relations of the United States, 1958-1960*, Vol. XII (Washington: U.S. Government Printing Office, 1993) pp. 17-32.

4 Noam Chomsky, *Towards a New Cold War*, (New York: Pantheon Books, 1982), pp. 97-98, citing presidential advisor George Kennan.

5 Cited in Noam Chomsky, *9-11*, (New York: Seven Stories Press, 2001)

6 John LeCarre, "A War We Cannot Win," *The Nation*, November 19, 2001

7 Scott Simon, "Reflections on the events of September 11," United Church of Christ's Team on Proclamation, Identity and Communication's 19th Annual Parker Lecture, Cleveland, Ohio, Sept. 25, 2001 (www.ucc.org/911/092701b.htm)

8 Robert Fisk, "The Wickedness and Awesome Cruelty of a Crushed and Humiliated People," *The Independent*, September 12, 2001

Chapter One

1 Address to Latin American diplomats, White House, Washington, DC March 12, 1962

2 George W. Bush, "Address to a Joint Session of Congress and the American People," United States Capitol, September 20, 2001 Office of the Press Secretary

3 Gerard Baker and Roula Khalaf, "A different script: The west appears to be losing the information war in the Arab world," *Financial Times*, October 13, 2001

4 Structural functionalism is a term used in sociology to describe a way of analyzing societies and their component features that focuses on their mutual integration and interconnection, emphasizing the way that social processes and institutional arrangements contribute to the effective maintenance and stability of society. Leading theorists of this approach include

Talcott Parsons, Herbert Spencer and Emile Durkheim. This approach, largely discredited in recent years, is often utilized to rationalize for the status quo and to oppose major social change.

5 See Samuel Huntington, "Clash of Civilizations," *Foreign Affairs*, Vol. 72, No. 3 (Summer 1993)

6 See Khalid Kishtainy, "Violent and Nonviolent Struggle in Arab History," in Ralph E. Crow, Philip Grant, and Saad E. Ibrahim, eds. *Arab Nonviolent Political Struggle in the Middle East* (Boulder: Lynne Rienner Publishers, 1990). Kishtainy cites the Prophet Muhammad's successor Abu Bakr al-Siddiq when he said "Obey me as long as I obey God in my rule. If I disobey him, you will owe me no obedience." Kishtainy also notes how such a pledge was reiterated by successive caliphs, such as Imam Ali, who stated that "no obedience is allowed to any creature in his disobedience of the Creator." (pp. 9-10)

7 Cited in Karl Vick, "In Arab World, Suppression of Dissent Sparks Extremism," *Washington Post*, October 28, 2001

8 Israeli Prime Minister Benjamin Netanyahu's address before a joint session of the U.S. Congress, July 10, 1996. See also Thomas Dine of the American Israel Public Affairs Committee, "Testimony before the House Appropriations Subcommittee on Foreign Operations," March 1, 1993

9 Salman Rushdie, *The Satanic Verses* (New York: Viking, 1989)

10 See Anouar Abdallah, *For Rushdie: A Collection of Essays by 100 Arab and Muslim Writers* (New York: George Braziller, 1994)

11 For example, the expanded academic index backfile 1980-1990 showed nearly 300 citations about the Rushdie affair as compared with less than fifty dealing with human rights violations by Middle Eastern governments allied with the United States.

12 Such accusations are often well-founded, though there have been a number of cases where the seriousness of the human rights situation has been greatly exaggerated.

13 Background briefing, Department of State, July 1995

14 *Country Reports on Human Rights Practices*, Report submitted to the Committee on International Relations, U.S. House of Representatives and the Committee on Foreign Relations, United States Senate, by the Department of State, 1991 and 1995. Omani Sultan Qabus bin Said's speeches justifying his country's lack of democracy as manifestation of its cultural traditions are reportedly written in English by his Western advisers and only then translated into Arabic.

15 Cited in Robert Fisk, "America's Morality has been Distorted by 11 September," *The Independent*, March 7, 2002. One reason concerns about Egyptian military tribunals were dropped may have been that, in the inter-

im, the United States had instigated military tribunals of questionable legality itself against fighters captured in Afghanistan.

16 Background briefing, U.S. Consular offices, East Jerusalem, May 1993

17 Or compensation if they refused return.

18 Jules Kagian, *Middle East International*, Dec. 17, 1993. See Thomas and Sally Mallison, *The Palestine Problem in International Law*, (Longman, 1986), ch. 4. See also Noam Chomsky *World Orders Old and New* (Columbia University Press, 1995), p. 219

19 U.S. Ambassador to the United Nations Bill Richardson, Emergency Special Session of the UN Security Council, Press Release SC/6611, December 16, 1998

20 Noam Chomsky has analyzed these double-standards in a number of his writings, including *Necessary Illusions: Thought Control in Democratic Societies* (Boston: South End Press, 1989) For an interesting Kurdish perspective on American double-standards towards that conflict, see Vera Beaudin Saeedpur, "Kurdish Times and the New York Times," *Cultural Survival* (Summer 1988)

21 See Stephen Zunes, "The Strategic Function of U.S. Aid to Israel," *Middle East Policy*, Vol. IV, No. 4 (October 1996)

22 See Stephen Zunes, "The United States in the Sahara War: A Case of Low-Intensity Intervention," in Daniel Volman and Yahia Zoubir, eds., *International Dimensions of the Western Sahara Conflict* (Westport, CT: Greenwood Press 1993.)

23 "Democracy Denied in Algeria," *New York Times*, July 24, 1992, p.A24. For an analysis of events that led up to the coup, see Stephen Zunes, "Behind the Fundamentalist Upsurge in Algeria," *In These Times*, January 29, 1992

24 "The Vengeful Ones," *The Economist*, March 9, 1991, p.39

25 Congressional Research Service, "Jordan-U.S. Relations and Bilateral Issues," June 13, 1993

26 Cited in Phyllis Bennis, *Calling the Shots: How Washington Dominates Today's UN* (New York: Olive Branch Press, 1996), p.33

27 Cited in Robert Fisk, "Farewell to Democracy in Pakistan," *The Independent*, October 26, 2001

28 Ibid.

29 Cited in Andrew and Patrick Cockburn, *Out of The Ashes: The Resurrection of Saddam Hussein*, (New York: HarperCollins, 1999)

30 Cited in Vick, op. cit.

31 Michael Klare, "Asking 'Why?'," Global Affairs Commentary, Foreign Policy in Focus, September 2001

32 Cited by Noam Chomsky, *World Orders Old and New*, op. cit., pp. 198-200; the Macmillan quote originated from his *At the End of the Day* (New York:

Harper & Row, 1973)

33 Quoted in Charles M. Sennott, "Doubts are Cast on the Viability Of Saudi Monarchy for Long Term," *Boston Globe*, March 5, 2002

34 Dilip Hiro, "The Gulf Between the Rulers and the Ruled," *New Statesman and Society*, February 28, 1993

35 Amnesty International, "Uzbekistan: Briefing on human rights situation," October 11, 2001

36 Cited in Abid Aslam, "Central Asia: On the Periphery of a New Global War," Global Affairs Commentary, Foreign Policy in Focus, September 2001

37 Secretary of State Colin Powell, Testimony before the Senate Finance Committee, Feb. 12. 2002

38 United Nations Security Council resolutions 353 and 354 (1974)

39 President Bill Clinton, in nationally-televised address announcing the NATO bombing campaign against Yugoslavia, March 24, 1999

40 Kevin McKiernan, "Turkey's War on the Kurds," *Bulletin of Atomic Scientists*, March/April 1999 Vol. 55, No. 9

41 Cited in Ibid.

42 Nicholas Burns, Press Briefing, Department of State, June 12, 1997

43 King Hassan organized what he called the "Green March," where over 300,000 Moroccans nonviolently walked several miles into the Spanish Sahara as a symbolic display of claiming the desert territory. However, there was a simultaneous armed invasion away from the media spotlight that was far more significant.

44 Fourth Geneva Convention, Article 41 (1949)

45 Stanley Meisler, "Failure Feared for W. Saharan Truce," *Los Angeles Times*, March 7, 1992, p. A6

46 This is certainly not a unique phenomenon. During the Cold War, repressive right-wing dictatorships would often join U.S.-led efforts to condemn human rights violations by Communist governments and, likewise, various left-wing dictatorships would join the Soviet Union in condemnation of rightist regimes.

47 See Stephen Zunes, "Israel's Blank Check: How Congressional Liberals Support Israeli Human Rights Abuses," *The Progressive*, November 1989

48 Human Rights Watch, "Question of the violation of human rights in the occupied Arab territories, including Palestine," Human Rights Watch Oral Intervention at the 57th Session of the UN Commission on Human Rights, March 28, 2001.

   The Foundation for Middle East Peace reports that Israeli Knesset member Mossi Raz warned just five weeks before the outbreak of the Palestinian uprising that the settlers' intention was "to cause an outbreak of violence in the territories that will harm the chance for an agreement." He accused the Israeli government of "groveling surrender to the criminal settlers." The report noted, however, that most of the settler activities were coordinated with the Israel Defense Forces. "Sharon Government Violates Pledge not to Establish New Settlements," *Report on Israel Settlements,* January-February 2002]

49 Interview, NBC's *Meet the Press,* October 8, 2000

50 A Dahaf poll taken May 5-6, 2002 showed 56% of the public said that such an international force would raise their hopes, a much higher percentage than those who said that their hopes would be raised by IDF responsibility for security in Palestinian cities.

51 Human Rights Watch, "Independent Inquiry Needed in Israeli-Palestinian Bloodshed," October 7, 2000

52 Deutsche Presse-Agentur, October 3, 2000, cited by Noam Chomsky, "The Current Crisis in the Middle East: What Can We Do?," lecture at the Massachusetts Institute of Technology, Dec. 14, 2001

53 Amnesty International, "Israel/Occupied Territories: Findings of Amnesty International's Delegation," Oct. 19, 2000

54 House Concurrent Resolution 426, 106th Congress, Second session

55 The death of Isaac Saada, a teacher at Terra Sancta school in Bethlehem, was cited in a special report from Gershon Baskin of the Israel/Palestine Center for Research and Information in Jerusalem, July 18, 2001

56 United Nations Commission of Enquiry: 16 March 2001

57 Cited in James Zogby, "Israel's Assassinations: The U.S. Debate," *Washington Watch,* August 13, 2001

58 Al-Jazeera TV, August 2, 2001

59 Office of the White House Press Secretary, "President Bush, Secretary Powell Discuss Middle East," Remarks by the President and Secretary of State Colin Powell, the Oval Office. Washington, DC

60 Gwen Ackerman, "Barak Assassination of Abu Jihad," Associated Press, July 4, 1997.

American troops were also sent to guard a sixth man, Palestinian Authority finance chief Fuad Shubaki, arrested for attempting to smuggle arms from Iran. The U.S. position has been that while it is legitimate for the United States to send arms to facilitate the Israeli occupation, it is illegitimate for the Palestinians to import arms to resist the occupation.

61 Amnesty International, "Israel And The Occupied Territories: The heavy price of Israeli incursions," AI-index: MDE 15/042/2002 April 12, 2002

62 House Resolution 392, 107th Congress, 2nd session

63 Senate Resolution 247, 107th Congress, 2nd session

64 Prepared statement, "Senators Feinstein and McConnell Urge Sanctions

Against Arafat PLO over Palestinian Suicide Bombings," April 18, 2002

65 Office of the House Democratic Leader, Gephardt Statement to National Rally in Solidarity with Israel, April 15, 2002

66 Uri Avnery, "Something Stinks," *Gush Shalom Billboard*, April 20, 2002

67 See *The New Republic*, April 17, 1995

68 CNN.com, "U.N. Security Council Give Nod to Jenin Probe," April 19, 2002

69 Dina Shiloh, citing article in *Yediot Ahronot* in "U.S. Promise on Jenin Won Arafat's Freedom," *San Francisco Chronicle*, April 30, 2002

70 Jim Lobe, "Poll Points Toward Peace," *Alternet*, May 13, 2002

71 Conference of High Contracting Parties to the Fourth Geneva Convention, convened on December 5, 2001 at Geneva
    The phrase "grave breaches" in reference to the Geneva Conventions is widely interpreted as diplomatic language for war crimes.

72 Office of the White House Press Secretary, The White House, "President Bush Calls for New Palestinian Leadership," Washington, DC June 24, 2002

73 Ali Abunimah, "Bush's Speech—A Vision of Permanent War," Common Dreams News Center, June 25, 2002

74 Office of the White House Press Secretary, "President Launches 'Lessons of Liberty,'" Remarks by the President in Announcement Of Lessons of Liberty Initiative, Thomas Wootton High School, Rockville, Maryland, October 30, 2001

Chapter Two

1 Quoted in Charles E. Nathanson, "The Social Construction of the Soviet Threat: A Study in the Politics of Representation," *Alternatives*, Vol. 13, No. 4 (October 1988), p. 443,

2 George W. Bush, Remarks to the United Nations General Assembly, UN Headquarters, New York, November 10, 2001

3 John Winthrop, *A Modell of Christian Charity (1630)*, Collections of the Massachusetts Historical Society (Boston, 1838), 3rd series 7:31-48.

4 Presidential address, Richard M. Nixon, October 30, 1970

5 Presidential address, Ronald Reagan, November 22, 1982

6 U.S. Department of State, "Foreign Operations, Export Financing, and Related Programs (Foreign Operations)," FY 2003 Budget Request

7 George Orwell, *1984*, (London: Martin Secker & Warburg, 1949), chapter 3

8 See Stephen Zunes, Lester Kurtz and Sara Beth Asher, eds. *Nonviolent Social Movements: A Geographical Perspective* (Malden, Mass.: Blackwell Publishers, 1999)

9   See Stephen Zunes, "Nonviolent Resistance and Islam," *Nonviolent Activist*, January-February 2002

10 Joan Bondurant, *Conquest of Violence*, (Berkeley: University of California Press), revised edition, 1965, pp. 131-144. See also Pyaralel, *A Pilgrimage of Peace: Gandhi and the Frontier Gandhi Among N.W.F. Pathans*, (Ahmedabad: Navajivan, 1950) and Eknath Easwaran, *Nonviolent Soldier of Islam: Badshah Khan, A Man to Match His Mountains* (Delhi: Nilgiri Press, 1998)

11 See Stephen Zunes, "The Israeli-Jordanian Peace Agreement: Peace or Pax Americana?" *Middle East Policy*, Vol. III, No. 4 (Spring 1995)

12 Congress reserved its loudest objections for the aid sent to the Palestinian Authority, even though none of it was for military purposes. The consternation on Capitol Hill was focused on the $400,000 sent for badly needed development projects in Palestinian areas.

13 Interview, May 12, 1992, Seattle, Washington.

14 Alan Kronstadt, et al, *Hostile Takeover: How the Aerospace Industries Association Gain Control of American Foreign Policy and Double Arms Transfers to Dictators*, (Washington: Project on Demilitarization and Democracy, 1995)

15 See www.politicalmoneyline.com

16 State Department International Affairs (Function 150) *FY2003 Budget Request. Summary & Highlights*, (Washington, DC: Department of State, 2002)

17 *Foreign Military Sales, Foreign Military Construction Sales and Military Assistance Facts: As of September 30, 2000*, published by the Defense Security Cooperation Agency (Washington: Department of Defense, 2000)

18 General Accounting Office, *Defense Trade: Information on U.S. Weapons Deliveries to the Middle East*, GAO-01-1078, September 21, 2001, with addition figures from Ibid.

19 Office of Trade and Economic Analysis (OTEA), *Trade Development, International Trade Administration* (Washington DC: U.S. Department of Commerce, 2002)

20 Joe Stork, "The Middle East Arms Bazaar after the Gulf War," *Middle East Report* November- December 1995

21 Robert Vitalis, "Gun Belt in the Beltway," *Middle East Report*, November- December 1995)

22 "Saudis Go for Broke on U.S. Arms," *Arms Sales Monitor*, (Washington: Federation of American Scientists), No. 30, July 20, 1995

23 Ibid.

24 U.S. Arms Control and Disarmament Agency, *World Military Expenditures and Arms Transfers, 1991-1992*, (Washington, DC, 1994) pp. 6-7 and pp.

22-23

25 Vitalis, op. cit.

26 "Arab Aid to Developing Countries Falls," *Middle East Economic Digest*, Dec. 18, 1992 (Vol. 36, No. 50, p. 4)

27 Cited in Michael Klare, "Making Enemies for the '90s: The New 'Rogue States' Doctrine," *The Nation*, May 8, 1995, p. 625

28 Anthony H. Cordesman, *Trends in Iran: A Graphic and Statistical Overview: Demographics, Economics, Energy, Military Spending, Arms Imports, Conventional Force Developments and Proliferation* (Washington: Center for Strategic and International Studies) June 20, 1999, p. 85

29 Sennot, op. cit.

30 Anthony Cordesman, "The Changing Military Balance in the Gulf," *Middle East Policy*, Vol. VI, No. 1 (June 1998) p. 27

31 Ibid.

32 Cited in Lora Lumpe, "Clinton Administration Watch," *Arms Sales Monitor #19*, March 1993

33 Gary Milhollin, "The Business of Defense Is Defending Business," *Washington Post National Weekly Edition*, Feb. 14-20, p. 23

34 Milton Viorst, "Changing Iran: The Limits of Revolution," *Foreign Affairs*, November/December 1995, p. 75

35 Cited in Appendix D: "International Atomic Energy Agency Safeguards," in Rodney W. Jones and Mark G. McDonough, eds. *Tracking Nuclear Proliferation: A Guide in Maps and Charts, 1998* (Washington: Carnegie Endowment for International Peace, 1998) p. 295

36 James Bill, *The Eagle and the Lion: The Tragedy of American-Iranian Relations* (New Haven: Yale University Press, 1988) p. 204

37 Seymour Hersh, *The Samson Option* (New York: Random House, 1991) pp. 209-214

38 Ibid., p. 268

39 Cited in Ibid., p. 283

40 Ibid., p. 291

41 Jane Hunter, "A Nuclear Affair," *Middle East International*, 24 June 1994, pp. 12-13

42 Helena Cobban, "Israel's Nuclear Game: The U.S. Stake," *World Policy Journal*, Summer 1988, pp. 427-428

43 Hersh, op. cit., p. 9

44 See, for example, House Concurrent Resolution 9, 103rd Congress, 2nd session

45 Zachary Davis, "Nuclear Proliferation and Nonproliferation Policy in the 1990s," in Michael Klare and Daniel Thomas, *World Security: Challenges for a New Century*, second edition (New York: St. Martin's Press, 1997) p. 112

46 David Albright and Mark Hibbs, "Hyping the Iraqi Bomb," *Bulletin of Atomic Scientists*, March 1991, Vol. 47, No. 2

47 Charles Glass, *New Statesman and Society*, February 17, 1998

48 William Blum, "Anthrax for Export: U.S. Companies Sold Iraq the Ingredients for a Witch's Brew," *The Progressive*, April 1998, p. 18

49 It is noteworthy that both Syria and Cuba remain on the list of terrorist supporters despite the failure of successive administrations to demonstrate any direct backing of terrorist groups by these countries for more than a decade.

50 Patrick E. Tyler, "Officers Say U.S. Aided Iraqis in War Despite Use of Gas," *New York Times*, August 18, 2002

51 Interview by Frank Sesno, "Bush: What we are Doing is Right," *Washington Post*, Nov. 16, 1990, p. A24

52 Chomsky, *World Orders Old and New*, op. cit., p. 26

53 Cited in Blum, op. cit., p. 20

54 Sheila Carapico, "Legalism and Realism in the Gulf," *Middle East Report*, Spring 1998, p. 5

55 Barton Gellman, "US Spied on Iraqi Military via UN" *Washington Post*, March 2, 1999, p. A1. After initial denials, the United States acknowledged in January 1999 that it had indeed used American weapons inspectors for espionage purposes, including monitoring coded radio communications by Iraqi security forces using equipment secretly installed by American inspectors [*Washington Post*, January 8, 1999]

56 Scott Ritter, "Saddam Hussein Did Not Expel U.N. Weapons Inspectors," *Washington Report on Middle East Affairs*, May 2002, pp. 23-24. Ritter was a former team leader of UNSCOM weapons inspectors in Iraq.

57 Institute for Policy Studies, "Iraq's Current Military Capability," February 1998

58 Berton Gellman, *Washington Post*, March 20, 1998

59 Ibid.

60 *Washington Post*, July 15, 1999

61 Cited by Rep. Cynthia McKinney, *News Hour with Jim Lehrer*, Public Broadcasting System, Feb. 10, 1998

62 Dr. Julian Perry Robinson, *The Independent*, March 7, 1998

63 Charles A. Horner, "Military Force Has Its Limits," *New York Times*, February 7, 1998

64 Tim Wiener, "'Smart' Weapons Were Overrated, Study Concludes," *New York Times*, July 9, 1996

65 Institute for Policy Studies, op. cit.

66 *Los Angeles Times*, May 9, 1991

67 Lecture at Georgetown University, Washington, DC, March 26, 1997

68 *New York Times*, November 23, 1997

69 Cited in Sarah Graham-Brown, "Sanctions Renewed on Iraq," MERIP Press Information Note 96, May 14, 2002

70 From Fox News Channel's *The O'Reilly Factor*, cited in David Corn, "Next Step Baghdad? Anti-War Warriors Say 'Whoa,'" *Alternet*, November 30, 2001. The substitute host, former Republican Congressman John Kasich bitterly countered by saying "I don't know anybody else that agrees with you, except a few of Saddam's friends."

71 Barbara Crosette, "Iraqis Will Face Blunt Terms in Weapons Talks at the U.N.," *New York Times*, March 6, 2002 p. A11

72 Brian Whiaker, "US wants to oust Saddam even if he makes concessions," *The Observer*, May 5, 2002

73 Thomas Walkom, "War on Terror Little to do with Terror," *Toronto Star*, June 18, 2002

74 George Monbiot, "US Tries to Remove Diplomat Standing in Way of War with Iraq," *Guardian*, April 19, 2002

75 Ibid. The United States accused Bustani of mismanagement but refused to present any evidence. See also, Peter Ford, "US Diplomatic Might Irks Nations: A Senior UN Chief who Policed the Chemical Weapons Ban was Voted Out Monday Night," *Christian Science Monitor*, April 24, 2002

Chapter Three

1 Osama bin Laden, "Declaration of War Against the Americans Who Occupy the Land of the Two Holy Mosques," August 23, 1996

2 This observation comes from a series of interviews during the author's visits to the Gulf region and with Gulf Arab scholars at international academic meetings between 1992 and 2000.

3 President Richard M. Nixon, "Address to the Nation on the War in Vietnam," November 3, 1969

4 Scott Armstrong, "Saudis' AWACS Just a Beginning of a New Strategy," *Washington Post*, Nov. 1, 1981

5 Cited in Klare, op. cit.

6 Revelations about the clandestine arms transfers in 1985-86 became the basis of the Iran-Contra scandal, which plagued the Reagan Administration during most of its second term.

7 Cited in Noam Chomsky, "What We Say Goes," *Z Magazine*, May 1991

8 Robert Pear, *New York Times*, July 5, 1988

9 There is a rather startling contrast between the desperate American rationalizations for the attack (most of which were later disproven by press investigations) and the major propaganda campaign waged against the Soviet Union following their downing of a South Korean airliner in

September 1983. Ironically, the Iranian airliner was on course over Iranian airspace at the time it was destroyed, whereas the Korean airliner was off course and flying over Soviet airspace near sensitive military installations.

In April 1990, the senior President Bush awarded the Legion of Merit award upon the commander and the officer in charge of anti-aircraft warfare of the *Vincennes* warship that shot down the plane. Despite being responsible for the attack, they were praised for their "exceptionally meritorious conduct in the performance of outstanding service" in the Gulf and for the "calm and professional atmosphere" during that period. [Associated Press, April 23, 1990]

10 Cited in Vahe Petrossian, "Iran: US Signals Sanctions War," *Middle East Economic Digest*, August 16, 1996

11 Ibid.

12 President George W. Bush, State of the Union address, Jan. 29, 2002

13 European Union, Statement by Commissioner for External Relations, Brussels, Belgium, July 31, 2001

14 A comparable situation would be the U.S. training and support of various right-wing groups in Latin America during the Cold War that went on to engage in terrorist attacks against civilians. While certainly sharing some responsibility, the U. S. government, in most cases, did not organize, plan or direct specific attacks.

One of the strongest cases the United States alleges regarding Iran's terrorist activities overseas was two major bombings of Jewish targets in Argentina: the Israeli embassy in 1993 and a Jewish community center in 1994, both resulting in scores of fatalities. As with many such charges, U.S. officials have not released any evidence. The most likely suspects are extreme right-wing elements of the Argentine military, which has a notorious history of anti-Semitism. There were a series of arrests in connection with the bombing, particularly among the *carapintadas*, a particularly seditious sector of the military that was blamed for as many as four coup attempts between 1987 and 1990. Virtually all of the suspects have been released for "lack of evidence," fitting a pattern of the expeditious vindication of well-connected suspects. However, the governments of the United States, Israel and Argentina all have their own political motivations for blaming Iran rather than domestic Argentine sources for the bombings.

15 Houman A. Sadri, "Trends in the Foreign Policy of Revolutionary Iran," *Journal of Third World Studies*, Vol. 15, No. 1 (April 1998)

16 Released by the Office of the Coordinator for Counterterrorism, U.S. Department of State, *Patterns of Global Terrorism - 2000*, Section I: Overview of State-Sponsored Terrorism, April 30, 2001

17 Anthony H. Cordesman, *Trends in Iran*, op. cit., p. 17

18 Jamie McIntyre, "Iran Builds Up Military Strength at Mouth of Gulf," www.cnn.com/WORLD/9608/06/iran.threat/, Aug. 6, 1996

19 Hooshang Amirahmadi and Nader Entessar, eds. *Iran and the Arab World* (New York: St. Martin's Press) 1993, p.127

20 Anthony Cordesman, "The Changing Military Balance in the Gulf," *Middle East Policy*, Vol. VI, No. 1 (June 1998) p. 82

21 Cordesman, *Trends in Iran*, op. cit., p. 31

22 A good summary of the quiet U.S. support for Iraq can be found in an article on the media coverage of the scandal: Russ W. Baker, "Iraqgate: The Big One that (Almost) Got Away," *Columbia Journalism Review*, March/April 1993. For a more detailed account, see Mark Phythian and Nikos Passas, *Arming Iraq : How the U.S. and Britain Secretly Built Saddam's War Machine* (Boston: Northeastern University Press) 1996

23 Interview with HRH Hassan, Royal Palace, Amman, Jordan, January 8, 1991

24 Jean Heller, "Photos Don't Show Buildup," *St. Petersburg Times*, Jan 6, 1991, p. 1A

25 "Osama bin Laden: The Truth About the World's Most Wanted Man," *The Sunday Independent*, September 16, 2001

26 Associate Press, January 14, 1990. However, the U.S. essentially had been awarding aggression for years by sending military and economic support for other occupation armies, such as Indonesian forces in East Timor, Moroccan forces in Western Sahara, Turkish forces in northern Cyprus and Israeli forces in its occupied Arab lands.

27 Roger Fisher, Elizabeth Kopelman and Andrea Kupfer Schneider, "Consider the Other Side's Choice," from *Beyond Machiavelli: Tools for Coping with Conflict.* (Cambridge, London: Harvard University Press, 1994) pp. 52-56.

28 In an interview with *BizLaw Journal*, Roger Fisher noted, "I believe President Bush wanted to defeat the army of Iraq militarily. He thought a war would do that, and I think he wanted a war." Fisher described how he had met with Kuwaiti leaders in exile prior to the war offering suggestions for negotiating strategy and, while they sounded positive to his suggestions, told him, "No, we can't afford to offend the United States and President Bush wants a military victory." [Interview with Brian Anderson, "*Getting to Yes*' Twentieth Anniversary," March 7, 2001]

This author has heard similar stories from scores of diplomats, journalists and academics in the Middle East.

29 Report from CIA director William Webster, cited in "Divided Debate on a Foregone Conclusion," *Bulletin of Atomic Scientists*, March 1991, Vol. 47,

No. 2

30 Based on observations from the author's visit to Iraq January 6-14, 1991, just prior to the outbreak of the war.

31 For example, see House Armed Services Committee chairman Les Aspin, "Gulf Diplomacy Needs Arms Threat to Succeed," Center for Strategic and International Studies, December 21, 1990 [http://www.fas.org/news/iraq/1990/901221-166452.htm]

32 The State Department film "Why Vietnam?," used to justify U.S. military intervention in that country, opens with a scene from the 1938 Munich conference when Prime Minister Neville Chamberlain gave in to Adolf Hitler's demand for a German takeover of Sudetenland (the German-speaking part of Czechoslovakia), a summit that has become emblematic of appeasement.

33 New Republic, September 3, 1990

34 The U.S. government, which has never been supportive of Arab unity, was probably quite pleased with the divisions that resulted.

35 Phyllis Bennis, "Command and Control: Politics and Power in the Post-Cold War United Nations," in Bennis and Michel Moushabeck, eds., Altered States: A Reader in the New World Order (New York: Olive Branch Press, 1993). The cut-off of aid came just three days after the Security Council vote. A U.S. representative was overheard on the UN broadcast system telling Yemeni ambassador Abdallah Saleh al-Ashtal minutes after the actual vote, "that will be the most expensive 'no' vote you ever cast."

36 Fourth Geneva Convention, Common Article III (1949)

37 Cited in Robert Jensen, "The Gulf War Brought Out the Worst in Us," Los Angeles Times, May 19, 2002

38 Based upon interviews of leading academics and government officials in GCC countries by the author in January 1992.

39 Barton Gellman, Washington Post, June 23, 1991

40 There is a wide range of estimates regarding both the civilian and military death toll on the Iraqi side. The figures used in this paragraph were cited in Bob Woodward's The Commanders (New York: Simon and Schuster, 1991)

41 John Donnelly, "US is Probing Cause, Degree of Civilian Toll," Boston Globe, January 19, 2002

42 The Shatt al-Arab is the 100-mile river formed from the convergence of the Tigris and Euphrates rivers that demarcates the southern end of the Iran-Iraq border. Iraqi resentment of this agreement, which resulted from pressure by Iran and the United States, is what precipitated Iraq's invasion of Iran four years later.

43 Daniel Schorr, "Ten Days That Shook the White House," Colombia Journalism Review, July/August 1991

44 President George Bush, cited by Robert Parry, *The Nation*, April 15, 1991

45 Charter of the United Nations Organization, Article 51

46 *Middle East International*, Oct. 21, 1994, p. 4

47 United Nations Security Council resolution 1154 (1998)

48 Laura Silber and David Buchan, *Financial Times*, March 4, 1998

49 "UN Rebuffs US on Threat to Iraq if it Breaks Pact," *New York Times,* March 3, 1998

50 "US Insists It Retains Right to Punish Iraq", *New York Times*, March 4, 1998

51 United Nations Children Fund, "Iraq Survey Shows 'Humanitarian Emergency,'" August 12, 1999 [Cf/doc/pr/199/29]

52 The higher estimates have been extrapolated from a 1995 report from researchers for the Food and Agriculture Organization and various reports from UNICEF. The lower estimates are from reputedly more scientific studies, including the 1999 report "Morbidity and Mortality Among Iraqi Children" by Columbia University's Richard Garfield, and "Sanctions and Childhood Mortality in Iraq," a May 2000 article by Mohamed Ali and Iqbal Shah in *The Lancet*, the journal of the British Medical Society.

53 CBS, *60 Minutes*, May 12, 1996

54 United Nations Food and Agricultural Organization, 1995

55 Confirmation hearings for Madeline Albright for Secretary of State, Senate Foreign Affairs Committee, 105th Congress, 1st session, January 8, 1997

56 Colin Lynch, "Humanitarian Goods Are Being Blocked, U.N. Chief Charges," *Washington Post*, October 25, 1999, p. A16

57 "Smart exit: The end of the smart sanctions," *The Economist*, July 7, 2001

58 "Can Sanctions Be Smarter?" *The Economist*, May 26, 2001

59 *The Financial Times*, May 28, 2001

60 Boutros Boutros-Ghali, Supplement to *An Agenda for Peace*, (United Nations: Office of the Secretary General, January 1995)

61 Reuters, March 20, 2001

62 United Press International, August 2, 2002

63 BBC radio, *Talking Point*, June 4, 2000

64 Translation of statement by Osama bin Laden, broadcast on Al-Jazeera, October 7, 2001

65 Cited in Robert Scheer, "President Bush's Wag-the-Dog Policy on Iraq," *Los Angeles Times*, May 7, 2002

66 Cited in Ibid.

67 Cited in Conn Hallinan, "A U.S. Cabal Pulling America to War," Foreign Policy in Focus, May 3, 2002

68 Paul Rogers, "The Coming War with Iraq," *Open Democracy*, February 20, 2002

69 Department of State, *Patterns of Global Terrorism, 2001* (Washington, Goovernment Printing Office. 2002)

70 BBC News, "Region Opposes Attack on Iraq," March 18, 2002

71 Cited in Julian Borger, *Guardian*, March 27, 2002

72 Mona Salem, "Beirut summit sets Iraq on long road back to Arab fold," *Middle East Times*, March 28, 2002

73 Howard Schneider, "Saudi Puts Faith in Iraqi Pledge," *Washington Post*, March 30, 2002

74 Salem, op. cit.

75 Donald Rumsfeld, *New York Times*, September 27, 2001

76 BBC News, "Region Opposes Attack on Iraq," March 18, 2002

77 Cited from an article in the February 16, 2002 *Financial Times* in Michael R. Gordon, "Cheney Rejects Criticism by Allies Over Stand on Iraq," *New York Times*, February 16, 2002

78 *Defense Week*, November 1998

79 Daniel Byman, cited in *Foreign Affairs*, Jan/Feb issue, 2000

80 Cabinet-level officials of two of these countries have acknowledged this in background briefings with the author, January 1992

81 Abdullah Al-Shayeji, "Dangerous Perceptions: Gulf Views of the U.S. Role in the Region," *Middle East Policy*, Vol. V, No. 3, September 1997, p. 5

82 Cited in Jee Kim, ed. *Another World is Possible: Conversations in a Time of Terror* (New Orleans: Subway and Elevator Press, 2002) p. 83

83 Most parents can probably identify with this phenomenon.

Chapter Four

1   While some apologists for the Israeli government still claim that the Palestinians left their country voluntarily, Israeli historians and others— using archival material from the Israeli government and its antecedents— reveal that there was indeed a calculated policy to force the bulk of the Palestinian population into exile. Perhaps the most famous work is Benny Morris' *The Birth of the Palestinian Refugee Problem, 1947-1949* (New York: Cambridge University Press, 1989)

2   This came in a vote by the Palestine National Council meeting in Gaza on April 24. This was confirmed in a PNC meeting on December 18, 1998 in the presence of visiting U.S. President Bill Clinton and was formally accepted by Israeli Prime Minister Benyamin Netanyahu.

3   Congressional Research Service, "Israel: U.S. Foreign Assistance," August 30, 1995, compiled by Clyde Mark, with subsequent annual appropriations added on to his $77 billion total. This amount is higher than even that of the widely quoted Soviet aid to Cuba in the thirty years prior to 1991.

4   For Fiscal Year 2001, Foreign Military Financing totaled $2.04 billion and Economic Support Funds totaled $720 million. Taking 1995 as an example, additional U.S. grants to the Israeli government not included in the FMF and ESF funding includes bank charges incurred by the U.S. government for lump sum withdrawal ($60 million); interest earned by Israel on ESF aid money reinvested in U.S. treasury notes ($90 million); supplemental State Department funded aid ($93.5 million); supplemental Defense Department items ($242.3 million); a contract with the Immigration and Naturalization Service ($17 million); assistance from the Commerce Department ($2.5 million) ["House Appropriations Committee Funds U.S.-Israeli Cooperation," *Near East Report*, Vol. XXXIX, No. 18, Aug. 14, 1995, p. 99 and Shawn Twing, "A Comprehensive Guide to U.S. Aid to Israel," *Washington Report on Middle East Affairs*, April 1996, p. 7]

5   In other countries that receive U.S. economic aid, there is an AID mission as part of the US Embassy that audits all the relevant expenditures. Without such a presence in Israel, there have been a number of scandals involving U.S. funds, such as when General Electric's manager for Israel was caught paying kickbacks to Israeli authorities responsible for procurement, or when General Rami Dotan was found to be siphoning off U.S. funds for his personal use.

6   Figures cited in Edward T. Pound, "A Close Look at U.S. Aid to Israel Reveals Deals That Push Cost Above Publicly Quoted Figures," *The Wall Street Journal*, Sept. 19, 1991, p. A16

7   Martha Wenger, "The Money Tree: US Aid to Israel,", *Middle East Report*, May-Aug. 1990, p. 12

8   Ibid.

9   Cited in Joel Bainerman, "Looking the Gift Horse in the Mouth: Israelis Ask if U.S. Generosity Might Actually Be Hurting their Country," *Washington Post*, Oct. 29, 1995, p. C4

10   Edward Sheehan, *The Arabs, Israelis and Kissinger: A Secret History of American Diplomacy in the Middle East* (New York: Readers Digest Press, 1976) p. 200

11   Despite these restrictions, the Palestinian delegates—consisting primarily of respected West Bank intellectuals—were, in practice, able to operate separately from the Jordanian delegation and work in close coordination with the PLO.

12   Background briefings, Washington, DC, March 21, 1995

13   The United States threatened to withhold all funding from the UN when the United Nations upgraded the PLO's observer status in 1989 (*New York Times*, Nov. 28, 1989). Also in 1989, the FAO faced a deep cut in

U.S. support because of its assistance to the Palestinians (*International Herald Tribune*, Jan. 10, 1990). In addition, the U.S. threatened to withdraw from the WHO when it considered admitting Palestine as a full member. One of the justifications for the U.S. withdrawal from UNESCO in 1984 was its educational assistance to Palestinian children.

14 The UN General Assembly passed a number of anti-Israel resolutions, particularly in the 1970s, which even critics of Israeli policies found to be one-sided, hypocritical and mean-spirited, in which the United States was joined by scores of other countries in opposition. The most notorious was the 1975 amendment to the establishment of the UN Decade Against Racism, when the General Assembly declared that Zionism was "a form of racism and racial discrimination." This was overwhelmingly repealed in 1991. More recent UNGA resolutions critical of Israel have had a far more solid legal foundation.

15 U.S. Permanent Representative to the United Nations Madeleine Albright, letter to the United Nations General Assembly, August 8, 1994

16 In a June 30, 1993 paper to the delegations in the Washington peace talks, the United States—for the first time—would not recommit to UN Security Council Resolutions 242 and 338, long considered the basis of Arab-Israeli peace.

17 Jim Lobe, "U.S. and Israeli Governments Out of Step with Public According to New Polls," Foreign Policy in Focus, May 13, 2002

18 Supporters of the Israeli occupation sometimes claim that the resolution spoke of "territories" rather than "the territories," implying that there is no obligation for a full withdrawal. However, the resolution's text in French (the other official language of the United Nations) does use the definite article. Furthermore, the authors of the original resolution—the American and British ambassadors—explicitly stated that they were thinking only in terms of minor and reciprocal adjustments of the jagged border that was based upon cease-fire lines in the 1949 armistice agreement.

19 Interestingly, these same statements generally have avoided references to human rights, international law or disarmament.

20 U.S. Secretary of State Warren Christopher, "Widening the Circle of Peace in the Middle East," Wye Plantation Policy Conference, October 15, 1993

21 Matti Peled, *New Outlook*, May/June 1975

22 Phil Reeves, "Humiliation of Palestinians triggers rush to war: Dying Peace Process", *The Independent*, October 9, 2000

23 Deborah Sontag, "And Yet So Far: A special report: Quest for Mideast Peace: How and Why It Failed," *New York Times*, July 26, 2001, p. A12

24 Gideon Levy, "Just When We Were About to Give Them So Much," *Haaretz*, June 17, 2001

25 Edward Cody, "Israel's Grinding Presence Fueled a Festering Palestinian Rage," *Washington Post*, Oct. 27, 2000, p. A30

26 Sontag, op. cit.

27 White House Office of the Press Secretary, President William J. Clinton, "Statement on the Middle East Peace Talks at Camp David," The White House, Washington, DC, July 25, 2000

28 Jane Perlez, "Impasse at Camp David: The Overview; Clinton Ends Deadlocked Peace Talks," *New York Times*, July 26, 2000, p. A1

29 United Nations Security Council resolution 242 (1967)

30 Robert Malley, "Former Peace Team Member Discusses U.S. Failures under Clinton Administration," lecture at the Center for Policy Analysis on Palestine, Washington, DC March 7, 2001

31 William J. Clinton, Interview of the President by Israeli Television, The White House, Washington, DC, July 27, 2000

32 Sontag, op. cit.

33 Ibid.

34 Hussein Agha and Robert Malley, "Camp David: The Tragedy of Errors," *New York Review of Books*, August 9th, 2001

35 House Concurrent Resolution 426, 106th Congress, second session

36 Conference of the American Israel Public Affairs Committee, April 23, 2002

37 Dianne Feinstein, "Bold Leaders Needed in the Mideast," *San Francisco Chronicle*, April 29, 2002

38 Greg Myre, "Fearing Palestinian Attacks, Israel Keeps Up Quick Raids," *San Jose Mercury News*, May 27, 2002, p. 15A

39 House International Relations Subcommittee on the Middle East and South Asia, testimony of Assistant Secretary of State for Near Eastern Affairs William J. Burns, July 26, 2001, 107th Congress, second session. Throughout the hearing, Berman and other Democrats grilled the Republican appointee from the right, arguing that the administration was not supporting Ariel Sharon's government enough.

40 Members of Congress have found other ways to manipulate latent fears and mistrust carried by many Jews. For example, some members of Congress claim that the PLO Charter still calls for the destruction of Israel. In reality, it had been made moot by a series of PLO actions, such as acceptance of UN Security Council resolution 242 in the early 1980s, Chairman Arafat's unilateral recognition of Israel in 1988, and the Oslo Accords in 1993. More importantly, the Palestine National Council formally repealed it in 1996, a decision reiterated two years later, both of

which were formally acknowledged by the Israeli government. Other examples include claims of the widespread use of anti-Semitic textbooks as required reading in Palestinian state schools, which independent investigations have found groundless. Some Congresspeople have claimed that various statements by Arab leaders and organizations praising Palestinian "martyrs" in the struggle were referring to suicide bombers, when—in the vast majority of cases—they were referring to either Palestinian civilians killed by occupation forces or Palestinian militiamen battling Israeli soldiers in the occupied territories.

41 Quoted in Geoffrey Aronson, *Settlements and the Israeli-Palestinian Negotiations* (Washington: Institute for Palestine Studies, 1996). During the 1973 war in the Israeli-occupied Golan Heights, the settlements proved to be a security impediment by delaying the Israeli counterattack to the Syrian advance in order to first evacuate the settlers.

42 "Ariel Sharon Moves to Center Stage," *Report on Israeli Settlements in the Occupied Territories*, Foundation for Middle East Peace, Vol. 11, No. 2 (March-April 2001), p. 1

43 Jimmy Carter, "For Israel: Land or Peace?," *Washington Post*, November 26, 2002. Carter also noted that under the provisions of the Camp David Accords, Israel was required to have withdrawn from the entire West Bank and Gaza Strip "as soon as a self-governing authority has been freely elected by the inhabitants of these areas to replicate the existing military government." This would have been January 1996, when Arafat was elected president and 88 members of the Palestinian Council were elected in an election monitored by the Carter Center and approved by the Israeli government. However, even though the United States is the guarantor of the treaty, the U.S. government has refused to insist that Israel live up to its provisions.

44 Sontag, op. cit.

45 Interviews by author at Ben Gurion University in Beersheva, January 7, 1994

46 David Hoffman, *Washington Post*, June 10, 1993

47 Cable News Network, April 15, 2002

48 *Haaretz*, February 26, 2001; cited in *Report on Israeli Settlements in the Occupied Territories*, Foundation for Middle East Peace, Vol. 11, No. 2 (March-April 2001), p. 2

49 Declaration of Principles on Interim Self-Government Arrangements, Article IV September 13, 1992

50 Peled, op. cit.

51 Interviews by author with IDF reservists in 1981, 1994 and 1996.

52 Donald Rumsfeld, U.S. Department of Defense News Transcript, August

6, 2002

53 U.S. Department of State, International Information Programs, "Bush Praises Powell's Message of 'Hope and Peace' to Mideast," April 18, 2002

54 Meron Benvenisti, "A Committee of Moral Disgust," *Haaretz*, December 14, 2000

55 Report of the Sharm el-Sheikh Fact-Finding Committee (The Mitchell Report), May 20, 2001

56 Ibid.

57 House International Relations Subcommittee on the Middle East and South Asia, 107th Congress, second session. Testimony of Assistant Secretary of State for Near Eastern Affairs William J. Burns, July 26, 2001.

58 United States Information Agency, Department of State, "Cheney Says U.S. Goal is Clear: End Terror and Violence," March 18, 2002

59 Brian Whitaker, "Truce Plan Lets Israel Continue Attacks," *Guardian*, April 4, 2002

60 "Senators Urge Bush Not to Hamper Israel," *New York Times*, November 17, 2001

61 Gideon Samet, "In Uncle Sam's Cabin," *Haaretz*, February 9, 2002

62 Jackson Diehl, "The Catastrophe of U.S. Inaction," *Washington Post*, March 31, 2002, p. B7

63 Zbigniew Brzezinski, *News Hour with Jim Lehrer*, Public Broadcasting System, April 1, 2002

64 Jim Lobe, "Hawks Control U.S. Middle East Policy," *Alternet*, April 2, 2002

65 "A Clean Break: A New Strategy for Securing the Realm," Institute for Advanced Strategic and Political Studies, (June 1996), with Richard Perle as principal author.

66 Douglas Feith, "A Strategy for Israel," *Commentary*, September 1997

67 Alan Sipress, "Policy Divide Thwarts Powell in Mideast Effort," *Washington Post*, April 26, 2002

68 Cited in Edward Said, "A New Current in Palestine," *The Nation*, February 25, 2002

69 Samet, op. cit.

70 Cited in Jim Lobe and Tom Barry, "Enough is Enough," Global Affairs Commentary, Foreign Policy in Focus, April 5, 2002

71 Mouin Rabbani, "Bleak Horizons After Operation Defensive Wall," MERIP Press Information Note 93, April 30, 2002

72 Uri Avnery, "The Real Aim," *Maariv*, April 27, 2002

73 Serge Schmemann, "Ramallah: Palestinians Say Israeli Aim Was to Destroy Framework, From Archives to Hard Drives," *New York Times*,

April 16, 2002, p. A18

74 Rabbani, op.cit.

75 Barbara Plett, "Palestinian Society Lies in Ruins," BBC News, April 12, 2002, citing Ronni Skaked in *Yedioth Ahronoth*, Uzin Benziman in *Haaretz*, and Boaz Gaynor of the Israel Centre for Counter-terrorism.

76 Fareed Zakaria, "Colin Powell's Humiliation," *Newsweek*, April 29, 2002

77 United Nations Security Council resolution 1402 (2002)

78 Lobe, op. cit.

79 ABC *This Week*, April 7, 2002

80 Zakaria, op. cit.

81 United Nations Security Council resolution 1405 (2002)

82 Adam Entous, "'Troubled' Bush Demands Arafat Renounce Terror," Reuters, April 12, 2002

83 Rabbani, op. cit.

84 Graham E. Fuller, "As Killing Mounts, Who'll Blink First?", *Los Angeles Times*, April 3, 2002

85 Barbara Plett, op. cit.

86 Cited in Rabbani, op. cit.

87 Cited in Sandro Contenta, "Bush Speech Ignores Bloody Reality," *Toronto Star*, June 25, 2002

88 Cited in Lobe, "U.S. and Israeli Governments Out of Step," op. cit.

89 Ibid.

90 *Time*, April 29, 2002

91 Press Release, Office of the Press Secretary, The White House, "President Bush Calls for New Palestinian Leadership," June 24, 2002, Washington, DC

92 Ibid.

93 Shimon Shiffer, *Yediot Aharonot*, June 25, 2002

94 Cited by Gershon Baskin, "What is Behind the Bush Speech?," press release of the Israel/Palestine Center for Research and Information, June 25, 2002

95 Fuller, op. cit.

96 Cited in Gershon Baskin, "Surprise, surprise: Some More Political Observations and Thoughts," Israel/Palestine Center for Research and Information, July 5, 2001

97 Samet, op. cit.

98 Interview, May 12, 1992, Seattle, Washington

99 Cited in Kathleen Christison, "Who's Behind US Middle East policy?", *Middle East International*, March 8, 2002, p. 23

100 Uri Avnery, "The Great Game," February 9, 2002

101 Galia Golan, Shalom Achev, May 10, 2002. A Dahaf (Mina Zemah) poll,

conducted May 5-6, 2002, found that 63% said they did not believe that the problem of terrorism could be resolved without political negotiations and 62% of the respondents said that for them peace negotiations with the Palestinians would inspire hope or very much hope. According to 60% of the public, a withdrawal that was not acceptable to both sides would not lead to a peace accord with the Palestinians A majority of the respondents (59%) would support American guarantees for a withdrawal to the 1967 lines with minor mutual and agreed upon adjustments, evacuation of most of the settlements, compromise in Jerusalem and abandonment of the demand for right of return of the refugees.

102 This is not to imply that Israel's repression is anything near the scale of Stalin's Russia, they are comparative only in the sense that there is a tendency for ideological baggage to get in the way of a realistic assessment of the actual situation.

103 Michael Massing, "Deal Breakers," *The American Prospect*, March 11, 2002

104 Ibid.

105 For an elaboration of this argument, see Stephen Zunes, "The Roots of the U.S.-Israeli Relationship," *New Political Science*, Nos. 21-22, Spring-Summer 1992; See also, A.F.K. Organski, *The $36 Billion Bargain: Strategy and Politics in U.S. Assistance to Israel* (New York: Columbia University Press, 1990)

106 The United States, like other Western powers, has never been a strong supporter of Third World nationalism, including Zionism, except when it could be useful for its own geo-political interests. Nor has the United States pursued policies indicative of any great sympathy for the Jewish people. In the 1930s, the United States barred thousands of Jews desperately fleeing persecution in Europe from entering the country despite knowledge of the concentration camps. Even when the large-scale extermination of the Jews became apparent, the United States and its allies did not bomb the gas chambers or the rail lines leading to the extermination centers. Invading allied forces did not target the camps for early liberation. The lack of concern demonstrated by successive American administrations towards the plight of other oppressed groups, both domestically and worldwide, gives little credence to claims of ideological incentives for supporting Zionism.

107 This commitment to Israeli superiority often is cast in terms of compensating for the superior numerical strength of the combined forces of neighboring Arab states. However, not only are Israeli forces far better trained and more mobile, but the idea of large numbers of Arab states uniting to destroy Israel at this point is highly questionable at best.

108 Karen L. Puschel, *U.S.-Israeli Strategic Cooperation in the Post-Cold War Era: An American Perspective* (Boulder: Westview Press, 1993) p. 150

109 Glenn Frankel, *Washington Post*, Nov. 19, 1986

110 Cited in Stephen Green, *Taking Sides: America's Secret Relations With a Militant Israel*, (Brattleboro, VT: Amana Books, 1988) p. 250

111 The chronology of aid figures is taken from Wenger, op. cit.

112 Pound, op. cit.

113 Henry Kissinger, *Years of Upheaval* (Boston: Little, Brown, Company, 1982) p. 621

114 For example, when Great Britain and France sought to oust nationalist president Gamal Abdul-Nasser in 1956 to protect their commercial interests, they sent in the Israeli army to invade the Sinai Peninsula.

115 Interview, Film "Israel Faces the Future," Public Broadcasting System, 1987

116 Nathan Shaham, *Yediot Ahronot*, Nov. 28, 1996, cited in Noam Chomsky, *World Orders Old and New* (New York: Columbia University Press, 1994) p. 206

117 B. Michael, *Ha'aretz*, Nov. 11, 1983, cited in Ibid.

118 For example, see Cherie Brown, et al, "A Draft Policy on Jewish Liberation," *Ruah Hadashah*, #4 (1981); particularly, pp. 11-13.

119 This is based on the author's periodic experience lobbying for arms control and human rights on Capitol Hill since 1973 as well as anecdotes from colleagues who have had similar experiences.

120 Based on this author's interviews with a half dozen Arab foreign ministers and deputy foreign ministers between 1990 and 1994.

121 *Washington Post*, Sept. 13, 1991, p. A32.

122 Organski, op. cit., p. 28

123 Ibid., pp. 198-199

Even in cases where there has been a standoff, the reasons are not as clear-cut as they may appear. For example, there were a number of reports in the Israeli press that the initial decision to deny the $10 billion loan guarantee was not actually based on Israeli settlement policy as publicly announced, but out of an American desire to restructure the Israeli economy along a stronger free market orientation. Pioneered by one-time University of Chicago economist and then-Secretary of State George Schultz, the reported U.S. plan was that the Israeli government would severely weaken the Histradut (Israel's powerful trade union federation), abolish the minimum wage, privatize state-controlled enterprises, and lower taxes. Such economic restructuring has been a requirement for U.S.-backed loans to a number of countries as a means of creating a more favorable climate for U.S. investment, so it should not be surprising that

Israel would be held to such standards as well. The use of the settlements controversy as a cover, so goes this theory, was done to assuage allied Arab states into thinking that the United States was sincere about supporting the peace process.

124 Uri Avnery: Oct 21 2000 Disseminated through Avnery's website. http:home.mindspring.com/~fontenelles/avnery.htm

125 Cited in Sasha Polkow-Suransky, "War Now Peace Later," *The American Prospect*, April 16, 2002

126 Samet, op. cit.

127 United Nations Security Council Resolution 262 (1968), as well as 267 (1969)

128 Newstab PR Newswire, March 18, 1994 "Gore Reaffirms U.S. Policy Declaring United Jerusalem as Capital of Israel," quoting from a tele-conference between the vice-president and some American Jewish leaders.

129 Secretary of State Warren Christopher, Hearings of the Foreign Operation Subcommittee of the Senate Appropriation Committee, Wednesday, March 2, 1994

130 For example, see House Concurrent Resolution 20, 105th Congress, 1st Session, passed by a 406-17 vote on June 10, 1997 in honor of the thirtieth anniversary of Israel's conquest of the Arab half of the city.

131 For details on the Clinton Administration's support for Israeli claims on Jerusalem, see Stephen Zunes, "U.S. Policy Towards Jerusalem: Clinton's Shift to the Right," *Middle East Policy*, Volume III, Number 3, 1994

132 Donald Rumsfeld, U.S. Department of Defense News Transcript, August 6, 2002

133 American Israel Public Affairs Committee, transcript from 2002 Policy Conference, April 23, 2002

134 Transcript, *Hardball with Chris Matthews*, CNBC, May 1, 2002

135 James M. Inhofe, "An Absolute Victory: America's Stake in Israel's War on Terrorism," Senate Floor Statement, December 4, 2001. Inhofe, in his speech, cites Genesis 13:14-17. However, in Genesis 15, God promises Abraham's descendents all the land between what is now Egypt and Iraq, which would probably require—in the minds of Inhofe and other Christian fundamentalists in government—U.S. support for an Israeli conquest of much of the Middle East. In reference to the terrorist attacks on the United States the previous September, Inhofe argued, "One of the reasons I believe the spiritual door was opened for an attack against the United States of America is that the policy of our government has been to ask the Israelis...not to retaliate in a significant way against the terrorist strikes that have been launched against them." In his speech, which has been widely circulated among Christian conservatives, Inhofe also

claimed that Palestine—famous for centuries for its olive orchards, terraced vineyards, and citrus fruits—was actually an uninhabited wasteland before the Zionists settled the land during the previous century; he even claims those who call themselves Palestinians were actually migrants from other Arab countries wanting to take advantage of Jewish prosperity.

136 Interview by Nathan Gardels, Global Viewpoint, *New Perspectives Quarterly*, April 12, 2002

Chapter Five

1 Senate Concurrent Resolution 50, 105th Congress, 1st session

2 The United States and other Western nations interpreted Article 6 of UN Security Council resolution 713 that placed a military embargo on Yugoslavia applied to Bosnia-Herzegovina since it was passed on September 21, 1991, before Bosnia-Herzegovina declared its independence.

3 *Le Nouvel Observateur*, Paris, 15-21 January 1998

4 Mary Anne Weaver, "Blowback," *Atlantic Monthly*, May 1996

5 Bill Keller, "Last Soviet Soldiers Leave Afghanistan After Nine Years," *New York Times*, February 16, 1989

6 John F. Burns, "Afghan Capital Grim as War Follows War," *New York Times*, February 5, 1996

7 Cited in Alexander Cockburn, *The Nation*, January 27, 1997

8 Cited in Ahmad Rashid, *Taliban: Militant Islam, Oil and Fundamentalism in Central Asia* (New Haven: Yale University Press, 2000)

9 Robert Scheer, "Bush's Faustian Deal With the Taliban," *Los Angeles Times*, May 22, 2001

10 Cited in "The Deadly Pipeline War," *Jurist*, December 8, 2001. The title of the book translates as *Bin Laden, the Forbidden Truth*.

11 Most political observers believe that the hostage crisis was largely responsible for the defeat of President Jimmy Carter and the election of Ronald Reagan. Interestingly, most of the details of the final arrangement for the release of the American hostages in return for the release of frozen Iranian assets overseas and pledges of non-aggression from the United States had been worked out by that October, prior to the U.S. election. This would have almost certainly resulted in Carter's re-election. However, there is evidence to suggest that at least some leading operatives in the Reagan campaign, through contacts with elements of the Iranian government, successfully caused the delay in the release of the hostages until afterwards. See Gary Sick, *October Surprise: America's Hostages in Iran and the Election of Ronald Reagan* (Collingsdale, PA: Diane Publishing Company, 1991)

12 United Nations Security Council Resolution 425 (1978)

13 Jimmy Carter, *New York Times*, March 26, 1989

14 CNN All Politics, Press conference transcript, President Bill Clinton and Israeli Prime Minister Benjamin Netanyahu, February 13, 1997 [www.cnn.com/ALLPOLITICS/1997/02/13/transcript/]

15 Awad subsequently founded Nonviolence International and lives in Washington, DC. He continues to be an outspoken advocate for Palestinian rights, opposing the Israeli occupation and extremist Islamic groups as well as Arafat's administration.

Chapter Six

1 U.S. General Accounting Office, *Combating Terrorism: Threat and Risk Assessments Can Help Prioritize and Target Program Investments*, NSIAD-98-74, April 9, 1998

2 Background briefing with State Department officials, U.S. Embassy, Damascus, Syria April 1994

3 Viorst, op. cit. See also Joseph Kahn, "19 Countries Vow to Seize Bank Assets of Terrorists," *New York Times*, Feb. 10, 2001

4 Ironically, the United States had failed to recognize the authority of the International Court of Justice in another case involving terrorism just six years earlier. The court ruled 15-1 (with only the U.S. judge dissenting) that the United States had to cease its support of the Contras and other terrorist and paramilitary activity against Nicaragua and to pay $3 billion in damages.

5 See, for example, "Libyans Debate Post-Qaddafi Era," *Washington Report on Middle Eastern Affairs*, January 1994, p. 50, an account of the Center for Strategic and International Studies' conference "Post-Qaddafi Libya: The Prospect and The Promise" on November 28-29, 1993

6 U.S. Department of State, *Patterns of Global Terrorism 1994*, April 1995, p. vi.

7 Costa Rica and Venezuela are longstanding democracies with two of the freest and most credible judicial systems in Latin America. The evidence against the indicted suspects has been made public and appears to be quite credible.

8 Human Rights Watch, "Thirst for Justice: A Decade of Impunity in Haiti," September 1996, Vol. 8, No. 7 (B)

9 George W. Bush, Presidential Address, September 12, 2002

10 Dear Colleague letter signed by U.S. Representatives Albert Wynn, Edolphus Towns, Julia Carson, John Conyers, Cynthia McKinney, Maxine Waters and others, August 15, 2001

11 "Wrong Man for the U.N.," *Los Angeles Times*, September 17, 2001

12 United Nations General Assembly, A/RES/42/159, 94th plenary meeting,

December 7, 1987

13 Patrick Wintour, *Observer*, December 20, 1998

14 James Astill, "Strike One," *Guardian*, October 2, 2001

15 Werner Daum, "Universalism and the West," *Harvard International Review*, Summer 2001

16 Astill, op. cit.; see also Mark Huband, *Financial Times*, September 8, 1998

17 James Risen, "Angry at U.S. Attack, Freed Bomb Suspects, Officials Say," *New York Times*, July 30, 1999

18 David Rose, "Resentful west spurned Sudan's key terror files," *Observer*, September 30, 2001

19 Charter of the United Nations Organization, Article 51

20 John Pilger, "Bin Laden Extradition Offer Refused," *Daily Mirror*, November 16, 2001

21 Ivo Daalder and Michael O'Hanlon, "Bush and Powell Need to Remember the Lessons of Kosovo," *International Herald Tribune*, November 1, 2001

22 Julian Borger, "War About to Enter New Phase," *Guardian*, October 10, 2001

23 Amnesty International, "Afghanistan: Accountability for Civilian Deaths," AI Index ASA 11/022/2001 - News Service Nr. 189, October 26, 2001

24 Carl Conetta, *Operation Enduring Freedom: Why a Higher Rate of Civilian Casualties?* PDA Briefing Report 11 (Washington: Project for Defense Alternatives, January 15, 2002)

25 http://www.cursor.org/stories/civilian_deaths.htm

26 Conetta, op. cit.

27 David Corn, "Pentagon Denials and Civilian Death in Afghanistan," *Alternet*, December 7, 2001

28 Cited in Robert Fisk, "America's Morality has been Distorted by 11 September," March 7, 2002

29 Cynthia Cotts, "War Riddles: Ten Questions the Media Isn't Answering," *Village Voice*, February 25, 2002

30 Some segments of the Taliban may have actually had sophisticated anti-aircraft capability. One reason for the high number of civilian casualties was the U.S. decision to use jets instead of helicopter gun ships, which can more easily distinguish enemy forces from civilians. The justification for choosing the high-altitude aircraft was because the Taliban were believed to possess hand-held heat-seeking Stinger anti-aircraft missiles, which could be devastatingly effective against helicopters. The United States supplied these missiles and their launchers to the Islamic resistance in Afghanistan in the 1980s.

31 Paul Harris and Peter Beaumont, "Up to 60 die as US bombs tribal leaders

by mistake," *Guardian*, December 23, 2000

32 Mushahdid Hussain, "Opening a New Front," *Middle East International*, May 3, 2002

33 James Doran, "US Jets 'Fire on Wedding Celebration by Mistake'" *Times of London*, May 18, 2002; "Bombing Raid May Have Killed 48 Afghans: US General," Agence France Press, July 6, 2002

34 Carl Conetta, "Strange Victory: A Critical Appraisal of Operation Enduring Freedom and the Afghanistan War," Research Monograph #6 (Washington: Project for Defense Alternatives) January 30, 2002, p. 5

35 Cited in Jim Lobe, "One, Two, Many Afghanistans," Inter Press Service, March 7, 2002

36 Donald G. McNeil, Jr. "More and More, War is Viewed as America's," *New York Times*, November 4, 2001

37 Ibid., p. 10

38 Quoted from Richard Boudreaux and Tyler Marshall, "'Great Game II' has a Wealth of Players" *Los Angeles Times*, November 2, 2001

39 John Pilger, "Bin Laden Extradition Offer Refused," *Daily Mirror*, November 16, 2001

40 "Afghanistan: Amnesty International calls for urgent inquiry into violence in Qala-i-Jhangi," AI-index: ASA 11/036/2001 November 27, 2001

41 Brian Whitaker, "Raising the Double Standard in Afghan War," *Guardian*, November 26, 2001

42 Peter Dale Scott, "Heroin, Drug Warlords Reappear on Afghan Scene," Pacific News Service, Dec. 20, 2001

43 David Corn, "Bush's War in Afghanistan: A Case of Big Mission Creep?" *The Nation*, February 20, 2002

44 George W. Bush, presidential address, September 20, 2002

45 Jim Lobe and Abid Aslam, "Foreign Policy Shift: The Terrible Trade-Offs," Global Affairs Commentary, Foreign Policy in Focus Project, September 2001

46 Human Rights Watch, Letter to Secretary of State Colin Powell, September 24, 2001

47 Cited in Jim Lobe, "Human Rights Watch Scores U.S. 'Hypocrisy' on 'War on Terrorism,'" Inter Press Service, January 17, 2002

48 Conn Hallinan, citing U.S. special envoy Zalmay Khalizad (first quote) and Princeton University professor and Bush Administration advisor Bernard Lewis (second quote) in "A U.S. Cabal Pulling America to War," Foreign Policy in Focus, May 3, 2002

Chapter Seven

1 Many hundreds of Palestinians took part in prayer vigils, sent condolences

to the U.S. Consulate in East Jerusalem, and engaged in other acts of solidarity in the days and weeks after the September 11 attack.

2   One issue that sometimes appears as part of the grievances of terrorists involves the redistribution of wealth and power, which is not currently identified as a typically American value. In this era of globalization and the growing inequality, however, it is perhaps a concern that should be taken more seriously, both for its moral implications as well as for the long-term security of those states and societies that have accumulated great wealth at the expense of others.

3   "Terrorism and Human Rights," Commission on Human Rights, United Nations Economic and Social Council, June 27, 2001

4   Cited in Chuck Sudetic, "The Betrayal of Basra," *Mother Jones,* November/December 2001

5   Cited in Joel Campagna, "The Arab Press Sends Mixed Message," World Press Reveiw, November 2001 (Vol. 48, No. 11)

6   Barbara Kingsolver, "Reflections on Wartime," *Washington Post,* Nov. 23, 2001

7   Michael Klare, "Asking 'Why?,'" op. cit.

8   Prince Hassan, op. cit.

9   Chris Toensing, *Boston Globe,* May 5, 2002

Index

N

About the Author

Stephen Zunes is an associate professor of Politics and chair of the Peace & Justice Studies Program at the University of San Francisco. He also serves as a senior policy analyst and Middle East editor for the Foreign Policy in Focus Project and as a research associate at the Center for Global, International and Regional Studies at the University of California—Santa Cruz.

A native of North Carolina, he received his PhD. from Cornell University, his M.A. from Temple University and his B.A. from Oberlin College. He has since taught and lectured widely, holding faculty positions at the Ithaca College, University of Puget Sound, and Whitman College.

He served as founding director of the Institute for a New Middle East Policy and as a research fellow at the Institute for Policy Studies and the Institute for Global Security Studies.

Dr. Zunes was also a recipient of a National Endowment for the Humanities Fellowship on Middle Eastern and Central Asian Studies at Dartmouth College and a Joseph J. Malone Fellowship in Arab and Islamic Studies. He is an associate editor of *Peace Review* and is on the governing council of the International Peace Research Association. He has served as a fellow of the United States Institute of Peace on the study of international and regional organizations in conflict resolution. He is the author of scores of articles for scholarly and general readership on Middle Eastern politics, U.S. foreign policy, international terrorism and social movements. He is the principal editor of *Nonviolent Social Movements: A Geographical Perspective* (Blackwell, 1999) and the author of *Western Sahara: Nationalism and Conflict in Northwest Africa* (Syracuse University Press, 2004) and an upcoming book on U.S.-Israeli relations.

He lives in a co-housing community in Santa Cruz, California with his wife Nanlouise Wolfe and their children Shanti, Kalila and Tobin.